Bain Robert Nisbet

**The Pupils of Peter the Great**

A history of the Russian court and empire from 1697 to 1740

Bain Robert Nisbet

**The Pupils of Peter the Great**
*A history of the Russian court and empire from 1697 to 1740*

ISBN/EAN: 9783337299088

Printed in Europe, USA, Canada, Australia, Japan

Cover: Foto ©ninafisch / pixelio.de

More available books at **www.hansebooks.com**

# THE PUPILS

OF

# PETER THE GREAT

A HISTORY OF THE RUSSIAN COURT AND EMPIRE
FROM 1697 TO 1740

BY

R. NISBET BAIN.

AUTHOR OF "GUSTAVUS III AND HIS CONTEMPORARIES"; "CHARLES XII";
"HANS CHRISTIAN ANDERSEN: A BIOGRAPHY," ETC.

WESTMINSTER
A. CONSTABLE & Co.
1897.

# PREFACE.

IN the following pages it will be my endeavour to follow out, step by step, the early development of the modern Russian State from the latter years of Peter the Great to the death of his niece, the Tsaritsa Anne, and I propose at the same time, to draw a picture of the Imperial Court as it struck contemporary observers. The period chosen embraces, roughly speaking, the first forty years of the Eighteenth Century, and while I hope that serious political and historical students will find much in this volume to reward their attention and awaken their interest, I feel pretty confident that the curious scrutinizer of men and manners will not be altogether disappointed if he takes the trouble to peruse it. For the history of the Russian Empire throughout this period is, very largely, the history of the Russian Court, and, speaking from a large experience, I know of no other European Court which confronts us with such strangely original and eccentric types of character, such sharp and striking contrasts and such swift, sudden and tragical revolutions of fortune. I have prefaced my narrative with an introductory chapter on Seventeenth Century Russia, still, I regret to say, an historical *terra incognita* in this country.

I now proceed to set out my authorities. First come the contemporary despatches of the Foreign Ministers at St. Petersburg and Moscow contained in the voluminous *Sbornik*, or collections, of the Russian Imperial Historical Society, as follows: (1) *The Despatches and Correspondence* of the English Ministers, Whitworth, MacKenzie, Haldane, Norris, and Jeffries, 1704—1718; (2) *The Despatches* of the Prussian Minister Mardefeldt, 1721—1733; (3) *The Despatches* of the Saxon Minister Lefort, 1721—1730; (4) *The Despatches* of the French Minister Campredon, 1725—

1727; (5) *The Despatches* of the English Minister Rondeau, 1720—1739; (6) *The Despatches* of the French Minister Chétardie, 1740; (7) *The Despatches* of the English Minister Finch, 1740. To the same class of documents belongs (8) *Diario del viaje a Moscovia del Embajador el Duque de Liria*, forming Tome XCIII of the *Coleccion de documentos ineditos para la historia de España*. All these despatches are of great value as being the testimonies of eye-witnesses of the events described; but they are nevertheless open to the objection that they too often reflect not only the personal prejudices of the writers, but also the political bias of the governments by whom they were accredited. On the other hand, they can very often be made to serve as mutual correctives.

A second class of documents are the contemporary memoirs of the period, such as (9) *Tagebuch des Generals Patrick Gordon*, ed. Obolensky, containing many interesting personal details concerning Peter the Great; (10) *Mémoires du regne Catherine I*, La Haye, 1728, a work to be used with great caution; (11) *Lettres from a lady who resided some years in Russia* [*i.e.* Lady Rondeau] second edition. This little book, written in a most insinuating and piquant style, is one of our best authorities on the Court of Anne, and abounds with vivid pictures of its chief personage. The lady is a shrewd, but too often a superficial observer, and her strong partialities, which she makes no attempt to conceal, frequently render her judgments hasty and unjust. (12) *Mémoires sur la Russie par le Général Manstein*. This, in many ways an important work, is especially valuable for the light it throws upon the military operations of the young Empire, and the same may be said in a lesser degree of (13) "*Tagebuch des Grafen von Münnich*," descriptive of the Crimean Campaign of 1736.

The monumental work of Solovev (14) *Istorya Rossy* (History of Russia), of which I have utilised Vols. XVIII—XX, stands entirely by itself. It is not so much a history as an immense collection of original Russian historical documents of all sorts,—despatches, ukazes, protocols, manifestoes, etc.—a well-nigh inexhaustible mine of wealth to the historical student who has the courage and the patience to explore its labyrinths.

Next in order come a series of monographs, mostly Russian, such as: (15) Brückner: *Peter der Grosse*, an excellent work; (16) Grot: *Proiskhozdenie Imperatritsa Ekaterinui I* (Origin of the Empress

Catherine I) a very scholarly essay; (17) Semevsky: *Tsaritsa Ekaterina, Anna i Villem Mons* (Tsaritsa Catherine, Anne and William Mons) and (18) the same author's: *Tsaritsa Proskovya*, both somewhat scandalous works with a strong anti-Petrine bias which considerably lessens their historical value, but containing much important information not to be found elsewhere; (19) Zmakhin: *Koronatsy russkikh imperatorov* (Coronations of the Russian Emperors); (20) Bantuish Kamensky: *Biografy rosseskikh generalissumesov* (Biographies of the Russian Generalissimos); (21) Andreev: *Ekaterina Pervaya* (Catherine I); (22) Dolgoruki: *Graf A. I. Ostermann*; (23) Shcherbatov: *O povrezhdeniy nravov v Rossy* (On the Degeneration of Morals in Russia), a charming book with a delightful old-world flavour about it, containing, however, a severe indictment of the eighteenth-century luxury which the panegyrists of Catherine II find it very difficult to meet; (24) Geffroy: *Recueil des instructions données aux Ambassadeurs de France depuis les traités de Westphalie jusqu'à la Révolution Française;* (25) *Einrichtung der Studien Ihrs. Kays. Maj. Peter des Andern.*

I am finally indebted to the following works for much miscellaneous information; (26) Sipovsky: *Rodnaya Starina* (Our Ancient Fatherland); (27) Kostomarov: *Russkaya Istoria* (Russian History) Vol. II; (28) *Entsiklopedecheskiy Leksikon;* (29) *Polnaya historia zhizni Balakireva* (Complete History of the Life of the Jester Balakirer; (30) the valuable Polish publication: "*Slovnik geograficzny Krolestwa Polskiego*" (Geographical Encyclopedia of the Kingdom of Poland) and (31) Halem: *Lebensbeschreibung des Feldmarshalls B. C. Grafen von Münnich.*

If this study of the rise of the modern Russian State receive the encouragement which I think so novel and so interesting a subject deserves, I propose, in a subsequent volume, to continue the history of the Russian Empire through the epoch-making reign of the Empress Elizabeth, the contemporary and mortal antagonist of Frederick II, when the work of Peter the Great was finally consolidated.

R. NISBET BAIN.

## LIST OF ILLUSTRATIONS.

|  |  | PAGE |
|---|---|---|
| PETER THE GREAT | *Leroy*, 1717, *Frontispiece* | |
| ,, ,, ,, | *Kneller* (*Photogravure*) | 1 |
| CATHERINE I. | | 71 |
| PETER II. | | 120 |
| ANNE, EMPRESS | | 277 |
| ELIZABETH, EMPRESS | | 290 |

# CONTENTS.

PAGE

CHAPTER I.—INTRODUCTORY—SEVENTEENTH CENTURY RUSSIA . 1

The first Romanov—Misery of Eastern Russia, or Muscovy, in the 17th century—Partition of her dominions—Lithuania, or Western Russia—Her origin—Union with Poland—Condition of Poland at this time—Causes of her decline—Vicious constitution—Religious dissensions—The Protestants and the Jesuits—Struggle between the Jesuits and the Greek Orthodox Church—Origin of the Lithuanian Uniates—Increase of religious bitterness—Origin of the Cossacks—Description of the Ukraine—Rebellion of Bogdan Chmielnicki—His bloody wars with Poland—Tsar Alexius I—Peace of Kardis—Condition of 17th century Muscovy—Impediments to civilization—Byzantinism—Ignorance—Tyranny of custom—The Muscovite women—The Patriarch Nikon and his reforms—The new men Slavenetsky—Poletsky—Krijanić—Influence of Poland—And of the "Dutch Suburb"—Artamon Matvyeev—Tsar Theodore Aleksyeevich—The Tsarevna Sophia—Early years of Peter the Great—His first foreign tour—Horror with which his reforms were regarded in Russia—Revolt of the Stryeltsui—Peter's foreign policy—War with Charles XII—Peace of the Pruth—Murder of the Tsarevich Alexius—Internal Administration—The Tsardom of Muscovy becomes the Empire of Russia.

CHAPTER II.—CATHERINE ALEKSYEEVNA AND PETER THE GREAT. (1711—1725). . . . . . . . . . . . . . . . . . 36

Peter's pupils—P. A. Tolstoy—F. M. Apraksin—G. I. Golovkin—Anecdotes of his stinginess—P. I. Yaguzhinsky—A. D. Menshikov—His origin, career, and character—Rapacity of Peter's pupils—Anecdotes of Menshikov's greed—A. I. Ostermann—Early career and character—Diplomatic astuteness—Martha Skovronskaya—Peter's first acquaintance with her—His cruel treatment of his first Consort Eudoxia—Peter's ideal woman—His first mistress Anna Mons—Personality and character of Martha Skovronskaya—Her moral influence over Peter—Martha Skovronskaya becomes Catherine Aleksyeevna—Marries the Tsar—Devotion of Peter to her—Their affectionate correspondence—Ukaz fixing the succession to the throne—Execution of Nestorov—Coronation of Catherine—Description of the Regalia—The Mons affair—Last illness and death of Peter the Great—His character—Comparison with Charles XII.

CHAPTER III.—CATHERINE ALEKSYEEVNA ON THE THRONE.
(Feb. 1725—May 1727). . . . . . . . . . . . . . . 7

Who is to succeed Peter?—Presence of mind of Catherine—Energetic efforts on her behalf of Menshikov and Tolstoy—The higher clergy won over to Catherine—The Grand Duke Peter's Party—Debate in the Council Chamber—Violent Scenes—Catherine proclaimed Autocrat—Attitude of Moscow and the Army of the Ukraine—Conciliatory attitude of the new Empress—Troubles with her servants—Influence of Menshikov—Charles Frederick, Duke of Holstein— His early career and character—Institution of the Verkhovny Tainy Sovyet, or Supreme Privy Council—Domestic affairs—Distress of the people—Financial shifts—Prosecution and degradation of the Archbishop of Novgorod—Condition of European politics—Predominance of England—Causes of her hostility to Russia—Diplomatic contest between the two States—Attitude of France—The Hanoverian Alliance—English fleet despatched to the Baltic—Indignation of Catherine—Russia joins the Austro-Spanish League—Prussia—Denmark—Uncertain attitude of Sweden—Condition of that power—Chancellor Horn—Russian intrigues at Stockholm—Sweden joins the Hanoverian Alliance—Polish affairs—The Courland question—Maurice of Saxony elected Duke of Courland—Intervention of Menshikov—Yaguzhinsky in Poland—Corruption of the Poles—The question of the Russian Succession—Popularity of the Grand Duke Peter—Illness of the Empress—Critical position of Menshikov—He goes over to the Grand Duke's Party—Counter-conspiracy of Tolstoy—Last moments of Catherine—Disgraceful scene in the Antechamber—Arrest and banishment of Tolstoy and his accomplices—Death of Catherine I—Her character.

CHAPTER IV.—REIGN OF PETER II. (May 1727—Jan. 1730) . . 114

The will of Catherine I—Peter II proclaimed Tsar—His early years—Ostermann appointed his Governor—His pædagogic method—Its practical character—The Grand Duchess Natalia—The Tsarevna Elizabeth—Menshikov absolute—Departure of the Duke and Duchess of Holstein—Death of the Duchess—Wise and humane measures of the new Government—Betrothal of the Tsar to Menshikov's daughter—Tyranny of Menshikov—Violent passages between him and the Tsar—His quarrel with Ostermann—Fall of Menshikov—The Golitsuins—And the Dolgorukis—Difficult position of Ostermann—Re-appearance of the Tsaritsa Eudoxia—Peter II's coronation—Death of Menshikov—The Government transferred to Moscow—Character of Peter II—General demoralization—Foreign affairs—The Treaty of Seville—Decay of the Russian Fleet—Death of the Grand Duchess Natalia—Degradation of the Tsarevna Elizabeth—Supremacy of the Dolgorukis—Betrothal of the Tsar to Catharine Dolgoruki—His melancholy and discontent—Last illness and death of Peter II.

CHAPTER V.—ACCESSION OF ANNE OF COURLAND. (1730—1733). 158

Futile family council of the Dolgorukis—Apathy of the Tsarevna Elizabeth—Ascendency of Demetrius Golitsuin—His ambition and political views—Anne of Courland elected Empress—The Articles limiting the power of the Sovereign—Anne signs the Articles—Consternation at Moscow—Arrest of Yaguzhinsky—Arrival of the Empress—Her independent demeanour—The "Republican Gentlemen"—Anne under close surveillance—Preparations for a *coup d'état*—Cherkasky's petition to the Empress—Violent scenes at the Palace—Fall of the Oligarchs—The Empress declared Autocrat—Antecedents and character of the new Tsaritsa—Early marriage to the Duke of Courland—Liaison with Peter Bestuzhev—And with Ernest Johan Biren—Antecedents and character of the latter—First measures of Anne—Punishment of the Dolgorukis—Influence of Biren begins—The Löwenwoldes—Yaguzhinsky's elevation—Establishment of the Cabinet—Burkhard Münnich made Minister of War—His early career and character—Ascendency of the German Party—Insolence of Münnich—Unpopularity of Anne's Government—Causes of this unpopularity—Extravagant display at Anne's Court—Protest of Rumyantsev—Good points of Anne's character and government—Foreign affairs—French intrigues at the Russian Court—Münnich versus Ostermann—Triumph of the Austrian Faction—Polish affairs—Death of Augustus II.

CHAPTER VI.—THE WAR OF THE POLISH SUCCESSION. (1733—1735). 206

The Polish Primate, Theodore Potocki—France declares in favour of Stanislaus Leszczynski—The Convocation-Diet—Dissensions among the Poles—Protests of Russia—The Elective Diet—Russia and Austria support Augustus of Saxony—The Polish Diet elects Stanislaus King—Protest of the Minority—Flight of Stanislaus to Dantzic—Fruitless negotiations—Attitude of Prussia—And of Great Britain—A Russian army under Peter Lacy invades Poland—Antecedents of Lacy—He begins the siege of Dantzic—Arrival of Münnich—Unsuccessful attack on the Hagelberg—Arrival of a French force to aid Dantzic—It is captured and sent to Russia—Anne's courtesy to her captives—Fall of Dantzic—State of Europe—Victories of the French over the Emperor—Lacy sent to his assistance—Anti-Russian intrigues of the French at Stockholm and Stambul—Lord Kinnoul—Negotiations of Russia with Kuli Khan—War declared against the Porte.

CHAPTER VII.—THE FIRST CRIMEAN WAR. (1736—1739). . . . . 235

Theatre of the War—The Crimea—The lines of the Ukraine—Campaign of 1735—Campaign of 1736—Quarrel between Münnich and Lacy—Münnich's march across the Steppes—Skirmishes with the Tartars—Münnich's tactics—The Lines of Perekop—Münnich carries them by assault—Advance upon Koslov—Sufferings of the army—Advance on

Bagchaserai—Insubordination in the army—Return to the Ukraine—Lacy captures Azov—Terrible mortality in the Russian army—Indignation of the Empress—Her correspondence with Münnich—Vishnyakov—Campaign of 1737—General James Francis Keith—The siege of Ochakov—Münnich's blunders—Lacy ravages the Crimea—Peace Congress at Nemirov—Complaints against Münnich—Campaign of 1738—Sufferings of the army—Coolness between the Austrian and Russian Courts—France mediates between the belligerents—Campaign of 1739—Battle of Stavuchanakh—Fall of Chocim—Surrender of Jassy—Münnich's progress arrested by the news of the Peace of Belgrade—His indignant remonstrance—End of the War—Rejoicings—Reflections.

## CHAPTER VIII.—THE LATTER DAYS OF ANNE. (1735—1740) . . 277

Court of the Tsaritsa—Her personal appearance and mode of life—Peterhof—Amusements—Gorgeousness of the Court—Fairy Fêtes at the Summer Palace and the Winter Palace—The Carnival of the Calmuck Bride and the Ice Mansion—Anne's noble buffoons—Other Jesters—Luxury of the Court—The gaming tables—Morality of Anne's Court—The Tsarevna Elizabeth—Terror-stricken atmosphere of the Court—Servility of the Courtiers—Anecdote of Anne's caustic wit—Malign influence of Biren—He is elected Duke of Courland—A kidnapping anecdote—Biren's cruel persecution of the Russian nobility—Antagonism of Biren, Münnich and Ostermann—Unique position of the latter—Biren's dread of him—Yaguzhinsky—The strange and tragic history of Artemius Voluinsky—Alexius Bestuzhev—European politics—Ascendency of France—Rise of the Hat Party in Sweden—Murder of Major Sinclaire—England and Russia—Anne of Mecklenburg—Birth of Ivan VI—Illness of the Tsaritsa—The Regency question—Intrigues of Biren—Death of the Tsaritsa.

# INDEX.

## A

ADRIAN, *Patriarch of Moscow*, 28.
ALBERONI, *Cardinal*, 92, 256.
ALEXANDER, *King of Poland*, 4.
ALEXIUS I, *Tsar*, 15, 16, 20, 21, 22, 23, 24.
ALEXIUS, PETROVICH, *Tsar*, murder of, 32—33; 38, 43, 54, 55, 59, 106.
ALEKSYEEV (Peter). See PETER I, *Tsar*.
ALI PASHA, *Grand-Vizier*, 230, 231, 232.
AMBROSIUS, *Archbishop of Vologda*, 274.
ANNE, IVANOVNA, *Empress*, 43, 101, enamoured of Maurice of Saxony, 102—103; 122, accepts articles of Mittau, 166; arrival at Moscow, 169; independent attitude, 170—171; assumes autocracy, 175—176; early years and character, 177—182; dislike of Russian nobility, 183; coronation, 185; severity, 194; extravagance, 195—196; good points of character, 200; Polish policy of, 209, 214—215; courtesy, 224—225; sympathy, 252—253, 256; rewards Münnich and Keith, 260; 263, 268, 274, personal appearance and mode of life, 278—280; splendour, 281—283; cruel humour, 283—286; dresses, 287—288; introduces gambling, 288; morality, 289—290; kindness, 291—292; sarcasm, 298; 302, 304, abandons Voluinsky to Biren, 305—306; 310, 312, adopts Anne of Mecklenburg, 312; 313, last moments, 314—317.
ANNE, LEOPOLDOVNA, *Grand Duchess*, 290, character, 312; 314, 315, 316.
ANNE, PETROVNA, *Duchess of Holstein*, 59, 69, personal appearance, 83; 108, 110, 115; death of 125—126.
ANTHONY ULRIC, *Prince of Brunswick-Wolfenbüttel*, 256, character; 313, marries Anne of Mecklenburg, 313; Münnich's opinion of, 315; 316.

APOSTOL, *Cossack Ataman*, 127.
APRAKSIN (Alexius Petrovich), *Count*, 285, 286.
APRAKSIN (Fedor Matvyeevich, *Count*, early career and character, 38—39; venality, 45; 67, 77, 80, 86, 116, 124 death, 147.
AUGUSTUS II, *King of Poland*, 103, 146, 202, intrigues, 204—5; proposes partition of Poland, 205.
AUGUSTUS III, *King of Poland*, candidature, 211, 215; election, 219, 220; 230, 266, 268.
AZZARITI, *Dr.*, 67.

## B

BAKLUIREV, *Jester*, 285, cruel treatment of, 286.
BELGRADE, *Peace of*, 17, 38, 272.
BESTUZHEV-RYUMIN (Alexius Petrovich), *Count*, 285, 306, early career, 306—307; promoted by Biren, 307; 314, procures Biren the Regency, 315—317.
BESTUZHEV-RYUMIN (Michael Petrovich), *Count*, 99, responsible for Sinclaire's murder, 309.
BESTUZHEV-RYUMIN (Peter), *Count*, 97, liaison with Anne Ivanovna, 180; supplanted by Biren, 181.
BIDLO, *Dr.*, 155.
BIREN (Carl), 198.
BIREN (Ernst Johann), *Duke of Courland*, early career and character, 180—181; influence over Anne Ivanovna, 182; honours heaped upon, 185; 187, 188, 193, brutality, 199; venality, 201—202; 203, 204—205, 266, 289, immense wealth, 293; elected Duke of Courland, 293, 294; cruelty, 295—296; tyranny, 297; fears Ostermann, 298—299; promotes Voluinsky, 301; 304, ruins Voluinsky; 305, 306, ambition repulsed, 313; alarm on Empress's illness, 314; intrigues for Regency, 315—316; appointed Regent, 317.
BIREN (Gustav), 198, 274.
BIREN (Magnus), 249.
BIREN (Peter), 313.
BLUMENTROST, *Dr.*, 155.
BOURBON, *Duke of*, 94.
BREDAL, *General*, 261.
BULAVIN (Kondraty), 30.
BUTURLIN (Ivan Ivanovich), 76, 107, 108, 109, 110—111.
BUZHENINOVA (Anna), 284.

## C

CAMPREDON, *French Minister at St. Petersburg*, opinion of P. Tolstoy, 38; 49, 85, 111, 123.

CANTEMIR (Antiochus), *Prince*, 216, 217, 232.
CARLOS, *Infant*, 266.
CASTÈGE, *French Minister at Stockholm*, 204. 228.
CATHERINE, ALEKYSEEVNA, I, *Empress*, 46, origin, 51—52; personal appearance and character, 54—55; becomes Tsaritsa, 55; marriage, 56; correspondence with Peter I, 58—59; coronation, 61; 63, alleged liaison with William Mons, 65—66; accession, 77; 78, wise measures of, 79—80; hostility to England, 95—96; 104, 105, 107, last illness and death, 109—111; character, 112—113; last will, 115.
CATHERINE, ALEKSYEEVNA, II, *Empress*, 113.
CATHERINE, IVANOVNA, *Duchess of Mecklenburg*, 163, 173, 175, character, 179.
CATINAT, *Field Marshal*, 218.
CEDERCREUTZ, *Swedish Minister at St. Petersburg*, 147.
CHARLES VI, *Kaiser*, 106.
CHARLES XI, *King of Sweden*, 29, 82.
CHARLES XII, *King of Sweden*, struggle with Peter I, 29—30; 37, contrasted with Peter, 69—70; 75, 81, 82, 92, 202, 308.
CHARLES FREDERICK, *Duke of Holstein*, 64, early career and character, 81—83; married to Anne Petrovna, 84; 108, 115, expelled from Russia, 125.
CHARLES LEOPOLD, *Duke of Mecklenburg*, 163.
CHARLOTTE, *Princess of Brunswick-Wolfenbüttel*, 32.
CHERKASKY (Alexander), *Prince*, 296, 307.
CHERKASKY (Alexius Michailovich), *Prince*, 167, 173, 174, 184, 186, 187, 274, 314, 315.
CHERNUISHEV, *General*, 176.
CHÉTARDIE, *French Minister at St. Petersburg*, 288, 310—311, 317.
CHMIELNICKI, (Bogdan), *Cossack Ataman*, early career, 12; rebels against Poland, 13—14; final overthrow, 15; submits to Russia, 16; 127.
CHODKIEWICZ (Jan), 271.
CHURCHILL (John), *Duke of Marlborough*, 218.
COPENHAGEN, *Treaty of*, 1727, 97.
COSTA, *Jester*, 285.
CRIMEA, description of, in 1736, 237—238.
CZARNIECKI (Stephen), 15.
CZARTORYSKI, *Prince*, 213.

D

DE CROY, *Duke*, 218.
DEULINO, *Truce of*, 1618, 3.
DEVIER, *General*, 107, 108, 109, 110, 111—112.

DEWITZ, *General*, 246.
DOLGORUKI (Alexius Grigorevich), *Count*, 124, 137, 142, 149, 153, rapacity, 154; indecency, 155—156; plots to place daughter on throne, 159—160; banishment, 184.
DOLGORUKI (Catherine Aleksyeevna), *Princess*, 149, betrothed to Peter II, 152; 156, a candidate for the throne, 159—160; banishment, 184.
DOLGORUKI (George), *Prince*, 184.
DOLGORUKI (Ivan Aleksyeevich), *Prince*, 138, 144, 150, 152, 159, execution, 295.
DOLGORUKI (Ivan Gregorevich), *Prince*, 295.
DOLGORUKI (Michael Vladimirovich), 137, 159, 176, 295.
DOLGORUKI (Sergy Gregorevich), *Prince*, 159, 295.
DOLGORUKI (Vasily Lukich), *Prince*, mission to Sweden, 99—101; 102, 103, 124, character, 136—137; 153, 159, mission to Mittau, 164; 165, 171, 172, 174, appointed Senator, 183; degradation, 184; 189, execution, 295.
DOLGORUKI (Vasily Vladimirovich), *Prince, Field Marshal*, 137, imprisonment, 188; 295.
DONDUK-OMBO, 241.

E

ELIZABETH, PETROVNA, *Tsarevna*. 59, 82, 105, 108, 109, personal appearance at sixteen, and character, 121—123; 133, 140, frivolities, 149—150; persecuted by Dolgorukis, 151; refuses to snatch the crown, 160; 162, 171, beauty and profligacy, 290; 316.
EMANUEL, *Prince of Portugal*, 211.
EUDOXIA, LOPUKHINA, *Tsaritsa*, 32, character, 52; alleged amours, 53; Peter's dislike of, 53—54; 124, reappearance, 139—140; 142, at Peter's death-bed, 156.
EUGENE, *Prince*, 151, 227.

F

FAULKENER (*Sir* Everard), 232, 262.
FERDINAND, *Duke of Courland*, 101, 102.
FINCH (*Hon.* Edward), 229, 288, mission to Russia, 310—311.
FLEURY, *Cardinal*, 94, hostility to Russia, 308.
FORBES (*Lord* George), 215.
FRANCIS STEPHEN, *Duke of Tuscany*, 266.
FRANCIS II, *Prince of Transylvania*, 226.
FREDERICK II, *King of Prussia*, accession, 311.
FREDERICK WILLIAM, *Duke of Courland*, 101, 179, death, 180.

FREDERICK WILLIAM I, *King of Prussia*, 96, 97, 205, ambiguous policy; hostility to Russia, 221 :
FREDERICK, *King of Sweden*, 82, 147.

## G

GANDSCHA, *Treaty of*, 234.
GEORGE DASHKOV, *Archbishop of Rostov*, 116.
GEORGE I, *King of England*, foreign policy, 92—93; 95, 98, 146.
GOERTZ (Henrik von), *Baron*, 48, 82.
GOLITSUIN (Demetrius Michaelovich), *Prince*, 75, 76, 86, 116, 124, 133, character; 135, 140; political views, 161—163; ascendency, 164—165; constitutional projects, 166—167; 173, 177, appointed Senator, 183; 184, persecution of, 296.
GOLITSUIN (Michael Aleksyeevich) *Prince*, cruel treatment of, 283—285
GOLITSUIN (Michael Michaelovich), *Prince, Field Marshal*, 75, 78, character, 135; 140, 164.
GOLITSUIN (Sergy Dmitrovich), *Prince*, mission to Persia, 233.
GOLITSUIN (Vasily Vasilevich), *Prince*, 24.
GOLOVIN (Nikolai), *Count*, 90.
GOLOVKIN (Gabriel Ivanovich), *Count*, early career and character, 39—40; venality, 45; 67, 76, 86, 107, 116, 124, 140, 161, 163, 167, 170, 176, 180, 186, 187.
GOLOVKIN, *Russian Minister at Berlin*, 97, 147.
GORDON, *Admiral*, 223.
GORDON (Patrick), 25, 28.
GREGORY, GHIKA, *Hospodar of Wallachia*, 272.

## H

HARRINGTON, *Lord*, declines Russian alliance, 216; 227, 228.
HERRENHAUSEN, *Treaty of*, 1725, 94.
HESSE-HOMBURG, *Prince*, 188, 242, mutinous conduct in Crimea, 248—249; cowardice at Ochakov, 257; 261.
HORN (Arvid Bernhard), *Count*, pacific policy, 98—99; 147, 229, 303, fall, 309.
HORN, *Dr.*, 67.

## I

ISMAIL, *Grand-Vizier*, 232.
ISMAILOV, *General*, 242.
IVAN V, *Tsar*, 24, 26.
IVAN VI, *Tsar*, 312, birth; 314, accession, 316.

## J

JOACHIM, *Patriarch of Moscow*, 25.
JOHN, SOBIESKI, III, *King of Poland*, 271.
JOHN CASIMIR, *King of Poland*, 14, 15.

## K

KARDIS, *Peace of*, 21st June, 1661, 16.
KEITH (James Francis), early career and character, 255—256; gallantry at siege of Ochakov, 257—258; wounded, 260.
KINNOUL, *Lord*, ambiguous conduct, 231—232.
KIRIK (Luke), intrigues of, 231—232.
KOSTOMAROV, 291, 292.
KRIJANIĆ, 23.
KRUSE (Cornelius), 47.
KULI KHAN. See NADIR, *Shah*.
KURAKIN (Alexander Borisovich), *Prince*, 286.
KURAKIN, *Russian Minister at Paris*, 94, 146.

## L

LACY (Peter), *Field Marshal*, 214, early career, 218—219; besieges Dantzic, 220—222; 223, sent to the Rhine, 227; arrival in Ukraine, 1736, 240; differences with Münnich, 241; 242, 246, captures Azov, 1736, 250—251; 253, invades Crimea, 1737, 261; and 1738, 265; 274.
LA MOTTE PEROUSE, *General*, 223, 224.
LEFORT (François), 25, 42, 53.
LEFORT, *Saxon Minister at St. Petersburg*, 78, 104, 122, 126, 128, 134, 145, 147, 154—155.
LEONTIEV, *General*, 164, 239, 242, 246.
LESTOCQ, *Dr.*, 160.
LEVENHAUPT (Adam), 156.
LIRIA, *Duke of*, 50, 123, 136, description of, 141—142; 143, account of Grand Duchess Natalia, 148—149; 150, 151, 152.
LOBKOWITZ, *Prince*, 272.
LOUIS XV, *King of France*, 94, 123, 203, 220.
LÖWENWOLDE (Carl Gustaf von), *Count*, 185, 209, 314, 315.
LÖWENWOLDE (Friedrich Casimir), *Count*, 210, 211, 215.
LÖWENWOLDE (Reinhold), *Count*, 185.
LUBOMIRSKY, *Prince*, 212.
LYNAR, *Count*, 290.

## M

MACKENZIE, *English Minister at St. Petersburg*, 45.
MAGNON, *French Minister at St. Petersburg*, 201—202, 203.
MAKAROV (Alexius Vasilevich), 77, 124, persecution of, 296.
MAMANOV, *General*, 78.

MANSTEIN, *General*, as to Dolgorukis, 160; account of siege of Ochakov, 258—259; as to Russian soldiery, 261; as to Anne's Court, 288; 291.
MARDEFELDT, *Prussian Minister at St. Petersburg*, as to Tolstoy, 38; as to Golovkin, 40; as to Menshikov, 46; 50, 72, 87, 122.
MARIA, MNISHKA, *Tsaritsa*, 60.
MARY, LESZCZYNSKA, *Queen of France*, 94.
MATVYEEV (Artamon Sergyeevich), 24.
MATVYEEVA (Eudoxia Grigorevna), 24.
MAURICE, *of Saxony*, elected Duke of Courland, 104—105; 146, 182.
MAZEPPA, *Cossack Ataman*, 43.
MENA (Nikita). See Nikon.
MENSHIKOV (Alexander Danilovich), *Prince*, early career, 42—44; venality, 46—47; 52, 63, 64, 68, energetically supports Catherine I, 71—74; 75, 76, 80, great influence of, 81; 86, 90, 102, 103, 104, 105, 106, won over to Peter II, 107; ruins Tolstoy, 110—111; ascendency, 124—125; wise administration, 126—127; tyranny, 128; quarrels with Peter II, 129—130; and with Ostermann, 131—132; fall, 132—134; banishment and death, 142—143.
MENSHIKOVA (Daria Arsenevaya), *Princess*, 43, 134.
MENSHIKOVA (Maria Aleksandrovna), *Princess*, 128, 134.
MICHAEL I, *Tsar*, 3.
MIKHAILOV (Peter). *See* Peter I.
MININ (Kozma), 2.
MITTAU, *Articles of*, 164—165.
MOGILA (Peter), *Patriarch of Kiev*, 8.
MONS (Anna), liaison with Peter I, 53—54.
MONS (Wilhelm), alleged liaison with Catherine I, 65—66.
MONTI, *Count*, 207, 225.
MOSCOW, *Peace of*, 1686, 24.
MÜNNICH (Burkhard Christoph), *Count, Field Marshal*, 147, early career and character, 188—192; rapid rise under Anne, 192; ambition and arrogance, 193; intrigues of, 203; 204, 218, 219, besieges Dantzic, 221—222; 234, 237, 238, 239, campaign of 1736, 240; differences with Lacy, 241; advances through steppes, 242—243; storms Perekop, 244—245; advance through Crimea, 246—247; quells mutiny, 248—249; 253, 255, campaign of 1737, 256; storms Ochakov, 257—260; 262, campaign of 1738, 263—264; quarrels with Austrian Court, 265—266; wins battle of Stavuchanakh, 269—271; takes Chocim, 268; 271—272, 274, 276, vanity, 298; 314, supports Regency of Biren, 315.

# N

NADIR, *Shah of Persia*, victories over Turks, 231; arrogance towards Russia, 233; treaty with Russia, 234; usurps Persian throne, 264; expedition against India, 267—268.

NARISHKINOVA (Natalia). 24.
NATALIA, ALEKSYEEVNA, *Tsarevna*, 54.
NATALIA, ALEKSYEEVNA, *Grand Duchess*, 110, 116, description of, 122, 124, quarrels with Menshikov, 129; 138—139, 145, death 148—149.
NEMIROV, *Congress of*, 1737, 262.
NEPLUYEV (Ivan Ivanovich), 229, diplomatic zeal; 230—231; urges war with Porte, 232.
NESTOROV, execution of, 61.
NIKON, *Patriarch of Moscow*, early career, 20; reforms, 21—22.
NOSSOV (Jakob). 30.
NOVOKSHCHENOVA (Tatiana), 279.
NYSTAD, *Treaty of*, 1720, 48, 49.

O

OCHAKOV, *Siege of* 1737, 257—259.
ORDIN-NASHCHOKIN (Athanasius), 23.
OSTEIN, *Austrian Minister at St. Petersburg*, 181, quarrel with Biren, 26
OSTERMANN (Andrei Ivanovich), *Count*, early career and characte 47—49; services at Peace of Nystad, 49; Peter I's high opinio of, 49—50; diplomatic astuteness, 50—51; establishes Suprem Privy Council, 84, 86; hostility to England, 96; 105, 106, 10; 116, educates Peter II, 118—121; 124, 128, rupture with Men shikov, 131—132; 134; differences with the Dolgorukis, 137—138 139, 140, 141, 145, 148, 151, devotion to dying Peter II, 156; 161 165, services to Anne Ivanovna, 172; 183, establishes Cabinet, 186—187; 192, 193, 201, 202, 204, 216, 217, 226, 232, declares war against Turkey, 1735, 234; 252, 266, accepts mediation of France, 1738, 267; 268, declines England's advances, 1739, 276; commanding position, 1739, 298; the "Oracle" of Russia, 299, 311; last interview with Empress Anne, 316—317.
OZAROUSKY, 226.
OZTROZHKY (Constantine), *Count*, 7, 8.

P

PASSAROWITZ, *Peace of*, 272.
PEDRILLO, *Jester*, 285, 287.
PEREKOP, storm of, 244—245.
PESAREV (Gregory), 190—191.
PETER I, *Tsar*, accession, 24; early years, 25—26; first foreign tour, 26—27; cruelty, 28; struggle with Charles XII, 29—30; Turkish war, 31; murder of Tsarevich Alexius, 32—33; reforms, 34—35; opinion of Tolstoy, 38; hatred of venality, 44—45; punishes

Menshikov, 46—47; first meeting with Ostermann, 48—50; 52, hatred of first wife, 53; low ideals, 53; liaison with Anna Mons, 53—54; first encounter with Catherine, 54—55; his love for her, 55—57; correspondence with, 58—59; Ukaz against primogeniture, 59; coronation Ukaz, 60; brutality, 61; at Catherine's coronation, 62—63; last illness and death, 67—69; character, 69—70; relations with Duke of Holstein, 82—83; 178, fondness for dwarfs, 179; 180, employs Münnich, 190—191; 194, 195, 196, 218, designs Lines of the Ukraine, 238.

PETER II, *Tsar*, 59, 72, 73, 84, 105, 108, 109, 110, accession, 115; 116, early years, 116—117; education, 118—121; quarrel with Menshikov, 128—129, 130; final rupture with Menshikov, 132; 134, demoralized by the Dolgorukis. 138—139; 140, neglects study, 143—144; personal appearance, 144, 150; hunting exploits, 152; betrothal to Catherine Dolgoruki. 152; robbed by Dolgorukis, 153—154; last illness and death, 155—157.

PETER, *Duke of Holstein*, 126.
PETER, Petrovich, *Grand Duke*, 58—59.
POLETSKY (Simeon), 23.
POLYANKOVA, *Peace of*, 1634, 3.
PONIATOWSKI (Stanislaus), 207, 209, 213, 225.
POOL (Gerrit), 27.
POTOCKI (Nicholas), *Count*, 226.
POTOCKI (Theodore), *Archbishop of Gnesen*, character and policy, 206—207; energy, 208; 209, 210, 212, 213.
POTSYEI (Hypatius), *Bishop of Vladimir*. 7.
POZHARSKY, (Demetrius), *Prince*, 2.
PRASKOVIA, *Tsaritsa*, 163, 178, 180.
PROTASZEVICZ (Valerian), *Bishop of Wilna*, 16.

# R

RABUTIN, 106.
RADZIWILL, *Prince*, 212.
RADZIEWSKY, *Count*, 212.
RAZIN (Stenka), 17.
RONDEAU (Claudius), 50, 144, 146, as to Russian Navy, 147; 169, 186, 187, as to Anne's Court, 195—196; 215, 217, 223, 225, 232, 238, 254, account of storming of Ochakov, 259; 262, 310.
RONDEAU, *Lady*, as to Anne's Court, 176; 224, as to personal appearance of Anne, 278—279; 283, 291, 292, 312.
RTISHEHEV (Theodore Michaelovich), 22.
RUDOMINA, *Count*, 214—215.
RUMYANTSEV (Alexander Ivanovich), *Count*, courageous protest against Anne's extravagance, 197; 255.
RYEPNIN (Anicetus Ivanovich), 75, 76.

## S

SACKEN, *Herr von*, abduction of, 294.
SAGAIDACHNY, *Cossack Ataman*, 12.
SALTUIKOV, *General*, 133, 175, 279.
SANCHEZ, *Dr.*, 317.
SAPIEHA, *Count*, 115.
SAPIEHA (Leo), *Count*, 8.
SEVILLE, *Treaty of*, 1729, 146.
SHAFIROV, *Vice-Chancellor*, 48, 50, 64, 124.
SHAKOVSKY (Jacob), *Prince*, 297.
SHCHERBATOV, *Prince*, 287.
SHCHERBATOVA, *Princess*, 313.
SHEREMETEV, *Field Marshal*, 52.
SHEREMETEVA (Natalia), 279.
SIGISMUND III, *King of Poland*, 7.
SINCLAIRE (Malcolm), murder of, 309—310.
SKOVRONSKY (Samuel), 52.
SKOVRONSKAYA, (Martha). *See* Catherine I.
SKOVRONSKAYA (Sophia), 110.
SLAVENETSKY (Epiphanius), 23.
SOPHIA, ALEKSYEEVNA, *Tsarevna*, 24—25, 28.
SPIEGEL, *General*, 151, 242.
STANISLAUS I, LESZCZYNSKI, *King of Poland*, 202, 203, 204, 207, elected King the second time 208—209; 211, 212, 213, negotiates with Tsaritsa Anne, 214; 215, 217, besieged in Dantzic, 220—222; 225, 226, 228, 230, 266.
STAVUCHANAKH, *Battle of*, 1738, 269—271.
STEPHEN, BÁTORY, *King of Poland*, 11.
STOFFEL, *General*, 246, 261.
STOLBOWA, *Peace of*, 1617, 3.
STREITNER VON STERNFELD, 26.

## T

TAHMASH KULI KHAN. *See* NADIR, *Shah*.
TARLO (Adam), 208, 226, 227.
TATISHCHEV (Vasily Nikolaevich), 296.
TERLETSKY (Cyril), 7.
THEODORE I, *Tsar*, 1.
THEODORE II, *Tsar*, 23, 24.
THEODOSIUS YAVORSKY, *Archbishop of Novgorod*, 60, 62, 74; degradation, 89—91.
THEOPHANES, *Archbishop of Novgorod*, 62, 63, 68, 91, 166, 171, 173.
THEOPHYLACTUS, *Archbishop of Tver*, 117.

TIAGYA, *Seraskier*, 256.
TOLSTOY (Peter Andryeevich), *Count*, 33, early career and character, 37—38; 60, 67, 72, 74, 75, 76, 81, 86, rivalry with Menshikov, 107—108; 109, fall of, 110—111.
TREDYAKOVSKY (Vasily Karlovich), brutal ill-treatment of, 302—303.
TRUBETSKOY, *Prince*, 142, 173, 206, 242.

## U

USHAKOV, *General*, 295.
USUPOV, *General*, 173, 174, 175.
USUPOVA (Praskovia), cruel persecution of, 296—297.

## V

VALI, *Pasha, Seraskier*, 269.
VANATOVICH, *Metropolitan of Kiev*, 292.
VASILY IV, *Tsar*, 2.
VIENNA, *Treaty of*, 1725, 94.
VIENNA, *Treaty of*, 1738, 266.
VILLENEUVE, *Marquis de*, 229, urges Porte to make war with Russia, 230; 231, 267, negotiates Peace of Constantinople, 273.
VISHNYAKOV, diplomatic activity at Constantinople, 254—255; 273, 274.
VOLKONSKY (Nikita Thedorovich), 285.
VOLKONSKAYA (Agrafina), 286.
VOLKOV (Euphemius), 179.
VOLUINSKY (Artemius Petrovich), *Count*, early career and character, 300; subsurvience to Biren, 301; brutal conduct to Tredyakovsky, 302—303; 304, execution, 305—306.

## W

WAGER, *Admiral*, 95.
WALPOLE (Horace), *Earl of Orford*, 216, 276.
WALPOLE (Robert), *Earl of Orford*, 217, 229.
WARD, *Mr.* 146.
WELCZEK, *Count*, 210.
WHITWORTH, *Lord*, 30, anecdote of Peter I, 56.
WIESNIEWICKI, *Prince*, 212.
WILLIAM III, *King of England*, 26.
WISNIOWIECKI (Jeremiah), *Prince*, 14.
WITTE, *Colonel*, 242.
WLADISLAUS IV, *King of Poland*, 12.
WOODWARD, *Mr.*, 217.
WRATISLAW, *Count*, 151, 217.

## Y

YAGUZHINSKY (Paul Ivanovich), *Count*, early career and character, 40—41; venality, 45; drunkenness, 48; 74, 75, 80, 86, 103, 104, 107, 124, 140, opposition to the Golitsuins, 167; arrest, 168; release, 176; made Senator, 184; influence, 186; envoy to Berlin, 187; 201, 202, 215, 299, 300, death, 300.

## Z

ZAGRYAZHSHAYA (Eudoxia), 279.
ZEIKIN (János), 117.

Peter the Great.

# THE PUPILS OF PETER THE GREAT.

## CHAPTER I.

### INTRODUCTORY—SEVENTEENTH CENTURY RUSSIA.

THE first Romanov—Misery of Eastern Russia, or Muscovy, in the 17th century—Partition of her dominions—Lithuania, or Western Russia—Her origin—Union with Poland—Condition of Poland at this time—Causes of her decline—Vicious constitution—Religious dissensions—The Protestants and the Jesuits—Struggle between the Jesuits and the Greek Orthodox Church—Origin of the Lithuanian Uniates—Increase of religious bitterness—Origin of the Cossacks—Description of the Ukraine—Rebellion of Bogdan Chmielnicki—His bloody wars with Poland—Tsar Alexius I—Peace of Kardis—Condition of 17th century Muscovy—Impediments to civilization—Byzantinism—Ignorance—Tyranny of custom—The Muscovite women—The Patriarch Nikon and his reforms—The new men—Slavenetsky—Poletsky Krijanić—Influence of Poland—And of the "Dutch Suburb"—Artamon Matvyeev—Tsar Theodore Aleksyeevich—The Tsarevna Sophia—Early years of Peter the Great—His first foreign tour—Horror with which his reforms were regarded in Russia—Revolt of the Stryeltsui—Peter's foreign policy—War with Charles XII—Peace of the Pruth—Murder of the Tsarevich Alexius—Internal Administration—The Tsardom of Muscovy becomes the Empire of Russia.

AT the beginning of the 17th century, the Tsardom of Muscovy, as Eastern Russia was then called, seemed to be in the throes of political dissolution. On the death of Ivan the Terrible's only son, Theodore I, in 1598, the line of Rurik, which had ruled Russia for centuries, came abruptly to an end, and within the next thirteen years, no fewer than four usurpers, most of them men of unusual ability, vainly endeavoured to govern the thoroughly demoralized nation. With the disappearance of the last of these usurpers, Vasily IV (Shuisky), into a monastery (1610), the horrors of an interregnum were added to Muscovy's other troubles, and, during the next three years, her ever hostile neighbours, Sweden and Poland, disputed with each other for the possession of the disintegrated realm. But deliverance was at hand. In Kozma Minin, a man of lowly origin, and in Prince Demetrius Pozharsky, Muscovy found at last liberators from the yoke of the foreigner. In October 1612, the Polish garrison was compelled to abandon Moscow, and in February 1613, the boyars assembled in the *Krasnaya Ploshchad*, or "Beautiful Square," of the "Golden Headed City,"[1] to elect a native Tsar. Their choice fell unanimously on Michael Romanov, a gentle and God-fearing youth of sixteen, much more fitted to be a monk than a monarch, especially in those troublous times, but possessing the sovereign merit, in the eyes of the electors, of being a descendant, in the female line, of the ancient Ruriks. Amidst the joyful tears of his long-suffering subjects, the new monarch proceeded from his estate at Dumnina to Moscow. All along the line of route he was greeted by mobs of half-famished wretches, who had been rendered homeless by the predatory bands of the Swedes and Poles and their own countrymen, and whose rags scarce concealed the horrible wounds and mutilations they had suffered at the hands of their tormentors. Ruin and desolation met the eyes of Michael on every side. The country houses of the gentry, the churches and monasteries, were without roofs, doors and windows; the *isbas*, or huts of the peasantry, had everywhere been burned to the ground. The land

[1] Moscow was so called from the number and beauty of the golden domes and cupolas of its churches.

swarmed with freebooters, most of the towns lay in ashes, Moscow itself was half in ruins. Trade and commerce had quite died out, even agriculture was ceasing, for the peasants were perishing by hundreds in the midst of the cornfields they had not the strength to reap. Fortunately, the young sovereign had by his side, during the first thirteen years of his reign, a prudent and influential counsellor, in the person of his own father, the Patriarch of Moscow, Philarete, who did something to heal the nation of its deadly wounds, and nurse it into convalescence. The first care of the new government was to get rid of the foreigner, but this could only be done at a heavy cost. The enemies of Muscovy had indeed, by this time, dismissed, as impracticable, the original project of partitioning her vast domains amongst them, but they determined, at least, to make her perfectly innocuous for many generations. Poland would be satisfied with nothing less than the whole of White Russia and the Ukraine,[1] and the western part of Severia (truce of Deulino, 1618, and supplementary peace of Polyankowa, 5th June, 1634), while Sweden by the "eternal peace" of Stolbowa (17th Feb., 1617) acquired Kexholm, Carelia, and Ingria. These treaties threw Muscovy further back towards the East than she had ever been thrown before. She was now altogether cut off from the Baltic, the great water-courses of the Dnieper and Desna became the exclusive property of Poland, and a whole group of her ancient possessions, notably the venerable Kiev, the mother of all the Russian cities, and the chief centre of her nascent civilization, passed into the hands of the detested Latins. Nevertheless, these sacrifices gave to Muscovy the rest and quiet for want of which she was perishing, and thereby enabled her gradually to recruit her strength for future efforts and ventures. For the next half century or so, however, she may be said

[1] See Map.

to have lain in a heavy, though not always tranquil, slumber, knowing little of what was going on in the world around her, and of no account whatever in the councils of Europe. During this period her fate was being decided for her elsewhere, and it is to Western Russia, or Lithuania, that we must look, during the first five decades of the 17th century, for the causes which led to the gradual awakening, both politically and intellectually, of the mighty Muscovite colossus.

At the beginning of the 17th century, Lithuania was the name given to the eastern portion of the great Polish Republic which embraced the whole of the vast plain lying between Courland, Moldavia, the upper Desna and the Bug, a territory nearly half as large again as modern France. Originally, indeed, that is to say at the beginning of the 13th century, the confines of Lithuania comprised little more than the watershed of the Niemen, but her valiant pagan inhabitants, under the lead of an extraordinary succession of able Princes, rapidly extended her dominions at the expense of her Slavonic neighbours, to the south and east, so that by the middle of the 15th century she had grown into one of the most powerful states of Europe. By this time, too, the land had been partially christianized and civilized through the influence of Poland, with whom the Lithuanian Grand Dukes (for that was their title) had always been closely allied, and after the election of the the Grand Duke Alexander as King of Poland, in 1501, the two States continued to obey one and the same Sovereign, although it was not till the Union of Lublin (1569) that the two Governments were permanently and completely united. After this great event, Lithuania, despite a few peculiar rights and privileges, must, for all practical purposes, be regarded as an integral portion of the Polish Republic. By far the greater portion of Lithuania consisted of Russian territory, that is to say territory which had been wrested, from time to time, from the independent Russian Princes in the fourteenth and fifteenth centuries, such as White Russia, Black Russia, and Little Russia. The inhabitants of these provinces spoke a dialect closely akin to the language of Great Russia or Muscovy, and, like the subjects of the Tsar, were staunch adherents of the Greek Orthodox Religion. The Tsars of Muscovy, moreover, never abandoned the hope of recovering these portions of the original old Russian land, but this hope, at the beginning of the 17th century, had become faint indeed, for, to all appearance, Poland was destined to remain the great Slavonic power, and as such all Europe regarded her.

But, in reality, the brief period of Poland's greatness was over, and her swift decline had already begun. The primary cause of the ruin of the most chivalrous and romantic of Republics, was her incurably vicious constitution. On the death of the last Jagellon, in 1572, the Polish crown had been made purely elective, and the chief authority of the State was vested in the *Sejm* or Diet, a tumultuous assembly of noblemen and gentlemen (the towns had long ceased to be represented therein), every member of which enjoyed the unassailable privilege of instantaneously terminating its proceedings by interposing his individual veto, whereupon the assembly had to be adjourned, and all the previous resolutions, even those upon which the veto in question had no direct bearing, became *ipso facto* null and void. When towards the middle of the 16th century, the *liberum veto*, as it was called, was used so frequently that all legislation, and indeed the whole machinery of government, came to a standstill, the Poles hit upon a corrective, which proved infinitely more mischievous than the original evil. This was the right accorded to every member of the Diet to form an armed "Confederation" to support the views of the majority or minority of the *Sejm*, as the case might be, by force of arms if necessary, despite the interposition of the *liberum veto*, and thus the government of Poland gradually drifted into what can only be called a constitutional anarchy tempered by civil war. During the recesses of the Diet, the Senate, a council of magnates, held sway, and on the demise of the Crown, the Primate of Poland, the Archbishop of Gnesen, officiated as interrex till a new sovereign was elected. The so-called King was a mere state decoration. He could neither levy taxes, nor declare war, nor contract alliances, without being previously authorised to do so by the *Sejm*. He was not even consulted as to the choice of his successor, and was obliged to sign everything that his council chose to lay before him. Even treaties with foreign powers were concluded in the name of the King and of the Republic. And presently religious difficulties were superadded to this political confusion. Between 1548 and 1572, Protestantism made its way into Poland, and, so far from being regarded as a fresh danger, was tolerated, and even protected by the *Sejm*. From Poland it spread into Lithuania, where its inherent tendency to split up into sects, caused no small strife and dissension. Fortunately, its progress was speedily arrested by the growing influence of the Jesuits, who were invited into Lithuania within forty years after the establishment of their order by Valerian Protaszevicz, Bishop of Wilna. Their success was extraordinary. The splendour of their churches, the eloquence of their preaching, the excellence of the education they offered to all men, irrespective of class or creed, attracted general attention; the heroism they displayed in the time of the great plague of 1571, won for them whole hosts of grateful adherents; and their triumph over Protestantism was assured when the great Lithuanian magnates, the Radziwills, the Sapiehas, and the Chodkiewiczes, who had hitherto professed Calvinism, became their spiritual children. They soon proceeded to turn their arms against the Greek Orthodox Church, and their task seemed an easy one, especially when, in 1586, their pupil Sigismund III ascended the Polish throne. The Greek Church itself at this time was in a very unsatisfactory condition. The bishops, for the most part, lived in pomp and state like secular lords, quite neglectful of their pastoral duties, while the lower clergy were appointed at the will of the local magnates, and treated like serfs. So ignorant too was the bulk of the local clergy, that their own co-religionists among the laity were ashamed of what the more enlightened Jesuits scoffingly called "the serfs' religion." At last many of the Greek Prelates themselves, and even such men as the wealthy and intelligent Palatine of Kiev, Constantine Oztrozhky, who spent thousands of ducats in educating his fellow-countrymen and established costly printing-presses at his own castle of Ostrog, where the first Slavonic Bible was printed,—even such pillars of Orthodoxy as he began to despair, and look towards Rome. A step in this direction was taken by the Bishops of Lutz, Lemberg, and Pinsk, who petitioned the King for leave to open negotiations with Rome for a union of the Churches. In 1593 they won a valuable ally in the zealous and energetic Hypatius Potsyei, Bishop of Vladimir, a relation of Oztrozhky, who with Cyril Terletsky, Bishop of Lutsk, set off for Rome in 1595, where the Pope received them in solemn audience, "with unspeakable courtesy and kindness." After numerous conferences, they made a full confession of the Roman Faith on a copy of the Gospels, as the representatives of the Greek Uniates, as those desiring union with Rome were thenceforth called, and were formally received into the Church, with leave to preserve their own ritual. But it soon appeared that this so-called Union of the Churches had only introduced another element of discord into the already distracted Republic. The whole matter was submitted to the *Sejm* for confirmation, and ultimately sanctioned, but not till after scenes of violence which brought Poland and Lithuania to the very verge of a bloody civil war. Petitions were presented to the King and Diet to depose the prelates who had negotiated with the Pope, without the previous knowledge of their own Patriarch. Oztrozhky publicly declared that he would rather take up arms than acknowledge the apostates as true bishops. The orthodox prelates solemnly cursed their uniate brethren, and fiery sermons were preached against the Pope himself. Moreover, the attempts of the Uniate Bishops to drive their Orthodox rivals from their sees, and the audacity with which they appropriated their churches, caused intense anguish and bitterness throughout Little Russia and the Ukraine. A reaction in favour of Orthodoxy began. Even Count Leo Sapieha, the head of the Lithuanian Catholics, protested against the violence of the Jesuits. The Diet of 1622 confirmed the rights and privileges of the orthodox population, and forbade all ecclesiastical suits as only leading to unchristian hatred. The death of the fanatical Sigismund III (1632) gave the Orthodox Greeks fresh hopes, while the sweeping reforms and princely liberality of the great Patriarch Peter Mogila, who had the wisdom and courage to introduce schools and colleges on the Jesuit model, did much to revive the ancient glory of the Russian Church, and make Kiev a bulwark of Orthodoxy. Yet, for all this, the tide of Catholicism continued to steadily rise. The Jesuit schools superseded all other, except in the diocese of Kiev, and nearly the whole of the nobility and gentry of Lithuania and the Ukraine were gradually latinized. But the mass of the population still clung, with true Slavonic tenacity, to the faith of their fathers; the gap which already divided the upper and lower classes in Lithuania, was still further widened, and the Lithuanian serf's natural hatred of a hard master, was intensified by the growing conviction that that master was an infidel and a heretic, as well as a tyrant. Thus the materials for a terrible *jacquerie* were already to hand, and it needed only a spark of fanaticism to kindle the conflagration. This spark was at last supplied by the rebellion of the Cossacks, which reduced the fairest provinces of Poland to a desert, and shook the Polish commonwealth to its very base.

But first it is necessary to say a word of explanation as to the origin and early history of those picturesque freebooters—the Cossacks.

At the beginning of the 16th century, the vast steppes stretching south-eastward of Poland, from the Dnieper to the Don, had no settled population. Hunters and fishermen used to frequent the banks and forests of the Dnieper, from spring to autumn, returning home laden with rich store of fish and pelts, while runaway serfs occasionally settled, in small communities, beneath the shelter of the line of fortresses built, from time to time, to guard the southern frontiers of the Republic. The incursions of the nomadic Tartar hordes made the Ukraine,[1] as that borderland was called, unsafe to dwell in; but gradually, as the lot of the Polish serf grew more and more intolerable, the steppes of the Ukraine became a place of refuge for all who loved liberty better than life itself. There, at any rate, the fugitives found freedom, plenty, and little to do. The climate of the Ukraine, for seven months out of the twelve, was superb. Its famous black soil, the most fertile in Europe, could produce fifty, seventy, and even a hundred fold. The succulent wild grass of the steppes grew so high that horses

[1] *Ukrain* is the Ruthenian word for a border or boundary, corresponding with the Russian *Okrain*.

grazing in it were invisible a dozen yards off, and only the tips of the horns of the cattle could be discerned above it. Rivers, alive with fish, intersected this new Canaan in every direction, and the forests that lined their banks were rich with every sort of game and fruit, and literally flowed with wild honey. Nor was the element of adventure, so dear to the true Slav, wanting to complete the happiness of the first settlers. Obliged, for fear of the Tartars, to go about constantly with arms in their hands, they gradually grew strong enough to raid their raiders, and sold the rich booty thus acquired, to the merchants of Muscovy and Poland. Nay, the Basurmán, as they called the Turks and Tartars, being the most inveterate enemies of Christendom, a war of extermination against them was regarded not only as an exciting pastime, but also as a sacred duty. Curiously enough, however, these champions of orthodoxy borrowed the name, which has stuck to them ever since, from their "dog-headed"[1] adversaries. The rank and file of the Tartar soldiery were known as Kazaks or Cossacks, and this title gradually came to be applied to all the free dwellers in the Ukraine. As time went on, the number of the Cossacks multiplied exceedingly, spreading all over the south-eastern districts of Poland. Their daring grew with their numbers, and at last they came to be a constant annoyance, not merely to the Tartar Khan, but to the Turkish Padishah himself. Their light cavalry swarmed throughout the Ukraine, while their swift *chaiki*, or sailing-boats, haunted the Sea of Azov and the Black Sea, ravaged the coasts of Asia Minor, and sometimes penetrated as far as Stambul itself. But their incursions were most frequently directed against the Tartars, and thousands of Christian captives were rescued by them from the slave marts and the Katorgi, or galley prisons, of Kaffa and other Crimean towns. The Polish

[1] "Dog-headed" was the usual epithet applied by the Cossack to the Tartar.

Government was quick to perceive the value of these hardy but restless freebooters, and endeavoured to organize them into a regular auxiliary force. The great Hungarian, Stephen Bátory, who sat on the Polish throne from 1575 to 1586, enrolled the pick of them into six regiments of 1,000 men, each with an allotted district, and fixed the town of Trakhtimirov as their head-quarters; but ultimately it was transferred to the island of Khortitsa, just below the falls of the Dnieper, and on the numerous islands of that broad river there gradually grew up the famous Cossack Republic, or *Zaporozhskaya Syech*. For the more prudent of the Polish rulers judged it necessary to leave the Cossacks as free as possible, allowing them, so long as they fulfilled their chief obligation of guarding the frontiers of the Republic from the Tartar raids, a liberal measure of self-government. The Cossack *Kosh* or Community, had the privilege of electing its *Koshevoi Ataman*, or chief of the *Kosh*, and his chief officers the *Starshins*, which election took place annually in the midst of the *Maidan*, or great square, in front of the church of the Syech. The *Koshevoi* received the insignia of his office [1] from the King of Poland direct; but he was responsible for his actions to the *Kosh* alone, and an enquiry into his conduct during his year of office was held at the expiration of that term in the *Obschchaya Skhodka* or general assembly, where complaints against him were invited and considered. In times of peace his power was little more than that of the responsible minister of a limited monarchy, but in warfare he was absolute dictator, and disobedience to his orders in the field was punished with death. Notable, indeed, were the services which the Cossacks rendered to the Polish crown. Thus, in 1620, to take only a single instance, when an innumerable

[1] They consisted of the *Bulawa* or bâton, the *Banschuk*, a pole with a horse's tail attached to it, a banner and a seal.

Turkish host suddenly appeared on the Dniester and besieged the Poles in Khotin, the great Cossack Ataman, Sagaidachny, hastened to their assistance, at the head of 40,000 men, and compelled the Turks to raise the siege. But though often a bulwark, the Cossacks were still oftener more or less of a menace to the Republic, and this was especially the case with the unregistered or "free Cossacks" who swarmed over the Ukraine in tens of thousands. Accustomed to a boundless liberty, they were impatient of the slightest restraint, and, regarding themselves as the sworn champions of the Orthodox Faith, they watched the progress of Catholicism with a jealous eye. Between 1635 and 1640, the efforts of the *Sejm* to reduce the numbers, and restrict the privileges of the Cossacks, led to two terrible revolts, which were only repressed with difficulty, and the most savage ferocity; but it was the great rebellion of Bogdan Chmielnicki which first revealed the real power of the Cossacks.

It was at the manor of Subbotova, near the little town of Chigirin, that the most terrible of all the Cossack Atamans was born. After receiving an, for those days, excellent education at a Jesuit Seminary, where he perfectly mastered the Latin and Polish languages, Bogdan entered the ranks of the Cossacks, was taken captive during his first campaign, and detained at Stambul for two years, where he taught himself Turkish and French. On returning home he found that a personal enemy had burnt his manor house, and abducted his wife, and, unable to obtain any redress at Warsaw, he invaded Lithuania, at the head of the Zaporogean Cossacks and a large auxiliary force of Tartars, and utterly routed two large armies sent against him. The chaotic interregnum which supervened in Poland on the death of Wladislaus IV, materially assisted him, and at the first summons of the fiery Ataman, who eloquently appealed to the religious prejudices of his ignorant hearers, the whole population of the Ukraine rose against their rulers, and a *Khlopskaya zloba*, or "serfs' fury" burst forth, the like of which is fortunately unknown in Western Europe. For hundreds of miles around the gentry were hunted down, flayed, burnt, blinded, and sawn asunder. Every manor house and castle was reduced to ashes. Every Uniate and Catholic priest that could be caught, was hung up before his own high altar, along with a Jew and a hog. Everyone who shaved his head after the Polish fashion, or wore Polish costume, was instantly cut down by the *haidamaki*, as Chmielnicki's savage bands were called. The panic-stricken inhabitants fled to the few strongholds, and soon the rebels were swarming all over Volhynia, Podolia, and Galicia. Even now, however, the Polish Government did not properly realize its danger. The army of 40,000 men that took the field in 1648, was composed entirely of nobles, and rather resembled a bridal procession than a battle array. These splendid cavaliers dressed themselves in magnificent ermine-trimmed mantles; heron plumes waved from their jewelled caps; their spurs were of gold and silver, and their saddles and shabracks ablaze with precious stones. For Chmielnicki and his host, they expressed the most sovereign contempt. "This rabble must be chased with whips, not smitten with swords," they cried. On 23rd Sept., 1648, the two armies encountered each other on the banks of the river Pilyavok, and, in a few hours, the gallant Polish pageant was scattered to the winds. The steppe, for miles around, was strewn with corpses, and the Cossacks reaped 10,000,000 worth of booty when the fight was over. All Poland now lay at Chmielnicki's feet, and a two days' march would have brought him in triumph to the defenceless capital. But he wasted two precious months before the insignificant fortress of Zamość, and then the newly elected King of Poland,

John Casimir, persuaded him to retire to Kiev, there to await the Polish commissioners who were to treat with him. In June 1649, Chmielnicki, mounted on a white horse, made his triumphal entry through the golden gates of Jaroslaw, and at the door of the Cathedral of St. Sophia, the Metropolitan and clergy saluted him as the new Moses who had freed the Ukraine from the Polish bondage. On the arrival of the commissioners, however, he imposed terms of peace far too humiliating to be accepted from a rebellious vassal, and war again broke out. This time Chmielnicki ordered a *levée en masse* of the population (only the women, children, and old men remaining at home) and, reinforced by the Tartars invaded Poland with a countless host. Fortunately for the Republic at this crisis, she found a champion in Prince Jeremiah Wisniowiecki, a fanatical Catholic convert, of heroic valour, and no mean military capacity, who kept the whole Cossack host at bay in the fortress of Zborow, while John Casimir, that strangely interesting Prince, who had already exchanged a Jesuit cassock for a royal mantle, and was to resign a throne for a monk's cell before he died, hastened to Wisniowiecki's assistance. For a whole month Chmielnicki besieged the Poles, giving them no rest night or day, and reducing them, at last, to such straits, that they buried themselves in holes "like toads," to escape his darts and bullets, and gladly fed on offal. But John Casimir was now fast approaching to relieve them, with 20,000 men, and, after a drawn battle on the banks of the River Stripa, Chmielnicki, who had become suspicious of his Tartar allies, concluded peace in the camp of the Polish King, exacting, indeed, his own terms, but, at the same time, respectfully doing homage to the monarch, on his bended knee. For the next two years Chmielnicki ruled little Russia and the Ukraine like a sovereign Prince. He divided the country into sixteen provinces, made his native place Chigorin the Cossack Capital, and levied taxes to maintain his government. But the pride of Poland could not brook for long such an insulting triumph, and, in 1651, a third war broke out between Suzerain and subject which speedily assumed the dignity and the dimensions of a crusade. Chmielnicki was now regarded not merely as a rebel Cossack Ataman, but as the arch-enemy of Catholicism in Eastern Europe. The pope granted a plenary absolution to all who took up arms against him, and sent John Casimir his benediction and a consecrated banner. But Bogdan also was not without ecclesiastical sanction. The Archbishop of Corinth girded him with a sword that had lain upon the Holy Sepulchre, and the patriarch of Kiev blessed the snow-white standard under which he rode forth to battle, dressed in purple and ermine, which bore upon it, in letters of gold, the inscription: "Peace to Christendom!" But Fortune, so long Bogdan's friend, now deserted him, and at Bereszteczko, on the banks of the Stuiva, he was utterly routed by the famous Castellan of Kiev, Stephen Czarniecki, who twice within two years had snatched his country from destruction, and now proceeded to sweep the Ukraine clear of the hordes that had ravaged it so long, and restore law and order with an iron hand. Chmielnicki fled to the Crimea. All hope of an independent Cossackdom was gone. But the wounds that Bogdan had dealt Poland were deadly if not immediately fatal, and not she herself, but her rival Muscovy, was to reap the fruits of her hardly won victory.

It was the surest symptom of the recuperation of Muscovy that during the reign of the second Romanov Tsar, Alexius Mikhailovich (1645—1676), her foreign policy was, on the whole, aggressive rather than defensive. Circumstances indeed singularly favoured her. Her neighbours and rivals, Poland and Sweden, were exhausting each other by mutually destructive wars, and the Cossack Rebellion gave her the long coveted opportunity of recovering part of the Ukraine. In 1654 Chmielnicki placed himself under the Tsar's protection, and, although the thirteen years' struggle with Poland, which consequently ensued, was not very glorious to the Russian arms, Muscovy ultimately contrived, by the treaty of Andrussow (1667) to recover the greater part of Red Russia, Black Russia, and the Ukraine, so that the Dnieper once more became the boundary between Poland and Muscovy.[1] On the other hand, a five years' war with Sweden (1655—60) had a very impotent conclusion, Tsar Alexius, by the Peace of Kardis (21st June, 1661) relinquishing all his conquests in Ingria and Livonia. And if still unequal to coping with her formidable northern neighbour, the Swede, Muscovy was anxious to avoid the very semblance of a dispute with her still more formidable southern neighbour, the Turk. Indeed her attitude towards the Porte, for the next sixty years, was one of almost abject deference. Thus, when the Don Cossacks, who were subject to the Tsar, just as the Dnieper Cossacks were subject to Poland, and had much the same origin,—when the Don Cossacks, I say, captured Azov from the Turks, and valiantly held it for five years (1637—1642) against all their efforts, the Muscovite Government not only refused to accept this important outpost from the victorious Cossacks as a gift, but even scolded them for taking it, apologised to the Sultan, and invited him to chastise, and, if necessary, exterminate "these robbers and runaway slaves."

But, in truth, Muscovy was much too rude and ignorant to properly realize her opportunities, or utilize her immense if latent resources. Her very vastness, so often her political salvation, was a serious impediment to her progress in civilization. The relatively sparse population, scattered over a vast area, with few and simple wants and abundance of land, preferred dwelling in myriads of rural communities

[1] See Map.

to congregating in cities, where the heavy hand of an ingeniously extortionate bureaucracy was felt with its full force. It was, in fact, "an Empire of little villages," as a Russian historian aptly calls it. Trade was conducted only under the greatest difficulties, owing to the immense distances to be traversed, the almost insuperable difficulties of transit (except where the great water-courses supplied the place of the vile roads), the paucity of marts and fairs, and the successful competition of the privileged and more enlightened foreign merchants. Taxation, too, weighed heavily on the people, for the impoverished treasury could only be replenished by crushing impositions unmercifully levied; while the emigration of the over-burdened serfs beyond the Urals, or to "the quiet Don," was repressed by the Ukaz which chained them absolutely to the soil, thus making their condition materially worse than it was before, and leading ultimately to the horrible *jacquerie* of 1670, under the peasant leader Stenka Razin,[1] which was almost as mischievous to Muscovy, as Chmielnicki's rising was to Poland. Throughout the whole of the 17th century, indeed, the condition of Eastern Russia was unspeakably wretched.

The gross but self-satisfied ignorance of the ruling responsible classes, was another obstacle to improvement, an obstacle all the more insuperable as it seemed to have the sanction of religion. To begin with, Muscovy had received her Christianity from a tainted source, the decadent Eastern Empire. Her Byzantine teachers had taught her that asceticism was the only counsel of perfection, and the Slavs, naturally pious and docile, always apt to exaggerate, and knowing no better way (for, owing to unfavourable historical conditions, they were quite cut off from the

---

[1] This savage, but by no means incapable, ruffian, captured the wealthy city of Astrachan, waged war with Persia on his own account, and cost the Muscovites 100,000 men, and no end of treasure.

healthier influences of the West), attempted to regulate their daily life as closely as possible on the monastic model. The day was divided according to the canonical hours. Each hour had its allotted and rigorously observed religious exercises. All amusements, even the most innocent, were regarded with suspicion.[1] Feasting was the only pastime in which the Muscovite boyar could freely indulge without serious peril to his soul, and he feasted riotously. As time went on, this rigidly methodical system of observances intruded itself into every department of daily life. Never was custom so tyrannous as in old Moscow. The slightest divergence from the uses of antiquity, even in such trivial matters as the length and breadth of a beard,[2] the shape of a mantle, or the cut of a coat, was scouted as impious. Existence being made up almost entirely of functions and ceremonies, there was little time, and less inclination, for intellectual pursuits. Learning in seventeenth century Muscovy was at its lowest ebb. Apart from the clergy, very few even of the upper classes could read or write properly. Church books were the only books in common use. A clerk who knew Latin, was looked upon as a phenomenon—and a phenomenon to be avoided. For it was held that the learning of the *Nyemtsui*,[3] as the ignorant Muscovites indiscriminately labelled all foreigners, came of evil, and should be banished with anathemas from the midst of a God-fearing people. It was even dangerous for foreign scholars to reside in

---

[1] As an old Muscovite chronicler quaintly put it: "When dancing and the strife of fifes and fiddles begin, the good angels flee away, as bees before smoke, and the Devil and his angels rejoice."

[2] The priests refused to bless those of their flock whose beards were not of the regulation length and breadth of the ancient ikons. Peter the Great himself, who could do most things, was unable to abolish the beard, so he made money out of it by taxing it.

[3] Germans.

Moscow. Thus, for instance, a Dutch physician was banished for having a skeleton in his rooms for anatomical purposes; while a German astronomer was accused of sorcery because he was caught peeping through a telescope. Typography was also looked upon as a work of the Devil.

But it was the Muscovite ladies who suffered most from this exaggeration of Byzantinism. The forefathers of the modern Russians had a very poor opinion of their womenkind. In old Moscow woman was regarded as a moral and mental infant, naturally prone to all wickedness, and peculiarly liable to fall beneath the seductions of Satan. Such a silly and dangerous creature, it was held, must be kept safely under lock and key. Not fit to be the companion of her husband, she was little better than his slave. Imprisoned within the walls of her *terem* (as the women's apartments were called) she never quitted it except under a strict guard, and only appeared before her husband's guests to present them with liqueurs, or exhibit her rich dresses, in silence. In the society of men she was not allowed to open her mouth, and, even when she was ill, the doctor who attended her was not allowed to see her face. When she *took the air*, it was in peculiarly constructed coaches or sledges, like movable prisons. Longer journeys had to be taken in the night time, and even at church she was muffled up in the darkest part of the choir. Peculiarly distressing was the condition of the Tsarevnas. As it was considered derogatory for Princesses to marry subjects, and as their religion forbade their marrying foreigners, they were doomed from childhood to live in their palaces as in a convent, and pass their time in prayer and fasting. Three or four centuries of this state of things, was sufficient to stifle all healthy family life, and induce a condition of intellectual stagnation which is almost inconceivable. Some faint idea may, however, be given of the ignorance, fanaticism, and trivial turn of mind of the Russian people generally, at this period, by briefly relating the instructive story of the reforms of the Patriarch Nikon.

This remarkable man, whose family name was Nikita Mina, was born in the village of Vilimanov, near Nizhny Novgorod, in the year 1605. At an early age he showed a great fondness for books, and a vocation for the monastic life, but was persuaded to marry, and ultimately settled in Moscow. Here he lost his three children in quick succession, and, regarding this bereavement as a heavenly warning, persuaded his wife to take the veil, while he himself entered the Anzhersky Monastery, on a lonely island in the White Sea, removing subsequently to the still more desolate convent of Kozheozersk, whose igumen, or abbot, he ultimately became. In 1646 Nikon had occasion to go to the Capital on business, and there made the acquaintance of "the gentle" Tsar Alexius, who, himself more than half a monk, bowed before Nikon as to a stronger though a kindred spirit, and successively promoted him to be Archimandrite of the Novospasky Monastery, the burial place of the Romanovs, and Metropolitan of Great Novgorod, the second highest ecclesiastical dignity in the realm. The Archbishop's heroic repression of the great sedition of Novgorod in 1650, at the peril of his life, brought him still further into notice, and on the death of the Patriarch Joseph, in 1652, Nikon was elected his successor. But the stern monk refused to accept this supreme dignity, until the Tsar had solemnly sworn before the "Lord our Saviour, His Most Holy Mother, and all the Saints and Angels," to leave the ecclesiastical administration absolutely in his hands, for it was the darling wish of Nikon's heart to reform the abuses which had gradually crept into the Muscovite Church. An enthusiastic lover of rites and ceremonies, his efforts were chiefly directed to the outward forms of religion. He had discovered slight discrepancies between Muscovite practices and the ancient Greek canons, which convinced him that his branch of the Church had strayed away from Apostolic orthodoxy, and it was the ambition of his life to bring her back to the right path. Setting about the work systematically, he ordered more than five hundred ancient books and MSS. from Mount Athos and other parts of Greece, sent to Kiev for scholars learned in Greek, to help him to collate the old service-books with those actually in use, and, in 1664, held a synod at Moscow, to assist him in his labours. The result of all these investigations was a circular letter condemning, as heretical, the prevailing practices of crossing oneself with two fingers instead of three, of bowing to the girdle instead of to the ground, of using tetragonal instead of octagonal crosses, of spelling the name of Jesus in the service-books with one iota instead of with two iotas, and other points of equal importance. Moreover, all the ikons in use were also condemned as uncanonical, and the Patriarch ordered them to be seized and publicly burnt.[1] New liturgies and service-books were also printed to supersede the old ones. The questions here in dispute seem trivial enough now-a-days, but in an age when ritual was regarded as the essential part of religion, and the symbolism underlying it was little understood, these innovations, which after all, were only a return to genuine antiquity, were looked upon, by thousands of pious people, as terrific indeed. Many priests, on first hearing that in future they were to cross themselves with three fingers instead of two, felt "their hearts grow cold within them, and their knees knock together." A gasp of horror resounded through the Cathedral of the Assumption when Nikon tore the eyes out of the condemned ikons, and trampled them underfoot. The

[1] At the earnest entreaty of the Tsar, they were buried instead of being burnt.

monks of the great Solovetsky Monastery, declared that the insertion of an extra iota in the word Isyus (Jesus) was a sin too horrible to contemplate, refused to receive the new service-books, and resisted for eight years, an army sent to chastise them. The clergy, as a body, ultimately submitted when an assembly of Patriarchs at Moscow, in 1668, confirmed Nikon's reforms, while unjustly condemning and deposing Nikon himself, for alleged pride, presumption, and interference with the secular power; but a large section of the population, the so-called Starovyerui,[1] or Raskolniki,[2] from henceforth broke away from the national Church altogether, preferring to live like hunted wild beasts, rather than accept what they called the blasphemous teaching of Antichrist. They exist to this day, the most brutal and persistent persecution being absolutely powerless to eradicate them.

This semi-barbarous state of things was likely to last indefinitely, so long as Muscovy was unable to produce men sufficiently enlightened to see their country's needs, and sufficiently courageous to endeavour to supply them; but towards the end of the reign of Tsar Alexius, such men began to appear. Despite their intense hatred of all foreign ways, the conviction was slowly gaining ground among the Muscovites that Western civilization might still have some secrets worth knowing. In self-defence, they had already partially re-organised their army on European models, and hired scores of German, Dutch and Scotch officers to drill their recruits, and teach them how to use firearms. But for general instruction, they naturally turned, first of all, to their brethren in Little Russia and the Ukraine, who had no taint of latindom about them, and the more enlightened of the Boyars (such men, for instance, as the large-hearted Theodore Mikhailovich Rtishchev) summoned learned clerks from Kiev, to found schools in Moscow, and

[1] Old believers.  [2] Schismatics.

maintained them there at their own expense. Amongst these pioneers was Epiphanius Slavenetsky, who compiled a Greek-Slavonic-Latin lexicon for the use of Muscovites, translated many of the Latin fathers, and re-introduced the practice of preaching, which was a novelty in Muscovy in those days. His colleague, the amiable and witty Simeon Poletsky, wrote original verses, and even composed mystery plays for the court, a most daring innovation. The gentle and pious Tsar Alexius took very kindly to these dramatic entertainments, though tormented at first by grave doubts whether this novel pastime was not far too pleasant a thing to be otherwise than sinful: but his confessor reassured him, and he ultimately appointed Poletsky to be the tutor of his children. A still more remarkable man was the Serb Krijanić, who actually foresaw that Muscovy would one day reign over all, or most, of the Slavonic nations. But this audacious dreamer, who, moreover, had the fatal defect of being a Catholic priest, found little favour at Moscow, and was finally banished to Tobolsk, where he employed his leisure in writing works, which prove that his was the misfortune of being born at least a century and a half too soon. Polish influence, too, began to be felt very strongly at the Muscovite Court during the latter years of Alexius and the reign of his son Theodore, whose first wife was a Polish lady, especially in the matter of dress; but the all determining medium between semi-Asiatic Moscow and the rest of Europe, was the *Nyemetskaya Sloboda,* or "Dutch Suburb" of Moscow, as the Englishmen of those days called it, where the foreign merchants and artificers of all nations formed a little colony apart. It is not too much to say that the surest criterion of the intelligence of a 17th century Muscovite is the degree of his intimacy with the "Dutch Suburb." It was from there that Athanasius Ordin-Nashchokin, Russia's first diplomatist and statesman, in the modern sense of the term, and, in so many respects, the precursor of Peter the Great, learnt Latin, German, and mathematics. It was from there that Nashchokin's worthy successor, Artamon Sergyeevich Matvyeev, chose a Scotch wife (she was re-baptized Eudoxia Grigorevna) who taught him how to furnish his house in the European style, and cultivate a taste for pictures and china, strange and horrible luxuries in the eyes of a Muscovite of the old school. It was at Matvyeev's house that Tsar Alexius, after the death of his first wife, saw and fell in love with his second, the comparatively well-educated Natalia Naruishkin, the future mother of Peter the Great, who scandalized her ladies, soon after her marriage with the Tsar, by driving out in an open carriage. A new spirit seemed about to prevail at the Muscovite Court, when Alexius died suddenly (1676), leaving the throne to his eldest surviving son by his *first* marriage. Theodore was a sickly youth of fourteen, during whose minority the reactionary party gained the upper hand, and Matvyeev and the party of progress were banished on a charge of sorcery. Theodore, on attaining his majority, gave promise of being an enlightened Prince; but he died in 1682, without leaving issue, whereupon his brother, Ivan V, a weak-witted lad of fifteen, and his half-brother Peter I, now in his tenth year, were proclaimed joint Tsars under the regency of the Tsarevna Sophia, one of Tsar Alexius' daughters by his first wife, a young woman of extraordinary force of character, who, with equal craft and courage, quelled two dangerous rebellions of the Stryeltsui, or native Russian Court Infantry, at the beginning of her regency, and summoned to her side, as Chief Counsellor, the accomplished and experienced Prince Vasily Vasilievich Golitsuin, one of the very few great Russian nobles who belonged to the "new men." Sophia's chief political triumph was the Peace of Moscow (1686), whereby Poland finally relinquished Kiev in exchange for 146,000 rubles, and a promise of help against the Turks, which was never kept; but when, three years afterwards, she presumed to usurp the title of Autocrat, with the avowed intention of reigning *along with* her two brothers, Peter, now seventeen, supported by the foreign officers and the "Dutch Suburb," openly broke with her, and, after a brief struggle, deprived her of her power, and compelled her to retire to a monastery. To those who bear in mind that centuries of suppression and seclusion had degraded the Russian woman into a mere domestic chattel, the Tsarevna Sophia must always appear a prodigious phenomenon; she was, in fact, the harbinger of that succession of high-spirited Princesses who, during the 18th century, were to metamorphose Russia, and astonish Europe.

For some time after the Revolution of 1689, Peter had but little authority. The reactionaries, under the bigoted Patriarch Joachim, again gained the upper hand, and the young Tsar, left to himself, consorted with foreigners, and began that long course of self-instruction, which, never terminated, was only interrupted by his death. His chief teachers and associates at this time, were the accomplished and upright Scotch royalist refugee, Patrick Gordon, and an amiable, clever but shallow French adventurer, Francis Lefort. Peter, indeed, did not disdain to learn from anyone who had anything to teach, and it is recorded of him at this time, that during a visit to Archangel, he compelled a Dutch sailor there to show him how to climb the masts, and adjust the rigging of a ship. Navigation, indeed, had already become a passion with him, and on the little lake of Pereyaslavl, about twenty miles from Moscow, and subsequently on a larger scale at Voronezh, he superintended the construction of a flotilla by Dutch shipwrights, working himself in the dress of a ship's carpenter, axe in hand. From Gordon and Lefort, both military men, he learnt the rudiments of scientific warfare, and so confident did he already feel in himself and his troops that he conducted [1] two expeditions against Azov, which surrendered in July 1696, whereupon Peter set about converting it into a first-class fortress, and at the same time laid the foundations of the dockyard of Taganrog. In the course of 1696, the death of his half-brother Ivan left him sole Tsar, and a few months later (March 1697) Peter undertook a foreign tour to complete his education. There is no need to follow him on his travels, which have so often been described before. Suffice it to say that although the avowed object of the numerous Embassy in which he travelled, disguised as a Dutch sailor, was to consolidate existing alliances with a view to a combined attack upon the Turk, politics at this time occupied the young Tsar but little. The noble ambition of learning so that he might teach others, was his main object. It is remarkable, however, that his eminently practical mind took no interest in any but scientific or strictly technical subjects. William III complained that his Tsarish Majesty seemed quite indifferent to the beauties of architecture and horticulture; it was remarked in France that picture galleries made no impression upon him; while, at the German Courts, his ignorance of, and contempt for, the polite usages of society, produced a bad impression, especially upon the ladies. But the men of science received him with enthusiasm, and hailed him as one of themselves. The great engineer Streitner von Sternfeld, taught him gunnery at Königsberg. At Leyden he made the acquaintance of the celebrated anatomist Boerhave. Coehorn, the Dutch Vauban, gave him lessons at Delft in the science of fortification; and, whilst residing in Holland, he took lessons in mathematics,

[1] Strictly speaking these expeditions were under the command of Gordon, Lefort, and Golowin, whose resolutions, however, were subject to the sanction of the bombardier of the Preobrazhensky regiment, Peter Aleksyeev, *i.e.*, Peter himself, who had entered his own army in the lowest grade.

astronomy, drawing, and even dentistry. But ship-building was now, as ever, his darling pastime, and the most precious possession he took home, was the piece of paper given him by Master Gerrit Pool of Amsterdam, certifying that Peter Mikhailov, the name under which he travelled, had worked for five and a half months in his dockyard, thoroughly mastered the science of naval architecture, and was an able and competent ship's carpenter.[1] Peter's first foreign tour was now, however, brought to an abrupt conclusion. He had scarcely been absent from Muscovy eighteen months, when he was suddenly recalled thither by an event which, though it never, as is generally supposed, actually endangered his throne, showed only too plainly what an impassable chasm already divided him from his people—I mean, of course, the revolt of the *Stryeltsui*.

We who can have nothing but the deepest admiration for Peter's enlightened efforts to drag his benighted people out of the "swamp of Byzantine sluggishness" (whatever we may think of his methods), can scarce realize the horror and dismay with which the Russian nation regarded his conduct generally. The people, accustomed to look upon their Tsars as Grand Llamas or Demigods, who rarely appeared in public except in church processions, could not recover from the shock of seeing on the throne a mere man like themselves, who prostituted the sacrosanct imperial dignity by consorting with foreign mechanics, and trampled ruthlessly on the most cherished customs of his forefathers. What sort of a Tsar is this who eats "flesh on Fridays like a pagan Tartar?" cried the indignant peasants. "What a difference between this Tsar and the others," said a burgher's wife of the town of Dmitrov.

[1] It is worthy of remark, however, that Peter thought English naval architects far superior to the Dutch. "If I had not gone to England," he said, "I should have remained nothing but a ship's carpenter all my life."

"*They* made pilgrimages to the holy places to pray, *this* one goes to the Dutch Suburb to revel." They could only explain it by regarding him as a supposititious child of German parentage, or, worse still, as bewitched, and they pointed to the epileptic contortions, with which he was plagued all his life, as infallible signs that he was possessed by the Devil. But the head and front of his offending was his close friendship with foreign interlopers, and no class felt this more than the *Stryeltsui*,[1] or Russian native infantry, who, during the reigns of the last four Tsars, had gradually usurped the position of a Pretorian guard, but now saw themselves overlooked and set aside. During Peter's absence therefore, they revolted (1698) with the avowed intention of placing the Tsarevna Sophia on the throne, but were easily dispersed in less than an hour, by Patrick Gordon, and nearly all the ringleaders captured. Of the horrible vengeance taken upon them by the Tsar on his return, it is happily unnecessary to speak. Peter was naturally, or, rather, unnaturally cruel, and his ungovernable passion burst forth with maniacal violence at the slightest opposition to his plans. From henceforth torture on a gigantic scale became, under his personal supervision, one of his chief instruments of government,[2] and the people began to fear him as much as they had feared his prototype, Ivan the Terrible. This decisive success, purchased with streams of blood and the lasting hatred of his people, enabled the Tsar to work more energetically than ever for their future good. Ukaz after ukaz introduced a whole series of sweeping reforms. The practical supersession of the Patriarchate after the death of the Patriarch Adrian,

[1] Lit. Archers.

[2] A notable contrast to him, in this respect, was his great opponent Charles XII, one of whose first acts on ascending the throne, was to abolish judicial torture as irrational and inconclusive.

rendered harmless the secretly mutinous, but now leaderless, Church, and the laity was kept down with an iron hand. Hundreds of scientific foreigners and experts were imported into Muscovy, to teach the people the arts of war and peace, and hundreds of young Russians were sent abroad to be thoroughly educated, thus forming the school for a future race of statesmen, diplomatists, and generals.

And now, too, the necessities of his situation made Peter plunge into foreign politics with characteristic thoroughness. Muscovy was still, practically, without a seaboard, and till she had got a firm footing on the Baltic, could scarcely be said to belong to Europe. Sweden, however, barred the way, and Peter felt that it was only on the ruins of her empire that he could build up his own. That he should long have hesitated to attack a State renowned for her military efficiency, despite her inherent weakness, and still one of the great Powers, was only natural; but his opportunity seemed to have arrived when the wise and provident Charles XI died suddenly in 1697, and left his throne to a lad of sixteen. Peter at once joined the grand alliance against Sweden, and invaded Livonia, but the unexpected victories of the youthful Charles XII dissipated the anti-Swedish league, and brought the Tsar to the very brink of ruin. Fortunately for Muscovy, Charles was no statesman, and his extraordinary military exploits were nullified at every step by his still more extraordinary political mistakes. The young hero's crowning blunder was to imagine that a foe like Peter, who so readily ran away, might safely be neglected, and when, after pursuing chimeras for eight years through the fens and forests of Lithuania, he turned his arms, at last, against the Tsar, it was already too late. Peter had, by this time, firmly established himself in the Baltic Provinces, and laid the foundations of Petersburg. Nevertheless, for a moment,

the issue of the mortal struggle was doubtful, and it was
with despair in his heart, that Peter watched the irresistible
advance of his great opponent in 1708. Russian historians
themselves cannot sufficiently admire the wonderful way in
which the young Swedish hero flew rather than marched
from the heart of Saxony to the heart of Muscovy, carrying
everything before him, annihilating time and space, defying
climate, crossing broad rivers at the flood, and traversing,
with scarce an effort, forests apparently impenetrable, and
morasses that had ever been looked upon as impassable.
Nor was this all. Had Charles triumphed at Pultawa, Peter
might, or perhaps it would be better to say *must*, have
lost his life and throne in the general insurrection in Muscovy itself, which would inevitably have followed. Between
1705 and 1708, the indignation of the Muscovites at the
godless reforms of the infatuated Tsar, had found expression
in two terrible revolts which shook the Empire. Jakob Nossov,
with the aid of the *Raskolniki*, and the disbanded *Stryeltsui*,
seized Astrachan,[1] the third city in the kingdom, and the
Don Cossacks, under the able leadership of Kondraty
Bulavin, defeated the Tsar's troops at the pitched battle of
Liskovatka. Both rebellions were finally crushed, but they
gave much trouble to the Government at the time, and it
was known that on the approach of Charles, the whole
country was again in a ferment. But Charles's invasion of
Muscovy proved as fatal to him, as the invasion of 1812

---

[1] It is clear, from the despatches of the English Minister, Whitworth, that the revolt of Astrachan was induced by the brutality with which the Russian officials sought to enforce the edict enjoining the women to wear petticoats, instead of only a loose gown buttoned down before, and reaching to their heels. "The Governor of Astrachan," he adds, "placed officers at the doors of the churches, who cut off the women's loose garments from their middles, and pulled out beards of venerable persons by the roots... The mob found a peruke block with nose, mouth and eyes, which they carried in triumph through the town, exclaiming: 'Behold the god of the strangers, which we shall at last be condemned to worship.'"—*Sb. Imp. Rus. Ist. Ob.*, Tom. XXXIX.

proved to Napoleon, and Sweden's subsequent ten years' struggle against the banded might of Europe, heroic, unexampled as it was, only served to complete her exhaustion. Of all her numerous enemies, Peter was the most persistent, and at the final partition of her Empire (1720—1721) the lion's share of the spoil fell to him by right of conquest.

Only in one direction was Peter's foreign policy still unsuccessful. Ever since the capture of Azov (1696) the relations between the Porte and Muscovy had been strained, and it was therefore a comparatively easy task for Swedish diplomacy, after Pultawa, to bring about a rupture. Overconfident for the first and only time in his life, Peter advanced into the enemy's country, without taking sufficient precautions, was completely cut off from his communications by a Turkish army ten times stronger than his own, and only saved from destruction by the cowardice and the cupidity of the Grand Vizier. The Peace of the Pruth (1711) relieved him indeed from his embarrassment, but he was thereby compelled to relinquish Azov, and dismantle Taganrog.

But for this comparatively trifling check in the South, Peter was more than compensated by the commanding influence he gradually won in the North, after the battle of Pultawa. Hitherto Muscovy had been regarded by the rest of Europe with an indifference closely bordering on contempt; but without her aid, a partition of Charles XII's German possessions would have been impossible, and Peter gladly seized the opportunity of pouring army after army into Poland and Germany. From 1712 to 1717, he himself was actively engaged on the Continent, contracting fresh alliances, and consolidating his conquests; but his phenomenal success had already excited universal apprehension and alarm. He had entered the European system only to disturb it.

On his return home in 1717, Peter completed his work by an act which utterly crushed, once for all, the reactionary party in Muscovy, but has, at the same time, left an ineffaceable stain upon his memory. I allude, of course, to the shocking murder of the Tsarevich Alexius. This unfortunate young man was the son of Peter by Eudoxia Lopukhin. Something must be said in the next chapter of Peter's infamous treatment of his first consort, here I need only premise that he and his wife were, in every way, an uncongenial couple, that Peter detested her from the bottom of his heart, and that he transferred his detestation to her son. Alexius Petrovich was the very antithesis of his father. He was by no means incapable, indeed his parts were good, and he was naturally studious; but he devoted himself almost entirely to theology, church history, and philosophy, took little interest in practical subjects, and regarded his father's reforms with an indifference which gradually deepened into repugnance. In many respects he greatly resembled his grandfather, the gentle Tsar Alexius, and, like him, was a friend of the clergy and a lover of religious ceremonies. As he grew up, the malcontents in Muscovy began to look up to him as the future restorer of the old system of things, and Peter, who was not ignorant of this feeling, treated his son more and more as a personal enemy. He had always neglected him. During his long absences abroad, he had left him, at the most critical period of his life, at Moscow in the company of drunkards and debauchees, and encouraged his governors and tutors to be hard and even cruel towards him. When a son, the future Peter II, was born to the Prince[1] in 1715, the Tsar became still more uneasy at the possibility of a reactionary policy after his death, and attempted to induce Alexius to resign his right

[1] Alexius, on 14th Oct., 1712, married the Princess Charlotte of Brunswick Wolffenbuttel, who died soon after giving birth to her son.

to the succession. Alexius was willing to do so, but his friends persuaded him to escape abroad, and he finally took refuge in Italy, whence he was inveigled home, under false pretences, by the diplomatist Tolstoy. There can be no doubt that, on his recapture, his father made up his mind to do away with him, as the shortest and surest way of preventing future complications. On 31st January, 1718, Alexius arrived at the Capital. On February 3rd he publicly renounced his rights to the succession. His adherents, known or suspected, were then arrested wholesale; but the most ghastly tortures could only bring to light a general desire, chiefly expressed in private conversation, for the death of the Tsar and the accession of the Tsarevich. Of anything like a conspiracy, there was no trace. On June 19th Alexius received 25 strokes with the knout, to extort something more definite, the only outcome of which was an autobiography explaining why he hated his father. On June 25th he received 15 more strokes, and the next day an extraordinary tribunal of 127 persons pronounced the capital sentence upon him for "*wishing* his father's death, and harbouring treasonable designs." At 8 o'clock on the following day, the helpless creature, now thoroughly broken (he is said, in his desperation, to have sought a temporary solace from his torments in drink), was tortured for the third time *in his father's presence*, and died the same evening in prison. The officially published account gave apoplexy as the cause of death, but each knouting that he had received was sufficient of itself to have killed a robust man (which he was not), and Peter was the only person who had a direct interest in his son's death. Such, in its baldest details, mainly [1] derived from a writer by no means favourably

---

[1] I have subsequently studied all the available documents relating to the affair. The duplicity of Peter throughout is even more offensive than his brutality.

disposed towards Alexius, is the painful history of this detestable crime. Peter the Great did not shrink from cementing the foundations of his Empire with the blood of his own child.

For by this time Peter had assumed the Imperial Title, and the whole system of his government began to assume imperial dimensions. The administration was gradually remodelled to correspond with the new order of things. The old consultative, purely passive, Council of Boyars was superseded by the Senate (22nd Feb., 1711) consisting of eight members, to be increased if necessary, who were to rule the State during the Tsar's absence, in his name, and with equal authority. The powers of the Senators embraced the administrative, legislative and judicial functions, and they had a comprehensive, almost unlimited right of supervision. In 1715 a Reviser-General, or Inspector of Ukazes, was appointed to superintend the execution of the Senate's decrees; and in 1718 the old-fashioned *prikazes*, or government offices, nearly fifty in number, whose cumbrous machinery and conflicting, often contradictory, jurisdiction had impeded rather than promoted the action of the government, were superseded by nine Colleges[1] or Departments of State on the Swedish model. The Presidents of these Colleges were to be native Russians, the Vice-Presidents, foreigners. The members of the Senate were the usual Presidents of the Colleges. In 1721 a Grand Herald was appointed to see that the nobility performed their obligations; and in 1722, a *Procureur-Général* was appointed to superintend the working of the Colleges, and report irregularities to the Senate. The "Table of Degrees" put an end to the influence of the privileged noble classes, and substituted an official aristocracy in its stead. Ecclesi-

---

[1] *E.g.*, The College of War, the College of Marine, etc., corresponding to the modern War Office and Admiralty; the Presidents of the various colleges corresponded to our Chiefs of Departments.

astical affairs were committed to the charge of the Holy Synod instituted in 1721. In every corner of the vast realm was felt the transforming hand of the great Emperor, who, all his life occupied with the grandest, the most far-reaching designs, yet suffered not the pettiest detail of administration to escape his ever watchful attention.

Thus, at last, the ambitious dream of Peter the Great was realized. Before he died he had rescued his people from barbarism, and familiarized them with modern ideas. The old Tsardom of Muscovy had disappeared in the new Empire of Russia.

## CHAPTER II.

### CATHERINE ALEKSYEEVNA AND PETER THE GREAT.

(1711—1725).

PETER'S pupils—P. A. Tolstoy—F. M. Apraksin—G. I. Golovkin—Anecdotes of his stinginess—P. I. Yaguzhinsky—A. D. Menshikov—His origin, career, and character—Rapacity of Peter's pupils—Anecdotes of Menshikov's greed—A. I. Ostermann—Early career and character—Diplomatic astuteness—Martha Skovronskaya—Peter's first acquaintance with her—His cruel treatment of his first Consort Eudoxia—Peter's ideal woman—His first mistress Anna Mons—Personality and character of Martha Skovronskaya—Her moral influence over Peter—Martha Skovronskaya becomes Catherine Aleksyeevna—Marries the Tsar—Devotion of Peter to her—Their affectionate correspondence—Ukaz fixing the succession to the throne—Execution of Nestorov—Coronation of Catherine—Description of the Regalia—The Mons affair—Last illness and death of Peter the Great—His character—Comparison with Charles XII.

PETER the Great not only laid the foundations of his Empire as solidly and as substantially as the tyrannical use of unlimited power could make them, but was at infinite pains to gather around him a chosen band of pupils and fellow-workers, able and willing to build upon the foundations he had laid. Judged even by a very low standard of morality, the men of his choice were, as a rule, odious and contemptible enough; modern statesmanship would dub them rascals, modern society, ruffians. But they were all, without exception, men of extraordinary energy, capable of doing any amount of work, difficult, dangerous, and even dirty, as it very often was, and enlightened enough to perfectly understand that the work required of them was for their country's benefit, although it may well be doubted whether anyone of them was ever a patriot in the truer and nobler sense of the word. Peter himself did not look for high morality in his servants; so long as they did what he told them, he was content. What he wanted was men of action, character, and intelligence, and he always got what he wanted. For his discrimination was wonderful. It may safely be said that in the selection of his tools and instruments, Peter never made a single mistake.

The most experienced of Peter's pupils, and the one who most skilfully succeeded in hiding his native barbarism beneath a showy veneer of western culture, was Count Peter Andryeevich Tolstoy. Born in 1645, and therefore 27 years older than his master, Tolstoy from an early age displayed unwonted ability. He was especially remarkable for his intellectual suppleness, and a peculiar receptivity for new ideas even at an age when most men settle down into fixed habits, and lose the faculty of taking fresh impressions. When past fifty, he went to Italy to study navigation (a sure way of gaining Peter's favour); but diplomacy was always his *forte*, and, as ambassador at Constantinople, he, for many years, rendered his master most important services. It was he who frustrated Charles XII's Turkish policy, and conceived the plan of secretly capturing and carrying off the Swedish King by a troop of light horse.

Tolstoy, too, was the intelligent bloodhound that hunted down the unfortunate Tsarevich Alexius, a deed for which the common people, and all the lovers of the old order of things, never forgave him. By his brother-diplomatists he was regarded as sly and vindictive, and Peter himself seems to have always stood on his guard against him. "Tolstoy," he is reported to have said, "is an able and intelligent man; but it is just as well when you have anything to do with him, to have a good big stone handy, that you may be able to break his teeth, in case it should suddenly occur to him to bite you." He was liked, however, by the diplomatists at St. Petersburg, and the French Minister Campredon, in particular, had a very high opinion of his abilities. "M. Tolstoy," he wrote in 1725, "is the best head in Russia. He has grown grey in affairs, and manages them with much policy and prudence. He affects no superiority over his colleagues, but, with all the address of a *politique rusé*, knows how to bring them round to the views he has elaborated beforehand."[1]

By the side of this astute and somewhat sinister diplomatist, the rough and homely figure of the bluff sailor, Fedor Matvyeevich Apraksin, seems almost attractive. Apraksin came of one of the oldest and noblest families in Russia, he was even connected by marriage with the Imperial family, one of his sisters having been the second consort of Tsar Theodore, Peter's elder half-brother. But it was for his services, not for his high lineage, that his master valued him. Apraksin was the first celebrated Russian Admiral, and the creator of the Russian fleet.

[1] "Despatches of Campredon. *Sb. Imp. Rus. Ist. Ob.*, Tome LVIII, p. 34. Elsewhere he says of him: "C'est un homme habile, discret, expérimenté... d'un esprit délié, solide, et adroit à donner le tour aux affaires qu'il veut faire réussir."—The Prussian Minister Mardefeldt is less favourable, and calls him "naturellment heimtückisch und vindictif," in the macaronic jargon of the day.—*Sb. Imp. Rus. Ist. Ob.*, Tome XV, p. 182.

During the Great Northern War, he defeated the incompetent Swedish general, Lybeker, in Ingria, captured Viborg in Carelia, and held the chief command in the Black Sea during the brief campaign against Turkey, which was terminated so disastrously by the Peace of the Pruth. In 1713, he materially assisted the conquest of Finland by his operations from the seaside, and in 1719—20 he personally conducted the descents upon Sweden herself, ravaging that unhappy country mercilessly with fire and sword, and thus extorting from her wretchedness the Peace of Nystad, whereby she surrendered the best part of her Baltic Provinces to Russia. For these great services he was made a Senator, and Admiral-General of the Empire. Strong professional sympathies, as well as personal liking, bound Apraksin to the Tsar, and, though frequently in well-deserved disgrace, as we shall see presently, he contrived to escape Siberia, and die in his bed, full of riches and honours.

It is less easy to determine the merits and the services of Gabriel Ivanovich Golovkin, but they must have been considerable, for he was one of the most confidential ministers of Peter the Great. The son of a high official, he began life as a page at the court of Tsar Alexius, became, at the age of 17, one of Peter's gentlemen of the bedchamber, and subsequently was raised to the rank of *Oberkammerherr*. At Narva, he was one of the few Russian officers who displayed great personal valour, for which he was rewarded with the ribbon of the newly instituted Order of St. Andrew, while the ability he displayed at Pultawa, won for him the rank of Grand-Chancellor, in which capacity he was in almost constant attendance on the Emperor. He was also the first created Russian Count. It was he who, on the conclusion of the war, acted as spokesman of the deputation which begged its Sovereign, in the name of the Russian people, to assume the titles of "Father of the Fatherland, Peter the Great, and Emperor of all Russia." During the latter part of his life, Golovkin devoted all his energies to the accumulation of wealth, not even shrinking from making money out of the misery of the people. Thus, it was his constant practice to store up immense quantities of corn in his granaries, wait till hard times, and then dispense the grain to the starving people at famine prices. He was also remarkably penurious, or, as the Prussian Minister, Mardefeldt, sarcastically puts it, "a great economist, who never wasted his substance." At last his stinginess became proverbial. He was never known to have given a banquet, within living memory, but once, and the circumstance was considered so extraordinary that Mardefeldt goes out of his way to record it. "I can relate to your Majesty," he writes to Frederick William I, "as a quite incredible and yet absolutely certain affair, that the Grand-Chancellor Golovkin has been safely delivered of a great feast, which he gave to his Majesty the Tsar, the Duke of Holstein, and the foreign Ministers inclusive. His Majesty the Tsar fell asleep after the entertainment, and the rest of us followed his example." [1]

Tolstoy, Apraksin, and Golovkin, all belonged to old boyar families, and were therefore aristocrats; but Peter had no regard whatever for the accident of birth unaccompanied by native talent. He picked out the best men wherever he happened to find them, and many of his servants were persons of base, and even vile, extraction. This was especially the case with two of them, Yaguzhinsky and Menshikov.

Paul Ivanovich Yaguzhinsky, [2] the *enfant terrible* of Peter

[1] Despatches of Prussian Min. Mardefeldt. *Sb. of Imp. Rus. Ist. Ob.* Tome XV, p. 195.
[2] See the article, "Anna Fedorovna Yaguzhinskaya," in "Russkaya Starina." Vol. XVIII.

the Great's "fledglings," was the son of the Lutheran organist at Moscow. The Tsar probably first met him in the Dutch Suburb, placed him in the Guards, and, greatly fascinated by the vivacity and good humour of the handsome stalwart youth, speedily made him one of his *denshchik*, or field-adjutants. From that moment Yaguzhinsky's fortune was made. At 28 he was already an adjutant-general, and a *kammerherr*. He was next employed diplomatically, and acquitted himself with great dexterity. After the Peace of Nystad, he was endowed with wealthy estates in Livonia, was the first appointed member of the newly constituted Senate, and subsequently, as Procureur-Général, exercised a sort of supervision over that august assembly, or, as he himself expressed it, became "the Tsar's Eye." Finally, after divorcing his first wife Anna Fedorovna, he reached the apex of distinction by marrying the wealthy daughter of the influential Chancellor Golovkin. Yaguzhinsky was of Lithuanian origin, and certainly his violent, impetuous, easily excitable temperament was far more suggestive of Sarmatian effervescence than of Muscovite phlegm. In some respects he was the most disreputable of all Peter's pupils, and when in liquor, to which he was much addicted, his language and general behaviour were brutal in the extreme. Yet, as *bonhomie* was, after all, the basis of his character, his enmities, though fierce and frequent, were never either very bitter or very lasting, and this reckless carouser, who was quite as often drunk as sober, actually contrived to *reel* safely through the four successive revolutions which engulfed, one by one, his more sober and circumspect colleagues.

"Old Peter," as the Tsar convivially called himself, had almost as high an opinion of his boon-companion Yaguzhinsky's drinking capacity as of official ability; but the man entirely after his own heart, the person whom, after his second consort, he loved best in all the world, was Alexander Danilovich Menshikov.

This extraordinary man, who became a Prince of the Holy Roman, as well as of the Orthodox Russian, Empire, a Field-Marshal, a Privy Councillor, and the omnipotent Minister of three successive sovereigns, was literally plucked from the gutter. His origin is so obscure that it is still a matter of doubt whether his father was a Lithuanian peasant, or a boatman on the Volga. The first absolutely certain thing we know of him is that, when about twenty years of age, he gained his livelihood as a costermonger, and sold meat pies in the streets of Moscow. It was while plying this honest, if somewhat modest, trade, that the merry looks and smart sallies of the bright, young, itinerant pieman attracted the attention of François Lefort, the Tsar's early companion and mentor, as he passed through the streets, and he stopped and spoke to him. The repartees of the youth vastly amused the witty Frenchman, and he took him, there and then, into his service. As Lefort's lacquey, Menshikov displayed unusual zeal and intelligence, although he was so ignorant that he could scarcely sign his name. It was at Lefort's house that Peter first saw him, immediately took a fancy to the lively lacquey, and prevailed upon Lefort to part with him. As the Tsar's attendant, Menshikov completely won his master's favour by his assiduity and tact, anticipating all the Tsar's commands, and enduring frequent ill usage with the most serene good humour. It was not long before he became indispensable, and accompanied Peter everywhere. The intelligence with which he grasped the leading ideas of the Tsar's reforms, and the cheerful alacrity with which he was ready to break with all old Russian habits and customs to please his master, still further endeared him to Peter. He ceased to be a servant, he became a friend. During the Tsar's first foreign tour, Menshikov worked by his side in the dockyards of Amsterdam, visited all the workshops and ateliers with him, and studied Dutch and German beneath his very eyes. The way in which the ex-vendor of meat pies adapted himself to the manners of polite society in England, was wonderful, and Peter, at last, could not make too much of a man who was able to turn his hand to anything at a moment's notice. Whatever the work or play required of him, Menshikov always plunged into it with enthusiasm. He was the companion of Peter's drunken orgies as well as the partner of his arduous toils. He could drill a regiment, build a frigate, chop off the heads of rebels, with equal facility. In 1706 he married, also by the Tsar's command, the beautiful and noble-minded Daria Arsenevaya, and was appointed Governor of the unfortunate Tsarevich Alexius, whom, again to please his master, he treated with ferocious brutality. Throughout the whole of the Great Northern War, Menshikov and the Tsar were inseparable, and, after the war was over, "His Most Serene Highness," for Menshikov now possessed that title, was appointed Administrator of the conquered Baltic Provinces. He superintended the construction of Cronstadt, was allowed to build for himself a superb palace in the mushroom city of St. Petersburg, besides a country house at Oranienbaum, and was decorated with the order of St. Andrew of the first class by the hand of his own master, and with the White Eagle by the King of Poland. The best part of Mazeppa's vast possessions in the Ukraine were bestowed upon him for his services at Pultawa ; it was from his house that Peter's niece, Anna Ivanovna, was married to the Duke of Courland, and, in 1719, the offices of High Admiral and War Minister were added to his other dignities. At the end of Peter's reign he was that monarch's mightiest Satrap, and indisputably one of the wealthiest men in Europe. His natural abilities were beyond all question, his energy and assiduity marvellous, and he had all that astonishing versatility which distinguishes the true Slav. Not much, however, can be said for his morality in any sense. Obsequious and cringing to the master he served and feared, he was outrageously insolent to his rivals and equals,[1] and treated all inferiors in station as so much dirt beneath his feet.

These five men, differing as widely in character and temperament as men can differ, secretly hating each other as rivals, even while obliged to work harmoniously together as colleagues, were bound together, nevertheless, by the constraint of a vice common to them all—a shameless rapacity, which greedily clutched at every opportunity of robbing the master they professed to serve. Venality had always, indeed, been the crying evil of Russian administration. Strong Tsars, like Ivan the Terrible, had done something towards extirpating the ill weed, but under the subsequent rule of the mildly indulgent Romanovs, it had found a congenial environment, and flourished more luxuriantly than ever. Peter the Great, himself a thoroughly honest man, in the strictly pecuniary sense of the term,[2] was determined that his servants should be as honest as himself, and employed his favourite weapon, intimidation, with cruel rigour, but very little permanent effect. "I'll have no peculation at all in my realm," he exclaimed on one occasion.—"Then your Majesty must be content to live in your realm all alone," replied the impulsive

[1] The English Minister, Whitworth, who saw him in 1715, was very unfavourably impressed. "Menshikov," he says, "is of very low extraction, extremely vicious in his inclinations, violent and obstinate in his temper. However," he adds, "by his assiduity and diligence he has gained such favour with the Czar, that no subject ever had the like."—*Sb. Imp. Rus. Ist. Ob.*, Tome XXXIX, p. 125.

[2] As a diplomatist and politician, however, he was so shamelessly dishonest, that his most ingenious apologists are often hard put to it to find excuses for him.

Yaguzhinsky, "for we all rob you. Some take only a little, some take a great deal, but all of us take something." Still Peter persevered. Now and then he made terrible examples of the more eminent and responsible delinquents, so as to deter the lesser swindlers.[1] In vain, the evil seemed incurable. Even the Tsar's most trusted servants, his messmates and cronies, were frequently in danger of losing their heads for their malpractices. Thus, in the course of 1714, the Grand-Chancellor Golovkin, the Grand-Admiral Apraksin, and his Serene Highness Prince Menshikov, were all arrested, and confessed to having been "unfortunately overreached by the subtlety of their agents, and thus surprised into practices they may not have adverted to be so hurtful."[2] They escaped this time with savage menaces, which nearly frightened them into an apoplexy, and the buoyant old Admiral, Apraksin, after being taken into favour again, assured the English minister, Mackenzie, with a sly chuckle, that the hazards he had escaped at sea were as nothing compared with the storms he had weathered since he got back into harbour.[3] But by far the worst offender in this respect was Menshikov. The greed and extortion of "little Alec"[4] were insatiable, and he presumed again and again upon the indulgence of his long-suffering master. In 1718 he was imprisoned for the maladministration of Ingria, and condemned to pay a fine

---

[1] See Eng. Minister Mackenzie's account of the torturing of three Senators for gross venality. He adds: "All or most of the persons in the first stations... are said to be in one way or other dipped in the practices which the Tsar is willing to reform."—*Sb. of Imp. Rus. Ist. Ob.*, Vol. XLI, p. 321.

[2] Eng. Min. Mackenzie's Despatches.—*Sb. of Imp. Rus. Ist. Ob.*, Vol. XLI, pp. 323 et seq.

[3] Yet only a few years later, he was again found guilty of gross malversation of funds, deprived of the order of St. Andrew, and compelled to pay an immense sum of money.

[4] Alyushka, Peter's pet name for him.

of 200,000 rubles [1] (£50,000). Yet very shortly afterwards the Prussian Minister Mardefeldt wrote to his Court, "The good Prince Menshikov has again been well plucked. The Tsar asked him how many peasants he possessed in Ingria. He confessed to 7,000, but his majesty, who was much better informed, told him he was welcome to keep his 7,000, but must give up all above that figure, in other words 8,000 more ... Menshikov, from anxiety and wondering what will happen to him next, has grown quite ill, and as lean as a dog; but he has saved his neck once more, and been pardoned till Satan do tempt him again." [2] On another occasion, the Tsar found out that Menshikov had not only been plundering the Treasury himself, but allowing his subordinates to do so. At this discovery, Peter was so incensed that he belaboured the favourite severely with his cane, and forbade him ever to appear before him again. But the Empress Catherine interceded for him, and he was forgiven once more. Peter, however, deprived him for a time of his immense estates in the Ukraine, and condemned him to pay another 200,000 rubles. It is said that when "Old Peter" paid "little Alec" a friendly visit a few days afterwards, he was surprised to find the furniture of the house poor and shabby beyond description. "What's the meaning of this?" roared the Tsar.—"Alas! your Majesty," replied the Prince, "I was obliged to sell all my rich furniture, in order to settle up with the Treasury."—Peter looked at him sternly for a moment, and then replied: "I know better: none of these games with me. If when next I come to see you, your house is not furnished as becomes your rank, I'll make you pay me as much again." [3]—It is needless to say that

[1] Eng. Min. Jeffrey's Despatches. *Sb. of Imp. Rus. Ist. Ob.*, Vol. XLI, p. 465.
[2] Mardefeldt's Despatches. *Sb. of Imp. Rus. Ist. Ob.*, Vol. XV, p. 200.
[3] Kostomarov, Russkaya Istorya, Vol. II.

on the Tsar's next visit, Menshikov's palace was more magnificently furnished than ever. Nevertheless, Menshikov, meanly relying on the affection of the Tsar, and the advocacy of the good-natured Tsaritsa, continued to swindle his master to the very last, and it is said that the total amount of the fines he had to pay on conviction, amounted to more than 2,000,000 rubles (£500,000).

It must, however, have been some slight consolation to Peter the Great to reflect that despite the gross, and all but universal, venality of his friends and pupils, he could still lay his hand on, at least, one faithful servant who was above even the suspicion of any such vice. This political paragon was Heinrich Johann Friedrich, or, to give him the Russian *prænomina* by which he is better known, Andrei Ivanovich, Ostermann.

As his name suggests, Ostermann was of German extraction.[1] He was born at Bochum in Westphalia, in 1686, of respectable and highly intelligent middle-class parents, and, after receiving an excellent education, made the grand tour, and, while in Holland, made the acquaintance of the Dutch sailor Cornelius Kruse, who had risen in the Russian service to the rank of Vice-Admiral, and had, besides, a standing commission from Peter the Great, to pick up promising young men for him, wherever he could find them. Young Ostermann became Kruse's secretary, and accompanied him, in that capacity, to Russia. In 1717 the Tsar came on board Kruse's vessel, and enquired if he had any young man among his crew, capable of writing a good business letter. Kruse at once recommended Ostermann, who, by this time, had learnt Russian thoroughly, and Peter was so pleased with Ostermann's performance on this occasion,

---

[1] The only existing biography of this eminent statesman is Prince Dolgoruki's "Graf André Ivanovich Ostermann," in Russian, contributed to Vol. II of "Russkaya Besyeda." It is a very sympathetic, but by no means uncritical, work.

that, after submitting him to the searching test of a four hours' examination, he appointed him his private secretary. Quickly discovering that his new *protégé* understood German, Dutch, Italian, French and Latin, as well as Russian, the Tsar transferred him to his Chancellery, as translator, where he speedily became the right hand of the Vice-Chancellor Shafirov, whom he materially assisted during the troublesome negotiations which terminated in the Peace of the Pruth. The diplomatic talent Ostermann displayed on this occasion, as well as on a subsequent mission to Berlin, to persuade Prussia to take active measures against Sweden, so impressed the Tsar, that he bound down the young diplomatist not to quit the Russian service till the conclusion of a general peace. Ostermann, together with General Bruce, represented Russia at the ultimately abortive Aland Conference, in 1718, when he had the privilege of fencing diplomatically with the Talleyrand of the 18th century, Baron Goertz, and was one of the two Commissioners sent to treat with Sweden at the Congress of Nystad, in 1720. The Tsar was so anxious to conclude peace on the basis of the cession of the Baltic Provinces, that he was willing to surrender the important Finnish fortress of Viborg, rather than break off the negotiations, and, at the last moment, sent Yaguzhinsky to the conference, with secret instructions to abandon the fortress, if necessary. But Ostermann, determined not to let Viborg go, and resenting, besides, the interference of Yaguzhinsky, persuaded Shuvalov, the Commandant of Viborg, to invite the new commissioner to a banquet, which he accordingly did. As Ostermann had foreseen, Yaguzhinsky was carried away from table helplessly drunk, and, while he was sleeping off the effect of his debauch, Ostermann presented an ultimatum to the Swedish commissioners, to the effect that the negotiations would be broken off, unless Viborg were surrendered within two hours, and so frightened them that he carried his point.[1] When the Treaty of Nystad was placed in Peter's hands, he joyfully exclaimed that Russia had never before concluded such an advantageous peace, and that the clauses of the treaty were as adroitly worded as if he had put a hand to it himself. For his services on this occasion, Ostermann was created a Baron and a Privy Councillor. And the Tsar's solicitude for his ablest minister went still further. On his return from Nystad, Peter slapped him familiarly on the shoulder, and said: "This is all very well, Andrei Ivanovich. So long as I am alive, you'll be rich and famous; but what will happen to you when I am gone? You are a stranger in Russia, with no family connexions. You must be more firmly established. I mean to choose you a bride myself"—and he had him married forthwith to the wealthy Martha Ivanovna Stoyeshnevaya, who made him an excellent wife. But Ostermann was to rise still higher. Counting by years, he was still a very young diplomatist, being scarcely three and thirty; but, in truth, he was one of those men who never can be said to have been young. Even in his teens he had been remarkable for his precocious subtlety and a cold passionless way of regarding life. The French Minister, Campredon, was right in describing him as devoured by ambition, and he had a perfect genius for attaining his ends by circuitous methods, dextrously removing rivals out of his way without seeming to move in the matter himself. He was also afflicted with irritating fits of forgetfulness, when he would, for the moment, lose all recollection of certain languages which it did not suit him to remember;[2]

[1] Dolgoruki: Count A. I. Ostermann, p. 14.

[2] Several instances are given by the French Minister, Campredon. On one occasion Ostermann so completely forgot his French, that he was unable to translate an inconvenient phrase of Campredon's, for the benefit of his colleagues.—It should be remarked, however, that Campredon detested Ostermann, and therefore does not do him full justice.

and he used his very maladies (gout, for instance, from which he suffered severely) as diplomatic subterfuges. "When Ostermann is not pleased," writes the English Envoy, Rondeau, at a later date, "he pretends to be sick, and, during his absence, all the members of the Council are at a stand; sit a little, drink a dram, and then are obliged to go and court the Baron."[1] The Spanish Minister, the Duke of Liria, describes him as a consummate dissembler, and so skilful in giving an appearance of absolute truth to what was directly opposed to it, as to deceive the most wary.[2] Mardefeldt, the Prussian Envoy, said that no diplomatist was even so often ill *par politique* as Ostermann.[3] Compared, indeed, with the rough and brutal ways of the *canaille* by which he was surrounded, Ostermann's methods seem almost feline. He was a quiet, noiseless, seemingly inoffensive man, who always guarded his tongue, and, as the Russian proverb has it, "was a knife in nobody's eye." But because he shrunk from violence, and hated a fracas, he was no poltroon, as some have supposed, and, as we shall see, could face danger, and death itself, with imperturbable composure. The great blot on his career was the treacherous part he played in the plot to ruin his official chief, Shafirov, whom he supplanted as Vice-Chancellor towards the end of the reign of Peter the Great. But this is the only crime that can fairly be brought against him, and he possessed many virtues which were quite unintelligible to his contemporaries. Thus, he was faithful in a faithless, clean-handed[4] in a

[1] Rondeau's Despatches. *Sb. of Imp. Rus. Ist. Ob.*, Tome LXVI, p. 23.
[2] Liria: *Diario*, pp. 365—7. In another place he calls him "Extraordinariamento furbo"—"pero", [he adds] "es un furbo de quien necesitamos, y sin el cual no haremos nada aqui." p. 97.
[3] Compare Despatches of Campredon, Mardefeldt and Lefort.
[4] He would not even accept the usual "gratifications" from Foreign Courts, without the consent of his own Sovereign. All the Foreign Ministers without exception, are agreed as to his absolute incorruptibility.

corrupt, and humane in a cruel, age. His abilities, both
as a statesman and a diplomatist, are beyond cavil or
question, and his services to the country of his adoption
were inestimable. He gave himself up, heart and soul, to
the service of Russia, and was always ready to sacrifice
his personal interests to her advantage. But, perhaps, the
highest tribute to Ostermann's zeal and capacity is to be
found in the eulogium pronounced upon him by his master,
on an ever memorable occasion. "Ostermann," said Peter
the Great to those gathered around his death-bed, "Ostermann is indispensable to Russia. He best knows her needs,
and he is the only one of us who has never made a
diplomatic blunder."[1]

But Peter the Great had one remaining pupil who was
far dearer to him even than "Little Alec," and to whom
he gave his confidence with an absolute unreservedness,
denied even to the faithful Andrei Ivanovich—this pupil
was his second consort, and eventual successor, Catherine
Aleksyeevna.

The true origin of this enigmatical woman was, until
quite recently, one of the most obscure problems in Russian
history, and its obscurity was not a little intensified by the
accumulation of later legends, invented by malice or curiosity, to explain the origin of the first Russian Empress. It
was reserved for the critical acumen of the Russian historian,
Grot,[2] to dissipate much of the mystery, and, thanks mainly
to his investigations, the outlines of Catherine's early
career are now dimly discernible through the misty atmosphere of fiction that still environs them.[3]

The future Empress came of a Lithuanian stock, and was

[1] Dolgoruki: Ct. A. I. Ostermann.
[2] *Proischozhdenie Imperatritsa Ekaterinni I.*
[3] Compare Andreev: *Ekaterina Pervaya*; Semevsky: *Tsaritsa Ekaterina, Anna i Wilhelm Mons*, and Solovev: *Istoria Rossya*. The so-called *Mémoires du Règne de Catherine*, La Haye, 1728, is an almost worthless production.

one of the four children of a small Catholic yeoman, Samuel Skovronsky by name. In all probability she was born in 1683, but her father died of the plague while she was still little more than a babe, the family scattered and disappeared, and little Martha, for so she had been christened, was charitably adopted by Pastor Gluck, the Protestant superintendent of the Marienburg district, who brought her up with his own children, seemingly more as a servant than as a companion, however, for no pains seem to have been taken to teach her, and when she left the Glucks she could neither read nor write. It is said that Frau Gluck grew jealous of the comely damsel as she grew up, and fearing, or suspecting, a liaison between Martha and one of her own sons, got the girl off her hands by marrying her to a Swedish dragoon named Johan. A few months later the Swedes were compelled to evacuate Marienburg by the Russians, and Martha, deserted by her husband, whom she never saw again, became one of Marshal Sheremetev's prisoners of war, and was brought into the Russian camp, wrapped in a corporal's cloak to hide her nakedness. Menshikov saw her at Sheremetev's, and purchased her as a servant for his wife, and it was at Menshikov's house that Peter the Great first beheld her.

Hitherto Peter's relations with the other sex had either been unfortunate or scandalous. While still a youth, he had been married, much against his will, to Eudoxia Lopukhina. This unfortunate lady, whose greatest misfortune it was to love[1] her husband in vain, was, no doubt, a model Tsaritsa of the pre-Petrine period, but she was certainly no fit wife for Peter the Great. She was handsome, but could have had no other attraction in his eyes. Gentle and god-fearing,

[1] There are some pathetic letters of Eudoxia extant, in which she complains that "her light" never tells her of his health, and implores him not to "despise her petition." Of these letters Peter took not the slightest notice.

accustomed to the monastic seclusion of the *terem*, her mental horizon did not extend much beyond her embroidery frame, or her illuminated service-book. She was, in fact, of those Princesses who were not allowed to receive the foreign ministers lest they should inadvertently commit themselves by saying something silly, and thus bring disgrace upon their husbands. Peter always hated her as a living embodiment of the stupid detestable old Muscovite system, that he would fain do away with, shamefully neglected, and purposely traduced, her,[1] and ultimately sought *his* ideal of womanhood among the "pot-house Phrynes" of the Dutch Suburb. The sort of woman Peter would be likely to admire was a buxom sturdy wench whose natural element was a revel, who could dance like a Maenad, and drink like a Dutch skipper, and whose fancy would be tickled, instead of alarmed, by the hardiest pleasantries. With his arm round the ample waist of such a Dulcinea, a pipe full of strong tobacco in his mouth, and a bumper of hollands before him, "Old Peter" was perfectly happy. It was not long before he fancied he had found what he wanted in Anna Mons, the pretty but disreputable daughter of a German vintner[2] in Moscow, to whom he was introduced by his indulgent mentor, François Lefort,[3] about 1692. Fräulein Mons' easy manners inflamed still further his dislike of his stiff and serious consort. Hitherto he had been only cold, now he became downright cruel to her. A week after his return

[1] When it became necessary to obtain a divorce, Peter invented, or caused to be invented, a whole series of gallant adventures attributed to Eudoxia. It was pretended that even in the monastery to which she was ultimately banished, she contrived to find a lover. These stories circulated freely, and got to be believed by the foreign ministers at the Russian Court. They come, however, from too suspicious a source to be seriously considered.

[2] Some say he was a goldsmith. It is quite possible that he united both businesses.

[3] Semevsky: *Tsaritsa Ekaterina*, who insinuates that she was the mistress of them both at the same time.

from his first continental tour, he tried to persuade Eudoxia to take the veil, and thus release him. But though he stormed and raved for four hours, it was all in vain. The Tsaritsa maintained that it was her first duty as a mother, to remain in the world, and look after her child. Then Peter, with the aid of his favourite sister, Natalia, took away Alexius by force from his mother, and sent her to the Pokrovsky Monastery at Suzdal, and thence to the fortress of Schlusselburg, where she remained a close prisoner till the reign of her grandson Peter II. The liaison with Anna Mons continued for six or eight years longer, and at last that "loyal friend," as she subscribed herself, made up her mind that she was to be next Tsaritsa. But the German lady had miscalculated her influence. Peter was already tiring of her charms, and when first he beheld the Lithuanian damsel, he felt that his true ideal was at last before him. Martha Skovronskaya was not perhaps of the severely classical type of beauty that would have commended itself to the fastidious taste of a Louis XIV, for instance; but she was a fine specimen of the dairy-maid type of loveliness, in the full bloom of youth; a plethoric ploughman would have considered her absolutely perfect, and Peter the Great was of the same mind as the ploughman. Her full red lips, ardent black eyes, round rosy cheeks, magnificent raven-black hair, noble bust, and massive build, all spoke of quite an extraordinary measure of health and vigour. At a later day, the fresh whiteness of her neck and shoulders were also much admired, and we can well understand that dressed in cloth of silver, or orange-coloured atlas, she was a brilliant apparition. Peter made love to her forthwith, after his own peculiar fashion. It is said that his rude pleasantries at first brought tears to the eyes of the coy and comely serving-maid: but he consoled her with a brimming bumper of Tokay, and packed her off to a richly furnished little house in the suburbs of Moscow, where he visited her regularly, but secretly, till after the birth of their first daughter Catherine, when he made no more mystery of their relations. For by this time the Tsar had resolved on the hazardous experiment of marrying his mistress. He had discovered in her qualities which he had never suspected in women, a robust common-sense which no sophistry could deceive, an unerring tact, an intelligent sympathy, a playful humour, and a boundless good-nature that never took offence. Her moral influence over him was already extraordinary, and she was the only person who had the skill and courage to soothe him in the fits of maniacal fury to which, in his earlier years, he was so subject. The premonitory symptoms of these attacks were convulsive twitchings of the corners of the mouth, and, on perceiving these ominous signs, Peter's terrified attendants would straightway run off to fetch Martha. She would at once go and speak to him, and the mere sound of her voice had always a magical effect.[1] She would then induce him to lay his head on her lap or breast, till the convulsions abated, and he fell asleep, always awaking quite refreshed, and free from the racking headaches which used to follow these attacks. No wonder then if she at last became so indispensable to him, that it was a torment to be without her. The first step towards regulating the relations of this strange pair of lovers was Martha's public reception into the Orthodox Church, when the little Tsarevich Alexius stood godfather, and she was re-christened under the name of Catherine Alekseyevna.[2] In 1710, she received the title of *Gosudaruinya*, only given to Sovereign Princesses, and in 1711 she was publicly married to the Tsar, and thus became the Tsaritsa. The ceremony[3] took place at seven o'clock in the morning, at a

[1] *Andreev.*
[2] *I. e.*, daughter of Alexius, Alexius being her godfather.
[3] See Despatches of Eng. Min. Whitworth. *Sb. Imp. Rus. Ist. Ob.*, Vol. LXI, pp. 145—146.

little chapel belonging to Menshikov. The Tsar was married in his quality of Rear-Admiral, and none but naval officers took an active part in the function, a Vice-Admiral and a Rear-Admiral being the bridegroom's sponsors, and the Empress Dowager, and a Vice-Admiral's lady, the bride's. The bridesmaids were two of the Empress's own daughters, aged respectively five and two, but as these Princesses were of too tender an age to bear the fatigue of the whole ceremony, their places were subsequently taken by two of Peter's nieces. An entertainment followed at the Palace, whither the company went in procession to the sound of trumpets and kettledrums; but before they got to the door, his Majesty slid out of his sledge, somewhat impatiently, that he might have time to hang up a sconce, with six branches of ivory and ebony, which he had turned himself, and which he now placed in the middle of the room, over the table.[1] The company was very splendid, the dinner magnificent, the best Hungarian wine flowed in streams, and, during the ball which followed, the Tsar drew Count Vizthum and Mr. Whitworth aside, and jocosely informed them that the wedding was a fruitful one, as, although he and his spouse had only been married a few hours, they had five children already.[2]

Henceforth the Tsaritsa was her husband's inseparable companion. She was with him during the whole of the campaign of the Pruth, and Peter always attributed the successful issue of that disastrous war to the courage and sangfroid of his consort.[3] She was with him, too, during

[1] "He told me," says Whitworth, "that it had cost him a fortnight's time, and no one else had touched it; the piece is indeed curious for the workmanship, as well as for the hand that made it."

[2] Catherine bore him eleven children in all, of whom two, the Tsarevnas Anne and Elizabeth, survived him.

[3] The precise nature of her services on this occasion, are not known. Many Russian writers think that Peter purposely magnified her devotion and patriotism, to prepare the way for her subsequent coronation—an innovation which even he durst not introduce without some decent pretext.

his earlier Caspian campaigns, and was obliged, on this occasion, to shave off her beautiful hair, and wear a close-fitting fur cap to protect her from the scorching rays of the sun. Simple in his own tastes, Peter loved to surround her with the utmost pomp and splendour, and spared no pains or expense to make her happy. He was miserable without her, she was even obliged to take a part in his drunken revels, though here, also, she exercised, on the whole, a salutary influence; and he frequently took her opinion on affairs of state. When he was absent from her, he wrote to her regularly every three or four days, and the slightest delay on the part of his "little Kitty" in replying to him, caused him the most poignant disappointment, although as Kitty corresponded under difficulties (she was no penwoman, and had to employ a secretary to compose her *billets doux*),[1] she naturally could not always be quite so prompt as her "old man" desired her to be. The whole correspondence, indeed, shows Peter in quite a new and amiable light. The terrible Tsar, whose abominable cruelties make human nature shrink and shudder, who half starved his lawful consort, and tortured to death his eldest son, here appears as an almost romantically affectionate husband, alternately tender and sportive. Peter evidently put his whole heart into this correspondence. Throughout the one hundred and eight letters that compose it, there is not a single angry or imperious expression. We find a reproach here and there, no doubt; but that is only because she sends him but three letters in reply to five of his. "It is now a week since I heard from you," he writes on another occasion, "and therefore I am not without suspicion." Catherine replies in the same jocose tone, that the rumour reaches her that his errand to the Baltic is not purely

[1] Yet she could *speak* fluently Russian, as well as High and Low Dutch. She was illiterate rather than ignorant.

political, but that "the Queen of Sweden is anxious to fall "in love with him." In his laconic but pregnant style, Peter tells her of all his adventures and experiences, small and great. Thus he remarks on the poverty of the common people in France, or alludes to the victories of the Austrians over the Spaniards, and then passes on to the reminiscences of some past revel, or drinking bout. He sends her knick-knacks and curiosities from all the places he passes through, parrots, canaries, clocks from Nuremberg, lace from Brussels, salmon from the Caspian, a dwarf from France. Sometimes these valentines, for so they might well be called, are of a more solid and substantial description, as when he forwards to her a good dozen of choice Burgundy, or nine barrels of "nice salt herrings," keeping only one for himself. Nay, sometimes, *mirabile dictu*, the correspondence of these robustly practical people, is lit up by a gleam of idyllic sentiment. Thus, on one occasion, he sends her a little mint and a few flowers from a garden at Reval, which she herself had planted, adding: "All is well here; only when I go into the garden, and don't find thee there, it is so dull and lonely."—"I thank thee, dear friend, for thy present," replies Catharine. "'Tis not dear to me because I planted it, but it pleaseth me as being a gift from thy hand." This letter was accompanied by a hamper of fruit, plucked by her from her own garden, and "God give thee health to eat it," she adds. The birth of their son Peter[1] was an additional bond of union, and many of the prettiest letters in the collection are about "Petrushka,"[2] as the doting parents called him. "I must beg my dear daddy to protect me against Petrushka, for he has had no small a quarrel with me on thine account. Especially when

[1] He was born the day after the death of Alexius' consort, Charlotte. He died when he was four years old.

[2] "Little Peterkin."

I speak of thee, and tell him that Dada is going away; he does not like at all to hear the words: Dada is going away!"

The death of this babe, whose portrait now hangs in the Petrine Gallery of the Winter Palace, had important political consequences. The last remaining male of the House of Romanov was now the Grand Duke Peter, the only son of the murdered Tsarevich Alexius. All Russia looked upon him as the one legitimate heir to the throne, but Peter the Great detested the very sight of his grandson, and, well aware that the reactionary Party looked upon the little Grand Duke as their future hope, resolved to exclude him from the succession. But who, then, was to succeed him? His own daughters, Anne and Elizabeth, were still mere children, and his nieces, the daughters of his brother Ivan, had married foreign Princes, and were living abroad. The Tsaritsa alone remained, and Peter determined to secure the throne for her whom he loved best in all the world. He prepared the way for this daring, this unheard of, innovation, by that curious document, the Ukaz of 1722. Time-honoured custom had hitherto reckoned primogeniture in the male line as the best title to the Russian Crown; in the Ukaz of 1722, Peter denounced primogeniture in general as a stupid, dangerous, and even unscriptural, practice. History, both sacred and profane, he argues, justified and even commanded sensible parents to make alterations in this respect, whenever necessary, and he concluded by making the succession to the Russian Empire in future absolutely dependent on the will of the reigning Tsar. "Thus," concludes the imperious lawgiver, "children or children's children, will not be tempted to fall into the sin of Absalom, and this Ukaz will be a curb upon them."

This Ukaz was itself but a preliminary step to a still more sensational event. On the 15th Nov., 1723, Peter issued a manifesto, in which, after explaining that from the days of Justinian and Heraclius to the present day, it had always been the custom of Christian Princes, both in the east and west, to crown their Consorts, he proceeded, at some length, and in very affectionate terms, to cite the services rendered to him by his Tsaritsa, in the past especially, during the Turkish War, when "with great self-sacrifice she shared all the trials and discomforts of a soldier's life, encouraging us, and our whole army, by her valour and heroism..." "Wherefore," proceeds the manifesto, "by the authority given to us by God, we have resolved to reward such great services of our Consort, by crowning her with the Imperial crown." That Peter himself should have considered some sort of an explanation necessary at all, is the clearest proof that he felt he was treading on dangerous ground. The whole nation listened aghast to the manifesto. The coronation of a woman, was, in the opinion of the Russian people, an unheard of, a scandalous innovation. The only Princess who had ever enjoyed that distinction, was Maria Mnishka, the consort of the False Demetrius, in the 16th century, and she, at any rate, was of noble birth. But what sort of a Tsaritsa is this? people asked each other. Who was she? Whence did she spring? Who were her father and mother? She had come to Russia not merely as a stranger, but as a captive, a half-naked captive, a slave who owed her very life to the clemency of the Tsar, her lord and master, and now, forsooth, this slave was to wear his crown, and sit upon his throne! Was it not clear that she was a witch who had cast her spells upon him? — But Peter was utterly regardless of the feelings and prejudices of his people in this respect. Theodosius Yavorsky, President of the Holy Synod, Archbishop of Novgorod, and the indefatigable Tolstoy, were sent to Moscow, six months beforehand, to make the necessary preparations on the grandest scale possible. The Court remained at St. Petersburg till March 1724, and a few weeks before his departure for the coronation festivities at the old Capital, Peter horrified the inhabitants of the new by a spectacle of a very different character. This was the public execution of the chief Fiscal, Nestorov, on the Vasilevsky island, where now the University stands, for peculation. All public officials, and especially Nestorov's subordinates, were under strict orders to be present, and the Tsar himself looked on from a window in the Revision-Department. Nestorov, who was condemned to be broken on the wheel, and then beheaded, suffered heroically. When both arms and legs of the unhappy wretch had been smashed, the Tsar sent his Adjutant-General Mamonov offering Nestorov "mercy," that is to say immediate decapitation, if he would make a full and complete confession of his misdeeds on the spot. Nestorov faintly replied that he had nothing more to confess, and that in his terrible position he could have spoken anything but the truth, is inconceivable. But Peter, who had a mania for full confessions, did not believe him, and furiously ordered the execution to proceed. So the delinquent's back was broken across the wheel, and, still breathing, he was carried to the scaffold, and there beheaded.

On 22nd March, 1724, Peter and Catherine set out for Moscow, and there, on the 7th May, the coronation took place with great pomp and magnificence. At an early hour in the morning, a signal gun fired from the Kremlin, summoned thither all who were to take part in the procession, and at ten o'clock, the Court, the Senate, the General Staff, and all the great Officers of State, escorted the Emperor and Empress to the *Yspensky Sobor*, or Cathedral of the Assumption,[1] which had been gorgeously decorated with scarlet and cloth of gold. In the centre of the nave a

---

[1] The best account of the coronation is to be found in Zhmakin: *Koronatsy russkick imperatorov*. Compare Semevsky: *Tsaritsa Ekaterina*, and Andreev: *Ekaterina Pervaya*.

throne had been erected with an ascent up to it of twelve steps all covered with velvet and gold galloon, and a canopy above it of the same materials. Beneath the canopy were two chairs for the Imperial Consorts, of antique workmanship, encrusted with precious stones. The way from the altar to the throne was covered with the most costly Persian carpets. At the door of the Cathedral, the clergy in full canonicals, headed by Theodosius, Archbishop of Novgorod, and Theophanes, Archbishop of Pskov, met the Imperial Consorts, who kissed the cross presented to them, and, after being censed and asperged, proceeded up the nave of the Cathedral, and, mounting the throne, sat down on their chairs amidst deathlike silence. Shortly afterwards the Emperor arose, holding his sceptre in his right hand, and, turning to the clergy, exclaimed in a loud voice: "Whereas it is our intention to crown our beloved Consort, and the reason whereof hath already been made manifest, complete now the ceremony according to the ordinances of Holy Church!"—The clergy then approached the throne, and Catherine, after reciting the orthodox creed aloud, knelt down on a cushion before the Primate Theodosius, who made the sign of the cross above her head and gave her his benediction. Then Theodosius, with the assistance of Theophanes, took the heavy imperial mantle from a table hard by, and laid it across the shoulders of the Empress, while Peter himself placed the crown on her head. Overcome with gratitude, and with the tears streaming down her cheeks, Catherine would have knelt before him and kissed his hand, but he lovingly restrained her. While the *Mnogolyetie*, or prayer for a long life, was being solemnly chanted by the choir, and salvos of artillery, and the pealing of all the bells in the city, announced the event to the people, the Emperor and Empress took their places in the chancel, and Catherine, removing her crown and mantle, knelt

## CATHERINE ALEKSYEEVNA AND PETER. 63

before the altar, was anointed with the Holy Chrism, and then received the Eucharist, whereupon Archbishop Theophanes, the most eloquent ecclesiastical orator of his day, preached a commendatory sermon. Peter, who had long been ailing, exhausted by the arduous ceremony, now quitted the Cathedral, and returned to the Kremlin; but the newly crowned Empress walked alone, at the head of a new procession from the Cathedral of the Assumption to the Archangel Cathedral, according to ancient custom, in full regalia, Menshikov walking by her side, and scattering handfuls of gold and silver among the people. The crown of Catherine, on this occasion, was the most costly and magnificent ever worn hitherto by a Russian Sovereign. It was made in Paris, on the model of the old Byzantine Imperial Crown, and was studded with no fewer than 2,564 precious stones. Each of the numerous pearls on it was worth 2,000 rubles,[1] and Peter had stripped his own crown of its finest diamonds, the better to adorn his consort's. But the most remarkable jewel of all was a ruby as large as a pigeon's egg, placed immediately beneath a cross of brilliants at the apex of the crown. This incomparable gem was purchased at Pekin by the Russian merchant Spafiry, at Menshikov's command, for 60,000 rubles.[2] The imperial mantle had also been made in France, of very heavy and costly materials, besides being literally encrusted with hundreds of large double-headed gold eagles. The Empress had a splendid physique, and her strength was prodigious,[3] yet on this hot spring day, a hundred and

---

[1] About £500. A ruble at this time was worth a crown English. See despatches of the Eng. Min. Mackenzie. *Sb. Imp. Rus. Ist. Ob.*, Tom. LXI, p. 270.

[2] £15,000. The whole crown was valued at 1,500,000 rubles (£375,000) and weighed four and a half pounds.

[3] It is said that at the marriage of young Count Golovkin, she held, in her outstretched right hand, her husband's massive bâton, which Peter's stalwart guardsman, young Buturlin, could not even lift.

fifty pounds of gold and purple hanging from her shoulders (for that was the weight of the mantle) was almost too much even for her powers, especially as the preceding three days' fast had somewhat reduced her, so that it is no wonder if she had to pause and rest once or twice during her passage between the two Cathedrals. After kneeling in prayer at the tombs of her ancestors at the Archangel Cathedral, and again at the Monastery of the Ascension, Catherine returned to the Kremlin, where the young Duke of Holstein,[1] then such a prominent figure at the Russian Court, received her at the foot of the Beautiful Staircase, and conducted her to the Granovitaya Palace, where a magnificent banquet was provided for the Foreign Ministers and the great Officers of State. Nor were the common people forgotten. While the banquet was proceeding, they were regaled, in the great square in front of the Kremlin, with two roast oxen of colossal dimensions, stuffed, to bursting, with all kinds of game and poultry, while two fountains, one running with white, and one with red, wine, played beside the platform on which the oxen were placed. Nevertheless, the coronation was not popular. Quite apart from the very intelligible dislike of the Russians for the upstart Tsaritsa, Peter himself had been more than usually harsh and tyrannical on the occasion. The best horses belonging to the merchants of Moscow, had been forcibly appropriated by Tolstoy, at the Tsar's command, to mount his guards in the procession, and, contrary to immemorial usage, no general amnesty was promulgated on the occasion. Nay, more, when Catherine, always merciful and indulgent herself, and fondly imagining that her consort could refuse her nothing on such a day as this, pleaded hard for the exiled ex-Vice-Chancellor Shafirov, Peter rudely repulsed her, and

[1] See chap. III.

bade her, with a frown, never to mention the man's name to him again.

Thus Catherine Aleksyeevna had been elevated, by her devoted consort, to a pedestal of glory so lofty, as seemingly to place her henceforth quite beyond the reach of the slings and arrows of outrageous fortune. Yet, such is the instability of human greatness, that, within a few weeks of this crowning triumph, her future prospects were suddenly darkened, and she was threatened with the loss of her consort's favour, and its inevitable consequence—utter ruin.

Amongst Catherine's attendants was Wilhelm Mons, the brother of Peter's former mistress, who was as handsome, and every whit as unscrupulous, as his sister. He was clever and assiduous however, made himself very useful at Court, rose to the rank of Kammerherr, and at last became a personage of some importance, the Foreign Ministers, and even Princes like the Duke of Holstein, not disdaining to approach, with bribes and caresses, the adroit and good-looking young German, who was known to possess the Empress's confidence, and suspected of enjoying her secret favour. I am inclined myself to think that Catherine's relations with Mons, though dangerously familiar, were perfectly innocent. [1] She was naturally an expansive, warm-hearted woman, always grateful for attentions paid to her, and, illiterate as she was, very much dependent on the good offices of her servants. On the other hand she was singularly shrewd and sensible, and well aware of the thorough system of

[1] The legends of Andreev on this subject are contrary to evidence. Semevsky's indictment in *Tsaritsa Ekaterina ... Anna i Wilhelm Mons*, is based indeed on a few facts, but facts transparently insufficient, often flimsy, and quite capable of a favourable interpretation. The whole tone of the book, too, is very scandalous and spiteful. The account of the matter in the Danish Envoy Westphalen's narrative (cited in full by the Duke of Liria in his *Diario*) deserves a little more attention, and certainly seems to point to great familiarity between the Empress and Mons, but nothing more, I think, for the reasons given in the text above.

espionage in force at Peter's Court. An intrigue with Mons could not possibly have escaped attention for long, and the consequences of detection being too terrible to contemplate, she would have hesitated to compromise herself, even if she had been inclined to do so, which I very much doubt, taking into consideration the indisputable affection she always entertained for her husband. That Mons, like all successful upstarts, may have presumed too far is very probable; but if he did so, he more than atoned for his folly by his death. Some opine that the Tsar's suspicions were first aroused by the vigilance of Yaguzhinsky, who publicly reproached Mons for his impudent conduct; but we know that secret spies and informers were at work long before the coronation festivities, though it was not till some months after the return of the Court to Petersburg, that the storm burst forth. At last, on the 5th Nov., 1724, Mons was arrested on a charge of receiving bribes, and all his papers were seized and carefully examined by the Tsar in person, at the Imperial Chancellery. The whole affair was conducted with the utmost secrecy, but after a rigorous examination, and frequent application of the question extraordinary in the torture chamber, the miserable Kammerherr was beheaded. We have it on fairly good authority that it was now that the Tsar, in an access of fury, destroyed a will whereby he had appointed Catherine his successor; but, however that may be, it is quite certain that for a few weeks after this mysterious catastrophe, there was a visible estrangement between the Imperial consorts.

But this estrangement did not last, and it must also be borne in mind that during this time Peter was unusually morbidly irritable. For some months he had been visibly ailing. Excesses of all kinds, recklessly indulged in from his earliest days, had not only undermined his magnificent constitution, but made it difficult for his intensely obstinate nature to submit even to the slightest, the most salutary, restraint. In 1722, during his Persian campaigns, appeared the first symptoms of the malady to which he was to succumb. During the next two years, he was almost constantly in the hands of the doctors; but, though he swallowed their drugs, he could not bring himself to obey their directions, and, despite their advice, gave himself up, as usual, to his exhausting labours, and his still more injurious relaxations. During the summer and autumn of 1724, he was seriously ill, and medicine began to lose its effect upon him. In the beginning of January 1725, he caught a violent chill by plunging into the half-frozen Neva to save the life of a drowning soldier,[1] and instead of keeping his room for a time, as advised, went about as usual. But what contributed, most of all, to kill him was his participation in a riotous debauch, when he drank to excess, and almost immediately afterwards, 20th January, was compelled to take to his bed.[2] For a time, indeed, his naturally robust constitution, assisted by the skilful treatment of an able Italian physician named Azzariti,[3] and of an English surgeon, Dr. Horne, who successfully performed a difficult and dangerous operation,[4] enabled the illustrious patient to rally to such an extent that, on Feb. 3rd, he was actually declared to be out of danger. On the same day Tolstoy, Golovkin, and Apraksin were admitted

[1] For Peter I's death, compare the Despatches of the Prussian Min. Mardefelt. *Sb.* of the *Imp. Rus. Ist. Ob.*, Vol. XV., pp. 250 et seq.; Despatches of Polish Min. Lefort, do., Vol. III., pp. 398—404; Despatches of Fr. Min. Campredon, do., do., Vol. LII., 415—440. See also Dolgoruki: Graf A. I. Ostermann, pp. 20—24.

[2] "La mort au vrai du Czar provient d'une maladie dont le flux à été arrêté par la débauche de l'élection du Knes-Papa, et qui a produit des ulcères qui ont pourri les vaisseaux et la gangrène y a mis fin."—Lefort. The election of the Knyaz' Papa by the way, was a profane parody of the ceremonies of the Church, accompanied and followed by liberal potations.

[3] See Campredon.

[4] For details, see *Campredon* and *Mardefeldt*.

to see him, and he ordered the old Admiral, who was deeply affected, to release some hundreds of political prisoners. He also enjoined his three Ministers to protect all the foreigners in the Capital, in case he himself should die. Fresh remedies, administered the same evening, seemed to still further strengthen him, and the doctors talked about letting him get up and walk about his room; but towards the evening of the 6th, there was a distinct change for the worse, and immediately after partaking of a little oatmeal gruel, he was attacked by such violent convulsions that the end was expected every moment, and the great Officers of State, the Senators, Heads of Colleges, and the Colonels of the Guard were summoned in hot haste to the Palace. Again, however, the patient rallied, and was even able to give a few verbal directions. Throughout his illness he had shown much irritability, and some fear of death; but he repeatedly expressed contrition for his past misdeeds, endeavoured, so far as he was able, to make reparation, and gratefully accepted the consolations of the Church, communicating thrice in seven days. On the 7th, Archbishop Theophanes shrived the Emperor, who exclaimed with great fervour: "Lord, I believe, help Thou my unbelief!" —Shortly afterwards he added, as if speaking to himself: "I hope God will forgive me my innumerable sins, because of the good I have tried to do to my people." The Empress who never quitted his side for an instant during his last illness, now besought him to make his peace with the Almighty, by forgiving Menshikov who had again fallen into disgrace for gross malpractices. Peter consented to do so, and the Prince was admitted, and pardoned, for the last time, by his dying master. Shortly afterwards, fever set in again, the patient became delirious, and was heard to mutter: "I have shed my own blood!—I have shed my own blood!"—On the night of the 8th February, however, he recovered consciousness, and his first words were: "Where's little Annie? I would see her."—His favourite daughter, the Tsarevna Anne, was at once summoned, but before she could arrive, her father was again delirious, and never recovered consciousness. The agony was long and terrible. Catherine, bathed in tears, knelt at the bedside all night, praying incessantly that her consort might be released from his torments. At last, between four and five o'clock, on the morning of the 9th, just as she had pronounced the words: "O Lord! I pray Thee, open Thy Paradise to receive unto Thyself this great soul!"—the Tsar expired. He died in the 53rd year of his age, and the 43rd of his reign.

Peter I had a singularly shrewd, lucid, and logical, but somewhat narrow, intellect. His mind was so intensely, so exclusively practical that it scarcely heeded, and made but small account of, anything that did not immediately subserve the business of life. Whole departments of knowledge were quite beyond his ken, and, in this respect, he was inferior even to Charles XII, who, though he, too, had little sense for art and literature, took, nevertheless, a keen and intelligent interest in speculative science, and was wont to amuse his rare leisure by disputing on the most abstruse philosophical subjects, with men of learning. But if Peter was master of but few ideas, he mastered these few thoroughly, and the marvellous energy of will, which enabled him to translate his ideas into action, was the real secret of his greatness. He was, indeed, a man of character rather than a man of genius. Morally, also, Peter seems, at first sight, to stand on an altogether lower plane than his illustrious antagonist. We find no trace in the Tsar of that profound piety, that unswerving veracity, that absolute self-command, that nobly austere sobriety, which are the salient features of the heroic young Swede's character, and his fairest titles to fame. Peter's piety was problematical, he had no regard whatever for truth, if it suited his purpose to tell falsehoods, and he was the slave of the vilest appetites and passions. "Here am I reforming a great Empire, and I cannot reform myself!" he cried on one memorable occasion. And yet, for all his noble qualities, Charles proved a scourge to his country, and, in all probability, his sudden death alone saved her from utter destruction, whereas the base and brutal Peter rescued *his* country from barbarism, and laid the foundations of the largest and strongest Empire in the world. But, in point of fact, Charles was quite deficient in that sense of public responsibility, which is the chief virtue of a good ruler. He never seemed to realize that his subjects had rights as well as duties. War was his one delight, glory his one ambition; to him Sweden was not so much a State, as a training school for soldiers. Peter, on the other hand, dedicated himself, from first to last, to the service of his people. Their welfare was always his first care. His political ideal was a new, a civilized Russia, and to the realization of this ideal he devoted himself with an enthusiasm, a single-mindedness, that have never been surpassed. That his sanguine over-eagerness often led him into serious blunders, is undeniable, that his methods were frequently cruel, and even scandalous, is only too true, but his aim was a lofty one, and even if he had only striven to attain it, and failed, he would still have deserved the name of Great.

Catherine I.

# CHAPTER III.

## CATHERINE ALEKSYEEVNA ON THE THRONE.

### (Feb. 1725—May 1727.)

WHO is to succeed Peter?—Presence of mind of Catherine—Energetic efforts on her behalf of Menshikov and Tolstoy—The higher clergy won over to Catherine—The Grand Duke Peter's Party—Debate in the Council Chamber—Violent scenes—Catherine proclaimed Autocrat—Attitude of Moscow and the Army of the Ukraine—Conciliatory attitude of the new Empress—Troubles with her servants—Influence of Menshikov—Charles Frederick, Duke of Holstein—His early career and character—Institution of the Verkhovny Tainy Sovyet, or Supreme Privy Council—Domestic affairs—Distress of the people—Financial shifts—Prosecution and degradation of the Archbishop of Novgorod—Condition of European politics—Predominance of England—Causes of her hostility to Russia—Diplomatic contest between the two States—Attitude of France—The Hanoverian Alliance—English fleet despatched to the Baltic—Indignation of Catherine—Russia joins the Austro-Spanish League—Prussia—Denmark—Uncertain attitude of Sweden—Condition of that power—Chancellor Horn—Russian intrigues at Stockholm—Sweden joins the Hanoverian Alliance—Polish affairs—The Courland question—Maurice of Saxony elected Duke of Courland—Intervention of Menshikov—Yaguzhinsky in Poland—Corruption of the Poles—The question of the Russian Succession—Popularity of the Grand Duke Peter—Illness of the Empress—Critical position of Menshikov—He goes over to the Grand Duke's Party—Counter-conspiracy of Tolstoy—Last moments of Catherine—Disgraceful scene in the Antechamber—Arrest and banishment of Tolstoy and his accomplices—Death of Catharine I—Her character.

AND now the question arose, who was to be the successor of Peter the Great—a woman or a boy? To all appearance the boy, that is to say the Grand Duke Peter, the only son of the Tsarevich Alexius, had by far the best chance. The vast majority of the aristocracy and the clergy, as well as of the nation at large, regarded him as the one rightful heir, while both the upper and the lower classes detested the upstart Tsaritsa, and would willingly have shut her and her daughters up in a monastery for the rest of their lives. The stern and ever increasing severity of Peter's system of government had, moreover, produced universal discontent, a discontent the more bitter and intense because, hitherto, it had had no opportunity of expressing itself, and with that system Catherine was inseparably associated. The army also murmured in secret, and with good reason. The pay of the soldiers was sixteen months in arrear, and they had been driven almost to desperation by the exhausting labours imposed upon them during the last years of the late Emperor's reign; in the construction of the Ladoga Canal, and other public works, for instance, their lives had been sacrificed by thousands. "According to all human appearances," wrote [1] the Prussian Minister Mardefeldt, the day after the Tsar's death, "it is all up with the prosperity of the widowed Empress."

But, as so often happens in human affairs, the apparently impossible turned out to be the easiest and most natural way out of the difficulty; yet it was certainly the energy and the presence of mind of Catherine herself, at least in the first instance, that saved the situation. As soon as she perceived that the malady of the Emperor must end fatally, she secretly instructed Menshikov and Tolstoy to sound the other Senators as to the succession to the throne, and to take measures on her behalf generally.[2] It was not so much personal ambition as the mere instinct of self-preservation, which made her look to these men for help

---

[1] Mardefeldt Desp. *Imp. Ist. Rus. Ob. Sb.*, Vol. XV, p. 250.
[2] Campredon Desp. *Imp. Ist. Rus. Ob. Sb.*, Vol LII, p. 458.

at this crisis. She knew right well that they *dare* not refuse to assist her. Neither Menshikov nor Tolstoy could hope to save themselves from destruction if a reaction set in, and a reaction was bound to set in if the Grand Duke Peter were now placed upon the throne. Their interests and their perils were therefore identical with those of the Tsaritsa. Both ministers, with characteristic energy, at once proceeded to smooth the way to the throne for the only candidate who was likely to maintain the existing Petrine reforms. Menshikov's first step was to win over the Guards who had always had an endless respect and devotion for their great Emperor. After taking the officers to the bedside of the expiring Tsar, he introduced them into the apartments of the Tsaritsa, who reminded them of the campaign they had gone through together, of the care she had always had for their welfare and comfort, and pathetically appealed to them, in conclusion, not to desert her. "I am sure," said she, "that you cannot find it in your hearts to desert me."[1] Moved by this appeal to their affections, the officers declared unanimously, with tears and sobs, that they would rather be cut to pieces at her feet than allow anyone but herself to ascend the throne. They then returned to their men, and informed them of what had happened. The soldiers were not behind their officers in enthusiasm. "We have lost our father," they cried, "but we have still our mother left!" But the Empress, always circumspect, did not put her whole trust in the generous sentiments of her soldiery. She had at her disposal other means of binding them to her, and she employed these means with prudent lavishness. The Guards were promised an increase of pay in future, and Catherine took the additional precaution [2] of sending money to the fortress of St. Peter and St. Paul, to pay the arrears due to the

[1] Mardefeldt.
[2] Campredon.

garrison. The sentinels before all the doors of the Palace were then doubled, and the streets of the Capital were patrolled by troops.

Menshikov, meanwhile, with uncommon prudence, had reconciled himself with all his enemies,[1] especially with Yaguzhinsky, whose devotion to the Empress was equal to his own, and, aided by Tolstoy, succeeded in bringing the higher clergy also over to Catherine's side. But here, indeed, he met with little difficulty. The archprelates of the Russian Church, Theodosius, Archbishop of Novgorod, Theophanes, Archbishop of Pskov, and the chief members of the recently instituted Holy Synod, were in very much the same position as himself. No novelties are so detestable to the people at large as ecclesiastical novelties, and both Theodosius and Theophanes had thoroughly identified themselves with the most offensive reforms of Peter the Great. The former had raised up for himself a whole host of foes by a zeal that had not always been according to knowledge, while the latter was hated even more because of his low birth and great learning.[2] He was also the author of the detested *Dukhony Reglament*, or new code for the regulation of ecclesiastical affairs. Both Archbishops felt that, at this crisis, they must stand or fall with Menshikov and Tolstoy.

All these measures had been taken not a moment too soon. When it became known that the Emperor was *in extremis*, the faction of the Grand Duke Peter assembled at the Palace. It included, as already mentioned, the larger portion of the old aristocracy and the clergy, at least half the Senate, although that was a purely Petrine institution, and some of the most distinguished officers in the army. The chief members of this party were the great families

[1] Mardefeldt.
[2] Solovev *Istorya Rossy*, Vol. XVII.

of the Golitsuins, the Dolgorukis, the Trubetskoys, the Baratinskys, the Narishkins, the Lopukhins, and the Ryepnins, who represented more than half the wealth of Russia,[1] and nearly all the influence that unofficial rank still retained in that country. But it was much weakened by the mutual jealousies of the Golitsuins and the Ryepnins, and though it numbered among its ranks many men of high character and considerable talent, it could boast of nobody with the administrative experience and phenomenal energy of a Menshikov, a Tolstoy, or even a Yaguzhinsky. Two military celebrities it possessed indeed, whom the opposite party greatly feared, and who might even have proved dangerous on an emergency, namely, Field Marshals Mikhail Mikhailovich Golitsuin, the one really notable Russian general that the Great Northern War had produced, and Anicetus Ivanovich Ryepnin, a blunt and straightforward soldier, who had not been afraid to tell the truth even to Peter the Great. But Golitsuin was absent in the Ukraine, 500 miles away, and Ryepnin had been somewhat under a cloud ever since Charles XII had defeated him, with a mere handful of men, at the Battle of Holowczyn. Nevertheless the preliminary debate in the Council Chamber was rude and fierce. The Magnates had barely assembled, when Prince Demetrius Mikhailovich Golitsuin arose, and proposed that the Grand Duke Peter should be proclaimed Emperor, with a Regency composed of the Tsaritsa and the Senate. Count Tolstoy at once objected that a minority was dangerous; that the Empire needed, above all, a firm and experienced ruler; that the Tsaritsa had been initiated into the art of government by her late consort; that she had already given ample and unquestionable proofs of her heroism, magnanimity, and capacity for affairs, and finally, that the mere fact of her coronation

[1] Dolgoruki: Graf A. I. Ostermann.

gave her an incontestable right to the throne. Tolstoy's words were warmly applauded by a group of officers of the Guards, standing in a corner of the room. How these gentlemen came to be in the Council Chamber at all, at such a moment, nobody knew, nor had anyone of the partisans of the Grand Duke the courage to enquire. When, however, a major of the Guards, General Buturlin,[1] proceeded to a little window overlooking the courtyard, and gave some order to the soldiers below, which was immediately followed by a muffled roll of drums, distinctly audible in the silence of the room, Marshal Ryepnin, unable to contain himself any longer at such a piece of audacity on the part of his subaltern, stepped forth, and angrily accosted Buturlin. "How dare you, Sir, give orders without my knowledge!" he exclaimed. "Do you forget that I am the Commander-in-Chief?"—"What I have done, your Excellency," replied Buturlin, "was done by the express command of our Sovereign Lady, the Empress Catherine, whom you and I, and every faithful subject, are bound to obey immediately and unconditionally."[2] Nevertheless the intervention of Ryepnin had revived the courage of the Grand Duke's faction, and an acrimonious discussion began which lasted till four o'clock in the morning. Demetrius Golitsuin proposed a conference between the two Parties, but Menshikov replied that no conference was necessary, as the only possible candidate for the throne was the Tsaritsa, who had indeed been actually crowned Empress seven months before. Golitsuin then proposed that the authority of the Empress should be limited, but this led to a terrible disturbance, in which both Tolstoy and Menshikov waxed very warm. At last Ryepnin, always jealous of the influence of the House of Golitsuin, agreed with Tolstoy that Cather-

[1] Menshikov had won over this able officer the evening before.
[2] Compare Dolgoruki, Campredon, Solovev, and Mardefelt.

ine should be elevated to the throne without any limitation of her authority, whereupon the Grand Chancellor Golovkin, who, up to that moment, had preserved a cautious neutrality, and remained absolutely silent, declared himself to be of the same opinion. After this there could be no doubt as to the issue of the debate, so that the Grand Admiral Apraksin felt himself to be perfectly safe in sending for Cabinet-Secretary Makarov, and inquiring whether his late Majesty had left any will appointing his successor. Makarov at once replied that he had not. "Then," cried Apraksin, "I propose that her Majesty be proclaimed Autocrat, with all the prerogatives of her late consort, and that a deputation be formed to wait upon her Majesty, and acquaint her with the wishes of her dutiful subjects."—A deputation of the Senate and Nobility accordingly waited upon the Empress, whom they found kneeling, bathed in tears, at the bedside of Peter the Great, who had just breathed his last sigh. Respecting her grief, the deputation withdrew, but presently, after closing the eyes of her dead consort, Catherine rejoined them in the Council Chamber, sobbing bitterly, and after pathetically lamenting the irreparable loss that both she and the Empire had sustained, recommended herself to their protection as "a widow and orphan." She had scarcely finished speaking when Apraksin fell at her feet, informed her of the resolution of the Senate, and declared that he and his colleagues were ready to shed the last drop of their blood in her behalf. The officers of the Guards, who were also present, confirmed the assurance of the Grand Admiral with loud plaudits, whereupon the assembly exclaimed with one voice: "Long live our beloved Empress! God grant her a happy and prosperous reign!" A few hours later all the Guards took the oath of allegiance, and the Senate followed their example. The reign of Catherine I had begun.

For the next few weeks, however, the Government felt uneasy and insecure. The new Capital was won, but the attitude of the old, or, rather, the real, Capital of Russia, Moscow, was still uncertain. Trouble was anticipated there, and General Mamonov was sent to keep order. But the fears of Catherine's partisans proved unfounded, or at least exaggerated. A few *raskolniki* had indeed to be knouted or roasted before they would take the new oath of allegiance, and many peasants and priests expressed their dissatisfaction at seeing a woman on the throne, but there was no serious disturbance of any sort. A much graver cause of anxiety was the supposed hostility to the new Government of Field Marshal Michael Golitsuin, who lay in the Ukraine with an army of 60,000 men. He had never been a friend of Peter's reforms, or of Peter's second family, and he was well known to be the most popular officer in the Russian army. The foreign Ministers shared the apprehensions of the new Government on this score. "If they can only gain Golitsuin in the Ukraine," wrote the Saxon Minister Lefort... "no trouble need be apprehended, but if not, God only knows what will happen.[1] —I see the throne tottering already," he adds. "The Empress has great need of good counsellors, and must take care what she is about." But this bugbear also disappeared. An officer of high rank was sent at once to the Ukraine, with an order to Golitsuin to return to St. Petersburg without delay. He was not informed of the Emperor's death until afterwards, and secret instructions were sent to his officers to arrest him on the slightest demonstration of mutiny. Happily it was not necessary to proceed to such extremities. Golitsuin took the oath without demur.

It is only due to the Empress to say that during this

[1] Lefort Desp. *Imp. Ist. Rus. Sb.*, Vol. III, pp. 404—405. Compare Campredon.

anxious time, she acted with great wisdom and prudence. Her safest policy, indeed, was a policy of conciliation, but it came naturally to her to be clement and generous, and her earlier measures produced a very favourable impression, and greatly improved her position. A general amnesty was proclaimed immediately after her accession. All political prisoners were released, including the Cossack deputies who had been thrown into jail by Peter the Great for petitioning for a renewal of their ancient privileges. Catherine now promised to confirm these privileges, and the Cossacks, in return, enthusiastically volunteered to serve their "great mother," in future, without pay. The severe poll-tax which weighed so heavily upon the unfortunate peasantry, that thousands of them, in order to escape it, fled every year to Poland, or to the steppes of the nomadic Bashkirs, was reduced by one-third, and a decree of the Senate forbade, in future, the employment of soldiers in the construction of the Ladoga Canal, an onerous and exhausting labour, which had always been the most bitter grievance of the army. Catherine, indeed, spared no pains to keep the army in a good humour. She held frequent reviews. She gave the Guards a new and splendid uniform. She frequently dined at the officers' mess in her capacity of Colonel, and gave the men drinks with her own hand. When Captain Chicherin of the Guards seriously injured himself by falling on his partisan, the Empress rose from table to attend to his wounds, and nursed him herself in one of the rooms of her palace, where he had the best medical advice procurable. She took care, too, to do away with many of the abuses that had disgraced the Court of her consort. All the foreign Ministers agree that the Russian Court, under Catharine I, was much more decent than it had been under Peter the Great. One no longer saw there the swarms of misshapen dwarfs, mountebanks and buffoons that had amused the leisure of the late Tsar. The gross abuse of making the ladies drink as much[1] as the men on public occasions, was also done away with. But Catherine's greatest difficulty was to keep the peace among her jealous and turbulent servants, who were perpetually flying at each other's throats. Only a few days after Peter the Great's funeral, there was a most disgraceful scene in full Senate between Menshikov and Yaguzhinsky. As usual, the latter was in liquor, and he reviled his Serene Highness with brutal violence. Menshikov threatened the tipsy Procurator-General with arrest, and even demanded his sword, whereupon Yaguzhinsky rushed off to the Cathedral where the clergy were singing a *panikhidion*, or requiem, for Peter's soul, and interrupted the solemn service by appealing for protection to the dead Tsar, as he lay in his tomb, against the violence and tyranny of the living. On another occasion, Admiral Apraksin informed the Empress that Menshikov had been giving himself airs, and begged her to keep him on an equality with his fellow-senators. "My lord Admiral," replied Catherine, "you must think me a very poor creature if you imagine me capable of giving any superior authority to the Prince. He is my subject as well as yourself, and I understand him better than you do. If I protect him, it is from compassion, as I know that you all hate him. Recollect, sir, that, before now, I have saved your life as well as his. Take care that you preserve it in future by your good conduct."[2] Still there can be no doubt that Catherine did favour Menshikov, and during her reign he was as powerful as a subject could well be. Nothing was

[1] Campredon. Of course there were exceptional relapses. Thus on the occasion of the marriage of one of Menshikov's daughters with young Sapieha, every gentleman present was forced to go down on his knees before the Empress, and drain to the dregs a huge bumper in her honour.

[2] Campredon.

done without his consent, his insolence and arrogance knew no bounds, and he had an offensive habit of silencing all opposition in the Senate, by suddenly rising, and declaring that the opinions he favoured where the opinions of the Empress. Nevertheless he was not so altogether omnipotent as many German historians have supposed. It was very natural that Catherine should wish to see nearest to her throne the man who had been her earliest protector, perhaps her lover, at any rate an intimate friend of fifteen years' standing. But she understood his character thoroughly, and, while appreciating and employing his energy and audacity, preferred in many things to follow the advice of other counsellors. Thus, Tolstoy likewise possessed her full confidence, much to the disgust of Menshikov, while the management of foreign affairs was confided almost entirely to the discreet and indefatigably industrious Ostermann. But Catherine had yet another confidant, who, young enough to be her son, hoped ere long to be entitled to call her mother, a youth in whom history has hitherto been unable to discover any extraordinary talent or virtue, but who was, nevertheless, at this time the object of no little curiosity, and some alarm, to Europe generally—I mean Charles Frederick, Duke of Holstein.

This unfortunate young man, all his life long the football of Fortune, was the only son of Hedwig Sophia, the best beloved sister of Charles XII, and Frederick IV, Duke of Holstein, who fell pierced through the heart by the side of his heroic brother-in-law, at the battle of Klissov. The young Duke was born and educated in Sweden, and there is very good reason to believe that Charles XII intended him for his successor. For nearly a hundred years the political interests of Sweden and Holstein had been absolutely identical. One of the chief causes of the fratricidal strife between Sweden and Denmark, was the protection afforded by the former power to the Dukes of Holstein. Charles X had married a Holstein Princess, and he took care to secure to his kinsman, the Duke, by the Peace of Roskilde (1658) the possession of parts of Schleswig. Twice during the minority of Charles XI, Christian Albert, Duke of Holstein, was driven from his dukedom; but, again through the efforts of Sweden, he regained it by the Treaty of Altona (1689), and his son Frederick IV was confirmed in its possession by the Treaty of Travendal, 1700. When, however, disaster overtook Charles XII, Denmark re-occupied the disputed Schleswig territory, and the young Duke found an asylum in Sweden. The death of Charles XII seemed to ruin the prospects of his nephew. Charles Frederick's mortal enemy, Frederick, Prince of Hesse, ascended the Swedish throne instead of himself, the Holstein party in Sweden was left without a head by the summary execution of its great leader, Baron Görtz, and Charles Frederick, now in his twentieth year, considered it advisable to cross the sea, and seek the protection of Russia. He is described, at this period, as a sickly, puny, heavy-looking young man of very moderate abilities; but as the pretender to the crown of Sweden, and the claimant of territory seized by Denmark, the Tsar regarded him as both a very useful hostage for the good behaviour of these malevolent powers, and as a political weapon in reserve for future use, and accordingly received him with open arms, and allowed him a pension and royal honours. The poor Pretender, whose ambition was out of all proportion to his abilities, had not been at the Russian court long, before he began intriguing for the hand of one of the two Tsarevnas. Peter himself, who loved his daughters "as his own soul," was against such a match, but Catherine, who took a fancy to the Duke from the first, persuaded her consort to look upon the matter in a favourable light, and it was finally arranged that Charles Frederick should be affianced to the elder[1] of the sisters, the Tsarevna Anne, by common consent, one of the most accomplished, beautiful, and virtuous Princesses of her day.[2] The lady herself was by no means enamoured of a *fiancé*, whom, in her heart, she despised, and who certainly was, in every way, her inferior, but she yielded at last, principally, it is thought, because she preferred even his society to the possible alternative of perpetual seclusion in a convent. The betrothal was postponed, however, in consequence of her father's death. Catherine's first care, on her accession, was to recommend the Duke of Holstein to the protection of the Senate, and, in the very beginning of her reign, he began to play a leading part in affairs. As a foreigner, indeed, he was regarded with suspicion and

[1] The young man himself had a preference for Anne's vivacious sister Elizabeth, "als welche," remarks Mardefelt, "ihre Lebhaftigkeit und Lustigkeit halber grosse Impression bei ihm gemacht." But she was considered to be too young for matrimony at this time.

[2] "I don't believe there is a princess in Europe at the present time, who could vie with the Princess Anne in majestic beauty. Her stature is much above the average, and though she is the tallest lady at Court, her figure is delicate and graceful. She is a brunette, but, for all that, of a vividly white, and yet quite unartificial, complexion. Her features are so perfectly beautiful that accomplished artists, judging them by the severest classical models, could desiderate nothing more. Even when she is silent, one can read the amiability and magnanimity of her character in her large and beautiful eyes... Her behaviour is without affectation, she is always the same, and serious rather than gay. From her youth up, she has striven to cultivate her mind, and has a preference for solid acquirements. She speaks French and German perfectly... She has a perfect horror of the drunkenness and swinish behaviour of the Muscovites." *Mardefeldt* Despatches. *Sb.* of *Ist. Rus. Imp. Ob.*, Vol. XV, 238—240. Then follows a detailed account of this amiable Princess's virtues, accomplishments and charms, in which not even her dimples are forgotten. As Mardefeldt was a warm partisan of the Holstein party, it is quite probable that this flattering picture may be a little overdrawn. But the extant letters of the Princess to her sister Elizabeth, to whom she was much attached, speak well for her goodness of heart, and we have the additional testimony of the Spanish Ambassador, the Duke of Liria (*Diario*) that she was *without doubt* one of the loveliest princesses in Europe.

jealousy by the Russian Ministers, while the people, at large, were distressed and indignant to see him take precedence of the little Grand Duke Peter, at the funeral of Peter the Great, and to hear his name mentioned in the prayer for the Imperial family before that of this unfortunate young Prince, who now seemed to be altogether neglected and set aside. But it must in fairness be admitted that Charles Frederick now displayed considerable tact and prudence. His personal character, too, was excellent. He was diligent, pious, courteous, painstaking, a kind master and a sincere friend. He also did his best to keep the peace between the magnates, and it was mainly due to him that Menshikov and Yaguzhinsky were finally reconciled. He also, by the advice of his chief minister, Bannewitz, tried to conform, as far as possible, with Muscovite customs, going even the length of frequenting their carouses, to the no small detriment of his weak head and feeble health. The Tsaritsa became so much attached to him, that she made him a sort of mentor, and even the great officers of state began to look upon him with less jaundiced eyes, especially as his growing influence seemed to them a sort of necessary counterpoise to the authority of Menshikov, whose overbearing insolence was becoming more and more intolerable every day. On May 21st, 1725, the Duke of Holstein was married to the Tsarevna Anne, with great pomp and splendour, and in February 1726, he became a member of the *Verkhovny Tainy Sovyet*, or Supreme Privy Council, which, as being the great administrative innovation of the reign of Catherine I, deserves a few words of explanation.

This Supreme Privy Council was Ostermann's idea.[1] It was not, as the French Ambassador Campredon supposed, a move in the direction of limited monarchy, by associating

[1] Dolgoruki.

the leading magnates in the government, after the model of an English Cabinet Council, but rather an attempt to strengthen the executive, by concentrating affairs in the hands of a few persons, instead of leaving them, as heretofore, to the care of a turbulent and distracted Senate. Menshikov warmly approved of the scheme, as presenting him with a convenient opportunity of degrading sundry of his rivals, and, after much secret deliberation between the Empress and her advisers, the Ukaz of February 26th established the *Verkhovny Tainy Sovyet*. It was to consist of not less than six, and not more than nine, members, under the presidency of the Empress, and its avowed object was to "lighten the heavy burden of government for her Majesty." Its powers were immense. No Ukazes were, in future, to be issued till they had received the approbation of the Council. The control over the three principal colleges, or government departments, namely, the War Office, the Admiralty, and the Foreign Office, was transferred from the Senate to the new Privy Council, and although the other Colleges were still left under the charge of the Senate, appeals were allowed from the Senate to the Council. Subsequently the Council received authority to revise the work of all the other Departments of State, without exception; even the election of Senators was subject to its approval. The Senate, moreover, was obliged to send regular reports to the Council, while the Council communicated with the Senate by Ukazes. The very name of the latter was changed from Administrative to High Senate, and it now became, to all intents and purposes, a mere subaltern department of state. The resolutions of the Supreme Privy Council were to be unanimous before they could take effect, but in case of difference of opinion, the matter was to be referred to the Sovereign, instead of being decided by the majority. Thus the authority of the Crown was left intact.

The first six members of this august and omnipotent body were Menshikov, Tolstoy, Apraksin, Golovkin, Ostermann, and Prince Demetrius Golitsuin. That the Procurator-General, Yaguzhinsky, "the eye" of the late Tsar, and one of his most indispensable and energetic servants, should have been left out, excited some surprise, and filled Yaguzhinsky himself with fury and despair. He naturally attributed his exclusion to the vindictiveness of Menshikov, and was scarcely comforted by being appointed Grand Equerry of Moscow, by way of compensation. Still greater astonishment was caused by the selection of Demetrius Golitsuin to fill his place. The aristocratic Golitsuins had always been secret opponents of Peter's reforms, they had always sympathized with the Tsarevich Alexius as much as they dared, and yet their leader was now chosen to sit in the Supreme Privy Council, amongst the disciples of Peter the Great! But what seemed a concession, was, in reality, a precaution. It was Ostermann who had suggested the reception of Demetrius Golitsuin into the Council. He knew that he would not only thereby earn the gratitude of the old Russian Party, but would now be able to keep an eye upon the Prince himself, and hold him fast in the Capital as a sort of hostage for the fidelity of his brother the Field Marshal. Shortly afterwards, by the command of the Empress, the Duke of Holstein was also made a Supreme Privy Councillor, to the intense disgust of his Most Serene Highness Prince Menshikov, who was obliged to yield precedence to one of royal birth, and take the second, instead of the first, place in the Council.

The inauguration of the Supreme Privy Council was characteristic of the times. It was to have met at the Palace on the first Saturday after its institution; but Menshikov invited all the members (except Ostermann, who pleaded illness as an excuse) to a great banquet at his house, in honour of his wife's nameday, and by the time the feast was over, their Excellencies the Supreme Privy Councillors were unable to sit round the Council Board, for the simple reason that they were all lying *beneath* it.[1]

There can be no doubt, however, despite the insinuation of Mardefeldt to the contrary, that the establishment of the new Council strengthened the Executive, and gave a fresh impetus to business. It was domestic affairs that gave the new Government the most trouble. The nation was suffering intensely from the immediate consequences of Peter's reforms, for like all hasty and sweeping reforms, however beneficial ultimately, their first effect was to disturb and unsettle. Catherine's government did what it could to relieve this suffering, but it could do but little. The grinding poll-tax was reduced, as already mentioned, and the peasants were permitted to pay one-half or two-thirds of it in provender and forage. One of the ablest of the local governors, Matvyeev, reported, however, that it was not so much the poll-tax in itself, as the harsh and corrupt way in which it was collected, that made it so bitter a burden to the peasantry. It was the old complaint of venality from which ancient Russia had suffered so severely, and which even modern Russia has not yet learnt to cure. Matvyeev was ordered to thoroughly investigate matters, and protect the people at all hazards; but the utmost he could do was to hang a dozen or two of the worst offenders, as soon as his back was turned, the exactions and extortions began again. To make up the financial loss caused by the reduction of the poll-tax, the only expedient the Government could hit upon was to reduce expenditure all round. To begin with, a large part of the army was disbanded, and two-thirds of the officers were discharged. Those officers in particular, who were also landowners, were ordered to live

[1] Mardefeldt. The Council, he tells us, "war ipso facto aufgehoben."

on their estates, during times of peace, at their own cost. The remaining third,[1] who remained with the army, consisted, for the most part, of foreigners who had no resources but their pay, and they did not always get that. The number of the officials in all the public offices was also reduced. Even these resources proved insufficient, and it was soon discovered there was not enough money to supply the most urgent needs. When Vice-Admiral Sievers wrote from Cronstadt for 30,000 rubles (£7,500) for the most necessary expenses, the Treasury could only send him 20,000, and that had to be borrowed from another department.[2] In the beginning of 1727, the needs of the Government became so pressing that it was compelled to issue 2,000,000 copper tokens of the nominal value of 5 copecks apiece. On this occasion, gross irregularities were discovered in the Moscow Mints, and Major-General Volkov, who was sent to investigate the matter, reported a wholesale plunder of gold and silver there for the uttering of false coins, besides other outrageous abuses and malpractices. The Government also endeavoured to assist the Treasury by removing many of the vexatious restrictions on commerce imposed during the last reign. Ostermann was for making commerce throughout the Empire as free as possible. Merchants were now allowed to trade where they liked; Archangel was made a free port, and it was ordered that in Siberia, pelts should, for a time, take the place of specie, as being more convenient to collect, and less liable to fall in value. Something also was done, though not much, to stimulate the copper and iron foun-

[1] In 1726 there were 5 generals, 19 major-generals, 22 brigadier-generals, and 115 colonels in the Russian army. Of these 2 generals, 3 major-generals, and 32 colonels were foreigners. Mardefeldt estimates the army of Russia at this time to be 200,000 and the population about 5,362,000.

[2] Solovev. For the same reason the digging of the Ladoga Canal, and other great public works, had to be suspended.

dries of Perm. The Government also had some care for the moral improvement of the people, and here again we trace the humane influence of Ostermann. Thus a Ukaz was issued to put a stop to the brutality of the *Kulachny boi*, or fist-fight. This popular game was not abolished, but those who chose to amuse themselves thereby, were to do so, in future, under police supervision, and were forbidden to use sticks, stones, knives and bullets, as supplementary weapons, or to throw sand in each other's eyes. The Church, moreover, was ordered to impress upon the people that murder, even if committed in the *Kulachny boi*, was both a crime and a sin. Something too was done to promote education. Hitherto the control of the national schools had been entrusted to the Synod, but the result had not been satisfactory, so they were now placed under the direct control of the State. The Church, indeed, gave the new Government no small trouble, and the one public prosecution which occurred during the reign of Catherine I was directed against the chief pastor of the Church, Theodosius, Archbishop of Novgorod. This energetic, but violent and rapacious, prelate was one of those persons who are willing enough to carry out reforms so long as those reforms do not offend their pride, or touch their pockets. He had supported the new Government at first because he hoped to see the Patriarchate revived, and himself made Patriarch; but his hopes had not been realized, and he not only became very angry, but was unable to conceal his anger. Accused of peculation in the latter days of Peter the Great, he had had to submit to a very vexatious investigation, and only the death of the Tsar had saved him from something much worse. He had made no secret of his joy at the death of his late master, and, his tongue no longer being tied by fear, he waxed bolder and bolder in his denunciations of the temporal

power, and more than once declared that it was an absurd
and unchristian thing for a woman to be the head of the
Church. In April 1726, Theodosius was driving towards
the bridge in front of the Empress's palace, when the sentry
on duty stopped the carriage, reminding the driver that
equipages were not allowed beyond the bridge. At this
interruption, Theodosius could not contain himself, and,
leaping out of his carriage in a great rage, shook his stick
at the sentry, exclaiming: "Let me tell you, I am a better
man than his Most Serene Highness Prince Menshikov!"
and so frightened the man that he let the Archbishop pass.
But the wrath of Theodosius was not yet appeased, and,
on reaching the Palace, he proceeded to brow-beat the
officer on duty there, enquiring why free access to her
Majesty was denied him, and calling him "a mangy sheep
who only deserved the stick." The officer reported the
affair, but no notice seems to have been taken of it. When,
however, a few days later, the Archbishop refused a twice
repeated invitation to the Imperial table, unless a special
messenger were sent to ask him again, Menshikov himself,
who had no great love for Theodosius, decided to take the
matter in hand; the other members of the Holy Synod
were consulted on the subject, and it came out that the
Archbishop had, for a long time past, been guilty of insolent
and improper language towards her Majesty, to say nothing
of frequent attempts on his part to usurp an authority in
the Synod which did not belong to him. An investigation
was at once ordered, and still more serious circumstances
came to light. It appeared that this ardent iconoclast and
enemy of all superstition, not content with simply removing
the ikons from the churches, had melted down their ornaments into bars of gold and silver for his own use; had
appropriated the vessels of the sanctuary for his own dining-
table, and been guilty of other irregularities. Finally, he

was condemned to death, and although the Empress mercifully remitted the capital sentence, he was deprived of all his offices and dignities, and banished to the distant monastery of Kovyelsky, near the mouth of the northern Dwina, with an allowance of 200 rubles (£50) a year for his maintenance. Theophanes, Archbishop of Pskov, was appointed, in his stead, Archbishop of Novgorod, and Vice-President of the Holy Synod, the constitution of which was now revised on a more liberal and economical basis. It was, however, subjected to the supervision of the Supreme Privy Council. I have already mentioned the concessions made by Catherine to the Cossacks, and, from henceforth, these hardy freebooters ceased to give the Russian Government any trouble. Mazeppa's was the last attempt at rebellion in the Ukraine. The collapse of Bulavin's rising, under Peter the Great, had taught the Don Cossacks also that a struggle with the central power was impossible of success, even under the most favourable circumstances. Henceforth the Cossack was to confine himself to his true vocation of guarding the frontier, and exercising his prowess on the broad steppes, in perpetual contests with the heathen Kirghiz and Karakalpaki. Speaking generally, we may say that as regards domestic affairs, Russia, during this reign, lost no ground, even if she gained none.

As to the foreign policy of Catherine I, if purely pacific and extremely cautious, it was nevertheless dignified, consistent, and independent. First, however, it will be necessary to say a few words about the condition of European politics generally.

For at least fifteen years after the conclusion of the Great Northern War, continental diplomacy was dominated by England, or rather, by the foreign Prince who sat upon the English throne, acting through an obsequious Whig

Ministry and Whig Parliament, who secretly despised, but yet could not dispense with, him. George I had succeeded in rounding off his Hanoverian electorate by despoiling Sweden in her direst extremity, but his territorial acquisitions had been so recent, so extensive, and so unexpected, that he was nervously apprehensive of losing them again, especially as his own throne was somewhat insecure. It was, therefore, his main object to form a league strong enough to maintain the existing state of things in Europe, against all possible disturbers of the peace. This policy led, as we shall see, to the most artificial combinations, and the most unnatural alliances. The most obvious confederates of George I were those states, which, like himself, had snatched something from the general scramble after Sweden's continental possessions, such as Prussia, who had appropriated part of Pomerania, and Denmark, who had occupied ducal Sleswig. Holland, too, now entirely given up to the accumulation of wealth, had no desire to injure her trade by competing with England for the mastery of the seas, while France, exhausted by the ruinous War of the Spanish Succession, and governed by a libertine with no regard for his country's glory, and an aged priest anxious only for her repose, was also pacifically disposed. The Empire and Sweden were doubtful powers to be watched or won, as the case might be. Spain, on the other hand, even after the fall of the restlessly ambitious Alberoni, was hostile towards England, for she could not yet accustom herself to the loss of Gibraltar, and the interests of Russia were also regarded as altogether inimical to those of the House of Hanover. The quarrel between England and Russia had begun when Peter the Great intervened in German affairs, after the battle of Pultawa. Without his aid, indeed, Charles XII's continental dominions could never have been partitioned, but, when the last Swede had been driven across the sea, the presence of the Russians in Mecklenburg and Pomerania, was felt as an intrusion, if not as a menace, indeed an actual rupture between George and Peter had only with difficulty been avoided. Peter's matrimonial alliances had also fluttered the German courts considerably. One niece of his had married the Duke of Mecklenburg, another the Duke of Courland. It was felt that there were too many Russian Princesses in the *Reich*. Then, too, as the new great northern power, Russia was an object of distrust and jealousy to England, especially as her Baltic trade had already suffered severely from the arbitration restrictions imposed upon it by the late Tsar. Finally, Russia had given an asylum to the exiled Duke of Holstein, and posed before all the world as his champion and defender, especially after he had become the Emperor's son-in-law by his marriage with the Tsarevna Anne. Now, if there was one thing more than another that George I feared, it was the reopening of the Sleswig-Holstein question. He had purchased Bremen and Verden from Denmark on the secret understanding that Denmark was to be put into possession of ducal Sleswig. If Denmark were forced to surrender Sleswig-Holstein, his own enlarged electorate would also be in danger. Thus Russia, by the mere force of circumstances, and with every desire to keep the peace, found herself, at the beginning of the reign of Catherine I, opposed to England, and a contest between the two powers began at all the courts of Europe, a contest in which British diplomacy, supported by British gold, almost invariable carried the day.

It was at the French court that this diplomatic contest first began.[1] France was by no means ill-disposed

[1] Compare despatches of Russian Minister at Paris, Kurakin, cited by Solovev; Receuil des instructions données aux ambassadeurs... de France, Vol. XIII, Danemark; also Vol. VIII, Russie.

towards Russia. Louis XV had assured the Russian Ambassador, Kurakin, of his unalterable attachment for the new Empress, and Kurakin endeavoured to unite the two Courts by contracting a marriage between the young monarch and the Tsarevna Elizabeth, a scheme which had been one of the favourite ideas of Peter the Great. But Cardinal Fleury and the Duke of Bourbon persuaded Louis to give his hand instead to Mary Leczsynska, the daughter of the ex-King of Poland, Stanislaus; and, moreover, there were two political questions on which, as it soon appeared, France and Russia were at hopeless variance. Count Marville, the French Minister for Foreign Affairs, plainly told Kurakin that whatever other alliances France might contract, she should not break with such an indispensable ally as Turkey. "The King," said he, "must not give the slightest cause of suspicion to the Porte." Yet Turkey was Russia's hereditary enemy with whom her relations were already strained almost to breaking. The other difficulty was the Holstein question, France, to please England, absolutely refusing to countenance the claims of the exiled Duke. Finally, a political event took place, which put an end to all hopes of an agreement. On the 30th April, 1725, Spain concluded an alliance with the Emperor at Vienna, which was looked upon as equally menacing to England and France.[1] The response to this step was the celebrated Hanoverian Alliance, concluded at Herrenhausen on September 3rd, 1725, between England and France, to which Prussia almost immediately acceded. This Alliance marked a reversal of the European political system along the whole line. The jealousies of the French and Spanish Bourbons had thrown the grandson of Louis XIV into the arms of the Hapsburgs; France saw herself desert-

---

[1] Since the refusal of Spain to give an infanta to wife to Louis XV, there had been an estrangement between the two Courts.

ed by Philip V, whom, at an incalculable cost of blood and treasure, she had placed upon the Spanish throne, and the two hereditary enemies, France and England, had united for their mutual defence. Russia was the first to have sensible demonstration of the bellicose energy of the Hanoverian Alliance. In the spring of 1726, England, startled by unfounded rumours that the Tsaritsa's Government was massing troops in Finland, and equipping her fleet to promote the interests of the Duke of Holstein, sent an English squadron, under Admiral Wager, into the Baltic, which anchored before Reval. Wager was the bearer of a letter to the Tsaritsa, from George I, in which his Britannic Majesty declared that the armaments of Russia, in times of profound peace, could not but arouse the suspicions of England and her allies, and compel them to take preventive measures. "Our fleet," continued this despatch, "has been sent to preserve the peace of the North, and prevent your fleet from putting to sea." The gratuitous insolence of this missive naturally incensed the Russian Court exceedingly. Catherine displayed great spirit. She declared that her fleet should put to sea, not only this year, but next year also, if only to destroy the poor opinion people seemed to have abroad of the reign of a woman. She said that, if necessary, she was ready to place herself at the head of an army of 20,000 men. Her reply to the unprovoked menace of the English Admiral was calm and dignified. She expressed her astonishment that such an ultimatum should only have been delivered to her at the very moment when the hostile fleet was at her shores. It would have been more in accordance with international courtesies if his Britannic Majesty had previously notified his complaints, and waited for an answer to his unjust and unfounded suspicions before taking the extreme step of sending an armed fleet against her. Such an act could only be regarded as a consequence of the persistent and long-standing ill-will of the English Ministry against her. She had no desire to dictate to others, but, as a free and independent Sovereign, she could not allow others to dictate to her. She would send out her fleet whenever she chose, without first asking the permission of England to do so, yet her chief aim would always be the preservation of that peace obtained with so much difficulty by her predecessor. This dignified protest had some effect, and Admiral Wager withdrew his fleet; but Vice-Chancellor Ostermann felt this attempt at domineering even more than the Empress. The only way to wound this impassible diplomatist was through his pride as a statesman, and his statesmanlike pride had been very deeply wounded. "If the English Ministers think they can treat us like children," he is reported to have said, "they will find themselves mightily mistaken." He met the menace of England by at once throwing himself into the arms of England's enemies. On the 6th Aug. 1726, the Empress, by his advice, joined the Austro-Spanish League, each of the three contracting parties engaging to guarantee each other's possessions, while Austria and Russia were to assist each other, in case of need, with 30,000 men.

Thus the Hanoverian Alliance found itself face to face with an Austro-Russo-Spanish League, and the League and the Alliance forthwith began competing against each other for the support of the rest of Europe. Prussia, as we have seen, was the first to accede to the Alliance, although the intimacy between the Courts of Berlin and St. Petersburg had always been, and still remained, cordial.[1] Frederick William I had sincerely lamented the death of his "dearest friend" Peter the Great, and the Prussian Court had been ordered to wear mourning for three months instead of the

[1] Despatches of Russian Minister at Berlin, Golovkin, cited by Solovev.

customary six weeks. Golovkin, the Russian Minister at Berlin, strongly advised the Empress to send Frederick William I another "batch of Goliaths," as the surest way of winning his heart, but even this contribution of "lange Kerlen" to his battalion of gigantic grenadiers, could not prevent the King of Prussia from hastening off to meet the King of England at Hanover, on the very first opportunity. On his return he frankly informed Golovkin that he had joined the Alliance, but assured him, at the same time, that it was purely defensive, and that he was quite willing to enter into a similar Alliance with Russia.

The Danish Government did not even think it necessary to make any such diplomatic excuses. So long as the Duke of Holstein found a refuge in Russia, the Court of Copenhagen was bound to be hostile to the Court of St. Petersburg.[1]

Bestuzhev, the Russian Minister at Copenhagen, reported "an unspeakable joy" at the Danish Court at the tidings of the death of Peter the Great. Everyone predicted anarchy in Russia as the immediate and inevitable consequence of the terrible Tsar's decease, and the Danish Royal Family, and the whole Court, were "in a high good humour" at the prospect. When the English fleet appeared in the Baltic, with the avowed object of coercing Russia, the King of Denmark and his Ministers went out of their way to caress and compliment their unexpected but most welcome guests, and Botmar, the Hanoverian Minister at Copenhagen, was offensively enthusiastic in his praises of the English seamen. After these demonstrations, it was only to be expected that Denmark would accede to the Hanoverian Alliance, and this she accordingly did by the Treaty of Copenhagen, 16th April, 1727, concluded for four

[1] Despatches of A. P. Bestuzhev, the Russian Minister at Copenhagen, cited by Solovev.

years, whereby both England and France promised to assist her against Russia, and assure her the tranquil possession of Sleswig.

Much more uncertain was the attitude of Sweden. That Power, although she had fallen considerably from her former high estate, was still an ally whose friendship was worth purchasing. Her Finnish frontier was perilously near the new Russian Capital; her German possessions, though a mere fragment of what they had been, gave her a vote and an influence in the affairs of the *Reich;* she was still the most considerable of the Scandinavian States, and her reputation for military prowess had survived the dire calamities of the Caroline period. By England, she had been treated very badly. George I had in 1719—20 intervened between her and her numerous enemies; but the so-called mediation had resulted in the ruin of her political greatness, and the Swedish Ministers bitterly complained, after the event, that the King of England had got more from Sweden by negotiation than all her other enemies had got by force of arms. Nevertheless the Swedish Chancellor, Count Arvid Bernard Horn, was amicably disposed towards England, of whose parliamentary institutions he professed himself to be an ardent admirer. In his youth, Horn had been conspicuous among the little band of heroes that surrounded the heroic Charles XII, and he had risen to his present commanding position quite as much by his martial prowess, as by his diplomatic dexterity. But the terrible sufferings of his country during the later years of the last reign, had disgusted the gallant soldier with war, and he was far too great a statesman not to perceive that, in her reduced circumstances, Sweden's best policy was a cautious neutrality, which would enable her to recover from her deadly wounds, and husband her limited resources. Still, Horn had opponents in Sweden itself, chiefly the members of the discomfited, but by no means dissipated, Holstein Faction, and the notoriously venal and turbulent *Riksdag*,[1] or Diet, had many unpleasant surprises in store for the all but omnipotent Minister. Sweden, therefore, was regarded as debatable ground by her neighbours, and the Russian[2] Government now did its best to get a firm footing there. Early in 1725 the Russian Minister at Stockholm, Michael Petrovich Bestuzhev, wrote home that the Swedes had hoped that Peter the Great's death would throw Russia into confusion, or, at least, lead to the dismissal of the Duke of Holstein, but that, since neither conjuncture had taken place, they had lowered their crests considerably. Nicolas Golovin, Bestuzhev's successor, reported that England and France were making incredible efforts to draw Sweden into the Hanoverian Alliance, and he was instructed to inform Count Horn that if such a thing were to happen, the Empress would be forced to take hostile measures. Horn replied that the Empress might do as she liked, but Sweden meant to contract alliances with the Powers with whom she had a community of interests. The situation now seemed so critical, that it was thought expedient at St. Petersburg to send to Stockholm a special envoy, the amiable and experienced Prince Vasily Lukich Dolgoruki, with 20,000 rubles (£5,000) in his pocket, to win over Russia's well-wishers, that is to say, the Holstein faction. On November 29th, 1725, Dolgoruki had his first audience, and began operations by presenting the captain of the royal yacht which conveyed him to the Palace, with a gold-headed sword, while the first lieutenant received

[1] After the death of Charles XII, the Swedish Crown had been made elective, and the Riksdag had almost absolute sway. It was a cumbersome political machine, consisting of four Orders or Estates, debating and voting separately in their respective Houses. See R. Nisbet Bain: "Gustavus III." Vol. I., Chap. I.

[2] See Despatches of Count M. P. Bestuzhev, Golovin, and Prince V. L. Dolgoruki, the Russian Ministers at Stockholm, cited by Solovev.

from him a silver tea-service, and every sailor on board a couple of ducats. Dolgoruki describes the Swedish Riksdag as "very much like a fair, everyone is bought and sold, and everybody knows to whom everybody else has sold himself, only they take good care that nothing comes to light before the tribunals, as the punishment for such doings is death." Dolgoruki himself kept open house at Stockholm during the session of the Riksdag, and entertained the leading Swedish politicians magnificently. On December 13th, he gave a banquet to the Senators and Ministers, and on the 15th, a grand ball and masquerade to the Court and City, which lasted from five in the evening till five the next morning. Five hundred guests were invited, and Dolgoruki took care that the Countesses Horn and Delagardie should be the queen and the vice-queen of the ball respectively. But neither of these ladies could be induced to accept any "gratification" from the hand of the Russian Ambassador, because they had expectations elsewhere. For England also spent her money on the Swedes, and she had more money to spend than Russia. Baron Sparre, the Swedish Minister, was home from London at this juncture, with his pockets well filled, and carried everything before him. Horn and his friend Delagardie each received a present of £4,000, and after that were ready "to be burnt alive for the King of England." Poor Dolgoruki was in despair. "I never anticipated such difficulties," he cries. "'Twould be easier to convert a Turkish mufti to Christianity, than to turn the hearts of this people away from the Hanoverian Alliance." Even when he did succeed in bribing some of the members of the Secret Committee to protest against the Alliance, Horn circumvented him by purchasing over again all the poorer members of that august assembly at from 500 to 1,000 ducats a head, and then locking them up from

7 o'clock in the morning till 8 at night, so that not another ruble could find its way to them, even by the most circuitous routes. As a last resource, he expended £4,000 more to try and create a disturbance in the Riksdag itself, but it was of no avail, and the Hanoverian Alliance was carried through in spite of him. The "haughty insolence" of the Swedes, and the high tone of Chancellor Horn, especially disgusted the discomfited Minister, and he advised his Government to keep an eye on Viborg, and look to their armaments, as Sweden evidently meant mischief at the first opportunity.

Thus English diplomacy had been victorious in Sweden, Denmark, France, and Prussia, but there was one large section of Europe to which the influence of the Hanoverian Alliance scarcely extended, and where Russia, consequently, had free play—the Polish Republic.

Apart from the chronic disputes between Russia and Poland as to the treatment of the Lithuanian Dissidents, the chief matter of dispute between them now was the Courland question. Ever since 1561, Courland had been a sort of fief of Poland, the last Grand Master of the Order of the Sword, Gotthard Ketteler, having in that year been invested first Duke of Courland by the Polish King. Ever since the Duchy had done homage to the Republic. So long as Russia was cut off from the Baltic, she had nothing to say in the affairs of Courland, but, after acquiring the bordering province of Livonia, she began to cast covetous eyes on the Duchy likewise, and when, in 1711, Anna Ivanovna, the niece of Peter the Great, married Frederick William, Duke of Courland, the influence of Russia began to compete with that of Poland in the Duchy. Frederick William had died almost immediately after his marriage, and his uncle and former guardian, Ferdinand, succeeded him as Duke. But Ferdinand was an absentee, and the widowed Duchess remained at the capital, Mittau, and practically ruled the Duchy. Now, Ferdinand being aged and childless, the question, who was to be elected his successor, agitated all the neighbouring states, for Russia, Prussia, and Poland had each their candidate ready. Such was the state of things, when who should come forward as an independent candidate for the ducal diadem but Maurice of Saxony, the illegitimate son of Augustus of Poland, by Aurora von Königsmarck. This brilliant, courageous, fascinating, and utterly unscrupulous adventurer, who from his twelfth year upwards had been fighting and flirting all over Europe, with a grace and a gallantry that no man could deny, and no woman could resist, in the course of 1726 suddenly appeared at Mittau. His handsome face, impassioned eloquence, and captivating manners, instantly and completely won for him the heart of the Duchess, and the suffrages of the Courlanders at the same time, and, before the neighbouring Powers were well aware of what was going on, he had been legally elected Duke of Courland by the Landtag, 18th June. The enamoured Duchess at once despatched a courier to St. Petersburg, begging the permission of the Empress to marry Maurice, but Catherine, who had intended to place Menshikov on the throne of Courland, was not best pleased at the tender petition of her kinswoman, and Menshikov and Vasily Lukich Dolgoruki were sent to Mittau forthwith, to bring both the Duchess and the Courlanders to reason. The Russian plenipotentiaries encountered, however, more difficulty than they had anticipated. The Estates of Courland absolutely refused to cancel the election of Maurice, and Menshikov, they said, could not be elected because he was neither of German origin, nor of the Lutheran faith, as the law of the land required. Stormy passages occurred in the Courlandish

Capital. Menshikov, with characteristic brutality, bullied the Duchess instead of reasoning with her, and that distressed Princess posted off to St. Petersburg, to lay her complaints at the feet of the Empress. Meanwhile Menshikov introduced Russian soldiers into the town by night, and Maurice was driven out, though not till after a display, on his part, of truly heroic valour, which added not a little to his reputation, and left the victors more profit than glory. Matters were still further complicated by the action of the Polish Republic, which, alarmed at the Russian progress in Courland, and equally disliking the candidature of Maurice and of Menshikov, expressed its determination to divide the Duchy into palatinates, or, in other words, reduce it to the rank of a mere subject province. The whole matter was to be submitted to the *Sejm*, or Diet, which met in August 1726, at Grodno, whither Yaguzhinsky was now despatched to represent Russia, at the head of a magnificent embassy. To please Poland, moreover, Catherine recalled Menshikov from Courland, where he had been threatening all and sundry with extermination and Siberia, and his candidature was abandoned; but at the same time Yaguzhinsky was to protest energetically against any attempts of the Republic to incorporate the Duchy. The Diet of Grodno, however, proved more than usually difficult to manage. For the first six weeks of its session, it did nothing but wrangle and rave, while its members and their wives put the most extravagant prices upon their ridiculous services. Yaguzhinsky reported that the ladies, who always played such a prominent part in Polish politics, were particularly fond of Siberian silks, and blue fox and ermine furs, while King Augustus had a decided weakness for Chinese curtains, and all sorts of "Persian carpets, the richer the better." Some of the magnates demanded presents from him, with the most unblushing effrontery, "the shameless Palatine of Troiczka asking me, every time I see him, if I have any furs for him, and seeming quite astonished that your Majesty should have forgotten him."[1] On the 30th October the Sejm broke up in the utmost confusion, after appointing a commission to settle Courland affairs, and Yaguzhinsky advised energetic measures against Poland, but the Russian Government, with the fear of England and Sweden before its eyes, forbore from active intervention, though it loudly protested when the Polish Senate first arrested the Courland Deputy, Medem, as a traitor, for petitioning for the maintenance of his country's ancient privileges, and then sent a small army into the Duchy itself, in the wake of its commissioners.

The hesitating and tentative policy of Russia towards effete and futile Poland, is only explicable when we bear in mind that Russia herself was now being agitated by a question so serious and anxious, as to dwarf all others— the question of the succession to the throne. "There can be no doubt that affairs go on very well under Catherine I," writes the Saxon Minister Lefort, "but the hearts of all men are turned towards the son of the Tsarevich." The universal popularity of this young Prince was indeed one of the most pressing dangers of the Government, and, although any expression of opinion as to his right was forbidden under pain of death, the voice of the people contrived to make itself heard nevertheless. Anonymous letters reached Catherine and Menshikov, denouncing woe against all who should set aside the rightful heir, and there were very many among the clergy like the Archimandrite of the Aransky Monastery, who, when mentioning the name of the little Grand Duke in the prayer for the Imperial Family, applied to him the epithet "*blagochestivyeeshy*,"[2]

[1] Yaguzhinsky's Despatches, cited by Solovev.
[2] Most pious.

given only to reigning monarchs, instead of the prescribed "*blagovyerny*."[1] It had been a comparatively easy task to raise the Empress to the throne while the Grand Duke was a minor; but both Menshikov and Ostermann began to recognise the fact that it would be impossible to ignore much longer his inalienable claims as the last surviving male of Peter the Great's line. Ostermann's way out of the difficulty was to bring about a marriage between the Grand Duke and the Tsarevna Elizabeth. Such a union, which the Greek, as well as the Roman, Church would have regarded as incestuous, he oddly enough attempted to justify by Scriptural arguments. "In the beginning," urged the Vice-Chancellor, "brothers and sisters had married each other, and that with the Divine Foreknowledge which had chosen that means alone to populate the world." But Menshikov, although his own Christianity was not very apostolic, was orthodox enough to revolt against such an unnatural expedient, and the idea of it was accordingly abandoned. Moreover, so long as the Empress remained strong and well, there could be very little immediate danger. The army was devoted to her, and the partisans of the Grand Duke, if numerous, were comparatively helpless. But towards the end of 1726, Catherine's health really began to fail. In December, she suffered from violent hemorrhage from the nose, and her legs began to swell ominously.[2] There were some who began to whisper that she was afflicted with the same secret malady that had been fatal to her husband, but her real complaint was an affection of the lungs. Her condition was not improved by a chill she caught through having to leave her bed-

[1] Orthodox. When remonstrated with, he boldly exclaimed: "They may chop my head off for it, if they like, but so I mean to pray for him who is the heir to the throne, and our lawful Gosudar."—*Solovev*.

[2] Compare *Mardefeldt*, *Lefort*, and *Campredon*.

room, suddenly and scarcely dressed, on a dark winter's morning, to escape the rising waters of the Neva. Early in January, 1727, indeed, her health seemed to be completely re-established, but her partisans had received a severe shock, and they thought it high time to begin to look out for themselves. The position of Menshikov, in particular, was highly critical. During the last four months, he had ruled almost like an absolute sovereign, and had had his own way in everything. The Duke of Holstein was now obliged to call him: "Papa!";[1] the Empress herself seemed to be a mere puppet in his hands. Some were even inclined to believe that he aimed at the imperial crown itself. On the other hand, his enemies were "as numerous as the hairs of his head," and his violence and tyranny had revolted them to the last degree. If he were to make a single false step, he was lost, and he knew it. At this juncture, his Most Serene Highness was approached by the Austrian Ambassador, Rabutin, with a project for securing the succession to the Grand Duke Peter. The Emperor Charles VI and the Tsarevich Alexius had married two sisters, wherefore the Kaiser took a personal as well as a political interest in the fortunes of his youthful nephew. Menshikov eagerly caught at his project, as the best possible means of emerging from his enormous difficulties. He stipulated for himself, however, the first vacant electorate in the *Reich*, and for his daughter Maria, the hand of the young Grand Duke, when he should ascend the throne. To these conditions, Rabutin cheerfully agreed. Ostermann, who had all along insisted on the impossibility of keeping the Grand Duke out of his rights, joined Rabutin and Menshikov, not so much from interest as from conviction, and it was his secret but powerful influence which ultimately gave the Austrian faction the victory. But even now

[1] Batyushka.

Menshikov was not out of danger. His astounding change of front had raised up against him a redoubtable adversary, whom he dreaded above all men. This adversary was the aged Tolstoy, who had even more reason to fear the accession of the Grand Duke than Menshikov himself, and who, by the desertion of his life-long colleague, or accomplice, now suddenly found himself completely isolated. Nevertheless he also possessed the confidence of the Empress, and he was determined that Menshikov should never triumph so long as he was alive to prevent it. Catherine had indeed already consented to the first point in the Austrian compact, namely, the marriage of the Grand Duke with Menshikov's daughter; but Tolstoy, taking with him the two Tsarevnas, obtained an audience, and represented to the Empress, in the most moving terms, the extreme danger that such a union must cause not only to her Majesty's faithful servants, but also to her loving children. He would rather kill himself, he added, than calmly await the frightful consequences of such an act. An affecting scene ensued. The two Tsarevnas threw themselves at their mother's feet, and implored her, with tears and sobs, to reconsider her decision. Catherine was deeply affected by the distress of her daughters, and the representation of Tolstoy; but she declared, at the same time, that, "for family reasons," she could not go back from her word. Nothing daunted, Tolstoy now tried to form a party of his own. His difficulties were overwhelming. Yaguzhinsky, Menshikov's most violent enemy, was far away in Poland, the Grand Chancellor Golovkin, cautiously held aloof. Ostermann, whom he hated as his supplanter in diplomatic affairs, was on the other side. He was compelled, therefore, to have recourse to the bolder spirits of the second rank, such as General Ivan Ivanovich Buturlin of the Guards, Devier, the son of a Portuguese jew, whom Peter the Great had picked up as a cabin-boy, and made Minister of Police and a Count, and a dozen others, who were willing to welcome any revolution as a means of promotion.[1] They all agreed that the marriage of Menshikov's daughter with the Grand Duke, would be dangerous to the State, inasmuch as Menshikov would thereby become even more powerful than he was at present. "Besides," added Tolstoy, "if the Grand Duke ascend the throne, he will release his grandmother Eudoxia from her monastery, and then she'll revenge herself upon me for my former rudeness to her,[2] and all the labours of the late Emperor will have been in vain." The only question was which of the two Tsarevnas should be chosen to succeed her mother as Empress. Buturlin and Devier were inclined to favour the elder Princess. The Tsarevna Anne, they said, had a much better temper, and a much finer intellect than her sister. Her gentleness and amiability too, made her less difficult to manage, and her morals were excellent. Tolstoy, however, objected that the elevation of Anne would give an undue influence to the intriguing Holstein faction, who cared a great deal for themselves, but very little for Russia. He was therefore in favour of Elizabeth, with a Council of Regency. The Duke of Holstein might be won over by being appointed Commander-in-Chief or War Minister, and the Grand Duke Peter should be "sent abroad to complete his education." Tolstoy then took upon himself the delicate task of laying his plan before the Empress, at the first opportunity. But the course of events was too swift for the conspirators, and the decisive moment was upon them before they were ready to profit by it.

On the 21st January, 1727, Catherine assisted at the ceremony of the benediction of the waters of the Neva, attired

[1] Solovev.

[2] Tolstoy had been one of the most cruel persecutors of Eudoxia and her unfortunate son.

as an Amazon in a tight-fitting jacket of cloth of silver, a petticoat trimmed with Spanish galloon, and with a white plume in her hat, and a marshal's bâton in her hand. This ceremony was followed by a review of 20,000 troops. Almost immediately afterwards, the Empress had to take to her bed, and not for two months did she appear in public again. She rallied once more in the beginning of April, but on the tenth the fever increased, and her frequent fainting fits soon left but little hope of her recovery. Menshikov at once took his measures. He surrounded the dying Tsaritsa with his creatures, and made it almost impossible for anyone else to approach her. He also constrained Catherine to sign [1] a will, appointing the Grand Duke Peter Aleksyeevich her successor, but not without difficulty, the dying Tsaritsa pleading hard for the rights of her own daughter, the Tsarevna Elizabeth.[2] On the 26th April the Empress was seized with such a violent paroxysm, that the end was momentarily expected, and the members of the Supreme Privy Council, the Senate, the Holy Synod, the Colonels of the Guards, and the Heads of Colleges, were summoned, as usual, to the Palace. Along with them came Count Devier, General Buturlin, and others of Tolstoy's partisans. They had been greatly agitated by the tidings of the Empress's dangerous illness, and had held another meeting to decide what ought to be done. The Duke of Holstein would have had Tolstoy make his way to the Empress's bedside, and there and then get her to declare her daughter her successor. But Tolstoy shook his head. "If her Majesty is really dying," said he, "it is too late."—"Then we are all lost," replied the Duke. Meanwhile the Empress's antechamber was filled

---

[1] The authenticity of this so-called will was afterwards strongly doubted, though never actually disputed.

[2] Campredon.

by a motley crowd of ministers, courtiers, lords and ladies, officers of the guard, dignitaries of the Church, and curious spectators of all ranks. The little Grand Duke and his youthful sister, the Grand Duchess Natalia, together with the two Tsarevnas and the Duke of Holstein, were also waiting there. Menshikov, Golovkin, Apraksin, young Count Sapieha, and some others, were at Catherine's bedside. The folding doors between the Empress's room and the antechamber were wide open, and Catherine, from where she lay, could see what was going on in the adjoining apartment, and even hear some of the conversation. Another paroxysm had seized the Empress, who suffered terribly, the whole Court was in the deepest distress, and many of the ladies, unable to bear the sight of her agony, had their handkerchiefs to their eyes, and were sobbing loudly, when a most disgraceful scene occurred in the antechamber. Count Devier, who was waiting there amongst the mourners, suddenly scandalized everyone by beginning to laugh and conduct himself in a most unseemly manner. He whispered something to the little Grand Duke, whom he took and dandled upon his knee, joked with the lacqueys, told the Tsarevna Anne, who was weeping close by, that she had better have a glass of wine instead of blubbering, and ended by taking the weeping Sophia Skovronskaya, the Empress's niece, round the waist, as if he were about to dance a jig with her. Menshikov, well aware that Devier was one of the Tolstoy faction, and his own personal enemy, skilfully seized this opportunity of suppressing the whole party. The same evening, the wretched man, who, it is charitable to suppose, was in liquor when he so misconducted himself,[1] was arrested, sent to prison, accused of *lèse-majesté*, and ordered to be put to the

[1] Unless, as some suppose, the whole incident was invented or grossly exaggerated by Menshikov.

torture. Twenty-five cuts with the knout extorted from him the names of his accomplices, and Tolstoy, Buturlin, and all their sympathisers were apprehended. The investigation was conducted with the utmost despatch, for a lucky conjuncture now enabled Menshikov to do as he would with his enemies without any fear of the consequences. Catherine, contrary to all expectation, rallied once more, and lived eleven days longer, and Menshikov, acting nominally at her command, although it is very doubtful whether the sick woman, though quite conscious, was fully aware of what was going on around her,—Menshikov, I say, succeeded in utterly crushing a conspiracy that aimed at crushing him. A special Ukaz banished Tolstoy and his son, for life, to the desolate island of Solovka in the White Sea, and Devier and Buturlin to Siberia. Their property was confiscated, they were deprived of all their offices and dignities, and Devier, as being the worst offender, was to receive, besides, a public flogging. This Ukaz was issued on the morning of the 16th May, and the same evening, between eight and nine, Catherine I expired. She is said to have died with great calmness and perfect resignation. Her two daughters were in constant attendance upon her to the very last.

"Catherine I," says Solovev, "was one of those persons whom everyone considers capable of governing till they have begun to govern." This verdict of the Russian historian seems to me somewhat exaggerated and unjust; anyhow, it can only apply, if applied at all, to the last six months of the Empress's reign, when her mind and will were weakened by the sudden collapse of her health and physical strength. The French Minister Campredon appears to me to come much nearer to the truth when he remarks that Catherine united to a masculine courage, all the intelligence necessary for a sovereign. And, indeed, a woman who, without any of the advantages of birth or education, could not only captivate and retain, for a long course of years, the good graces and the absolute confidence of a great monarch, the most difficult of mortals to manage, but could also, after his death, sustain the imperial dignity in her own person without dishonour, must have possessed at least some of the qualities of a great ruler. It is true she had some able counsellors, and not a few energetic champions; but then again it should be remembered that the counsellors were the men of her own choice, and it was only her tact and prudence that again and again prevented her champions from rending one another to pieces. Morally, also, Catherine is by no means an unattractive personage. That she was gross in her tastes and, at least in her later years, intemperate in her habits, is not surprising. No woman in the world could have cohabited with Peter the Great, for sixteen years, with impunity, and what was an utterly illiterate Princess to do with her almost unlimited leisure? She could not be always presiding over councils, or reviewing armies, and her consort never set her an example of self-restraint. It was something that she shut herself up in her apartments whensoever she was in her cups, and so, at least, spared the Court the spectacle of an open scandal. On the other hand, Catherine was altogether free from the vices of the vulgar *parvenue*. Her honesty and modesty were transparent. She was never ashamed of her lowly birth and early poverty, and would refer to her past career with the utmost frankness. In this respect she was much larger-minded than her daughter Elizabeth, who could never endure the reflection that the first husband of her imperial mother had been a common soldier. Nay, more, Catherine actually spared no pains to discover the whereabouts of all the members of her father's family, and succeeded in unearthing a number of poor relations, who lived handsomely upon her bounty for the rest of their days. She even made the most presentable of them, Sophia Skovronskaya, one of her ladies-in-waiting. Of her generosity and kindness, I have already spoken. She was, in truth, an open-hearted and liberal-minded woman, and, despite her many failings, infinitely superior, in all that constitutes moral worth, to her brilliant, fascinating and intellectual namesake and successor, Catherine II.

# CHAPTER IV.

### REIGN OF PETER II.

(May 1727—Jan. 1730.)

THE will of Catherine I—Peter II proclaimed Tsar—His early years —Ostermann appointed his Governor—His pædagogic method—Its practical character—The Grand Duchess Natalia—The Tsarevna Elizabeth—Menshikov absolute—Departure of the Duke and Duchess of Holstein—Death of the Duchess—Wise and humane measures of the new Government—Betrothal of the Tsar to Menshikov's daughter—Tyranny of Menshikov—Violent passages between him and the Tsar—His quarrel with Ostermann—Fall of Menshikov—The Golitsuins—And the Dolgorukis—Difficult position of Ostermann—Re-appearance of the Tsaritsa Eudoxia - Peter II's coronation—Death of Menshikov—The Government transferred to Moscow—Character of Peter II—General demoralization—Foreign affairs—The Treaty of Seville—Decay of the Russian Fleet—Death of the Grand Duchess Natalia—Degradation of the Tsarevna Elizabeth—Supremacy of the Dolgorukis—Betrothal of the Tsar to Catherine Dolgoruki—His melancholy and discontent—Last illness and death of Peter II.

AT 7 o'clock in the morning after Catherine's death, the members of the Imperial Family, the Supreme Privy Council, the High Senate, the Holy Synod, and the chief officers of the Guards, some three hundred people in all, assembled at the palace, to hear the will of the late Empress read. By this will, which was supposed to be signed by Catherine's own hand, although, as already stated, it is rather doubtful whether she knew anything about it,[1] the Grand Duke Peter Aleksyeevich was declared her successor, with all her powers and prerogatives. During his minority, the Government was to be in the hands of a regency composed of the Supreme Privy Council, now limited to nine persons, the Duke and Duchess of Holstein, and the Tsarevna Elizabeth. The new Tsar was to regularly attend the meetings of the Council, but all questions arising therein were to be decided by a majority of votes. Should the new Tsar die without issue, the crown was to devolve, in the first instance, to the Duchess of Holstein and her descendants, failing which, to the Tsarevna Elizabeth and her descendants, the males always taking precedence of the females. The document concluded with a denunciation against all who dared to oppose its provisions, and a benediction upon the Tsaritsa's "dear children," who were exhorted to live together in peace and unity. It will be seen that this will directly traversed the succession regulation of Peter the Great by fixing the succession to the throne two or three generations in advance, instead of leaving it to each individual to name his or her successor; but its provisions so completely gratified the desire of the people, and met the difficulties of the situation so excellently well, that none was disposed to question its authenticity for a moment. As soon as the will had been read, all present, beginning with the Duke and Duchess of Holstein, kissed the cross in token of their allegiance to the new Emperor, whereupon Peter II, at the head of his Ministers and Privy Councillors, descended into the street, and received

[1] Young Count Sapieha, whom scandal looked upon, though falsely, as her lover, and who was with her to the last, subsequently said that the Empress never saw this will. It so exactly expressed, however, the wishes of the nation that its authenticity was never questioned.

the homage of the Guards, who had already been drawn up outside the Winter Palace, and greeted their new Gosudar with loud applause, while the guns from the Fortress of St. Peter and St. Paul, the Admiralty, and the yachts lying in the Neva, saluted him with a threefold salvo.[1] The Emperor and the whole Court then proceeded to Mass at the Cathedral, which lasted an hour, when Peter returned to the Council Chamber, and, ascending the throne, held a meeting of the *Verkhovny Tainy Sovyet.* On his right hand sat the Duke and Duchess of Holstein, his own sister the Grand Duchess Natalia, and the Grand Admiral Apraksin; on his left, the Tsarevna Elizabeth, Menshikov, the Grand Chancellor Golovkin, and Prince Demetrius Golitsuin. Vice-Chancellor Ostermann, in his capacity of *Oberhofmeister,* stood beside the Imperial chair, with George Dashkov, Archbishop of Rostov, who represented the clergy. The will of the late Empress was then read a second time, and the Council decided that it should be carried out in its entirety. The minutes of the meeting were then signed by all present, beginning with the Tsar. After the Council rose, a great banquet was held, at which the new monarch was served by the chief magnates of the realm, on their bended knees. The self-confidence, dignity, and manly bearing of the young Prince, at this his first public function, caused no small surprise, and all who gazed upon his handsome, if somewhat melancholy, face, were filled with sympathy, and predisposed in his favour.

Peter II was still only eleven years old, but he was unusually tall and well proportioned for his age. Kept, from his childhood, in the strictest seclusion, his life had hitherto been anything but a joyful one. His grandfather,

[1] For an account of all proceedings, compare Solovev, and Mardefeldt's Despatches.

who hated him because he was his father's son, had systematically ignored him,[1] and was even suspected, at one time, of the deliberate intention of bringing him up in ignorance, so that he might not prove a too dangerous rival of Catherine's children. It is true that his earliest governesses were the wives of a tailor and a vintner, from the Dutch Suburb, and that these ignoble persons frequently whipped the little Prince, on the slightest provocation;[2] but it may be assumed, from what we know of his disposition, that he was a child who would be none the worse for a little chastisement, and, at any rate, he was likely to learn more from middle-class Germans, than from contemporary Russian gentlewomen. A sailor, called Norman, taught him the rudiments of navigation,[3] and the mysteries of the hornpipe at the same time; but, when he grew older, he was placed under the care of a Hungarian refugee, János Zeikin by name, who shirked accepting the charge, so long as he safely could, till a peremptory reminder from the Tsar, compelled him to set about his work at once.[4] Zeikin seems to have been a faithful and conscientious teacher, for even such a fanatical Xenophobe as Theophylactus, Archbishop of Tver, allows that his intentions were at least honest, and his morals unexceptionable. It is pretty plain, therefore, that Peter the Great did not absolutely neglect the education of his grandson, as some have supposed. Indeed, he may have thought he was doing the best he could for the child by surrounding him with unprejudiced foreigners. Still, it can scarcely be contended that the education of the future Emperor was conducted on anything like an imperial scale.

[1] Peter took so little interest in his studies, that he refused to attend his grandson's examination.

[2] Mardefeldt Despatches, *Sb.* of *Imp. Rus. Ist. Ob.,* Tom. XV.

[3] Ibid.

[4] Solovev.

To do Menshikov justice, it was his first care that the young Tsar should now be trained in a manner more befitting his exalted rank and sovereign responsibilities, and to Ostermann was entrusted the charge of his future training. A better Governor than the Russian Vice-Chancellor could not have been assigned to him. Judged even by a western standard, Ostermann was a man of superior education, and he devoted himself to his new duties with a zeal and a conscientiousness which do him infinite honour. Indeed, I may say at once that Ostermann's conduct, in all his relations with the new Emperor, was, from first to last, irreproachable. His pædagogic method has come down to us,[1] and is, in many respects, a very interesting document. We are told, in the preamble, that the young Tsar possessed a capacity for learning, and a quickness of apprehension, scarcely to be expected from one of his tender years. His general information, too, seems to have been by no means contemptible, for he already understood German, French and Latin, almost as well as his native tongue. Ostermann's plan aimed at giving his pupil an essentially practical education within the shortest possible time. For the next two years the young Tsar was to study four hours a day, two in the forenoon, two in the afternoon, for five days a week. His preceptors were, however, to proceed on the *Kindergarten* system. His studies were to be made as pleasant as possible. He was, at first, to be spared the drudgery of reading and writing, information being conveyed to him in the form of conversation so planned as to stimulate his curiosity, and lead him on, almost insensibly, from simple to more complex studies. He was also to be encouraged to keep a diary, as being the best way of teaching him an easy and natural style of composition. Especial care

[1] Einrichtung der Studien Ihro Kays, Maj. Peters des Andern... wie solche von Ihro Excell... Baron von Ostermann... angeordnet worden.

was to be taken not to weary or disgust him, and every hour of instruction was to be followed by a set period of recreation. As to the subjects to be taught, Ostermann divided them into two sections. First of all came the sciences "of immediate utility for the good government of States"—namely, (1) "Modern, or so-called Political, History," especially the history of neighbouring states; (2) "General Political Economy,"[1] comprising the constitutions of various countries, and the different varieties of government, with their respective advantages and disadvantages, and (3) the Science of War.—Ostermann considers of secondary importance those subjects whose chief use was to promote the better understanding of the above, or simply to divert the mind, such as (1) Ancient History, (2) The Elements of Mathematics, (3) Cosmography, comprising Geography and Astronomy, (4) Natural Science, (5) The Principles of Architecture, and (6) The so-called *Galant Studia*, that is to say, Heraldry, Genealogy, and Archæology, including Numismatics. These latter subjects were to be taught more briefly than the three principal subjects, it being considered sufficient if the pupil got a good general idea of them. A strong moral purpose is discernible throughout the curriculum. The history of each State from its origin was to be presented to the pupil, not in merely chronological sequence, but by order of the leading events, so as to emphasise the usefulness of good, and the worthlessness of vicious Princes. Especial care was to be taken to lay before his Majesty biographical descriptions of famous Kings, and a detailed account was to be given him of the life and deeds of his grandfather, "which will have the excellent effect of showing him, as in a mirror, the needs of his realm, and the means of satisfying them." The duties as well as the prerogatives of a ruler were to be circumstantially set

[1] "Allgemeine Staats Klugheit."

forth, and the superiority of a virtuous, peaceful, and happy reign, to the vainglory of useless, and often ruinous, military enterprises, was to be earnestly insisted upon. In studying ancient history, the names of those rulers who were little more than chronological points, were to be omitted as unworthy of the attention of an Emperor; but the praiseworthy deeds of good rulers were to be dwelt upon, as contributing to the honour and glory of the State; while the lives of openly scandalous rulers were to be particularly set forth, and "it should be pointed out that all their precautions to escape from the shame of their evil deeds, have come to nought, inasmuch as the description of their vices has come down, even to us, despite the flatterers they secured in their life-time." The jealousies and dissensions of the Greek Republics, as tending to the aggrandisement of Philip, were to be plainly indicated; while the foundation of Alexandria, the great metropolis of trade and the sciences, "was to be represented as a far greater deed of Alexander's, than his many conquests." The Roman Emperors were *not* to be taken seriatim; but the lives of the most notable among them were to be selected for his Majesty's better edification. Moreover, the most important passages in Livy were to be marked, so that he might be able, without difficulty, "to draw truth from the original source," when so disposed. Only the rudiments of arithmetic were to be taught, while astronomy [1] was to be regarded principally as a preservative against superstition. It would be sufficient if his Majesty learnt to recognise that eclipses, and other heavenly phenomena have their order fixed by God, once for all; only follow the laws of nature, and cannot possibly

---

[1] Ostermann grows almost enthusiastic at the contemplation of that noble science. "Es ist in alle Wege was anständiges," he says, "zu wissen nach was für Gesetzen die schöne und grösse Himmels-Cörper ihren Lauff einrichten, und warum sie uns Menschen zu einer jeden Zeit vielmehr auf diese als eine andere Weise erscheinen."

BKNNKR PINX.  COUPÉ, SCULP.

Peter II.

To face p. 120.

have any evil significance for the government of the day, as many ill-disposed persons have heretofore imagined. Ostermann also regarded a superficial knowledge, at least, of the natural sciences, including hydrostatics, hydraulics, aerostatics, optics, and the use of the magnet, as indispensable. These branches of knowledge, indeed, he looked upon rather as pastimes than studies, as they could be enlivened by so many pleasing experiments. They were capable too, of a moral application, as the pupil could be led thereby to a better knowledge of God and the Universe, and made to see that "the creature is a ladder leading up to the Creator."—This course of study was arranged to extend over two years, and was to be supplemented by lectures for two hours daily, the subjects chosen being the memoirs or biographies of great Kings and their ministers.

Ostermann seems to have easily and completely won the heart of his pupil, to whose service he devoted himself night and day. The young Tsar, who was naturally affectionate, soon got to love his Governor dearly, and trust him absolutely. The first thing he did on awaking, was to rush off, in his night-dress, to Ostermann's apartments, to wish him good morning, and it was observed that he listened to all he told him with the deepest attention. Yet Peter II had another more intimate and affectionate Mentor, who had been the sole companion of his lonely infancy, and was soon to be his guardian angel amidst perils and trials of which his infancy had never dreamed. This Mentor was his sister Natalia, one of the most lovable and pathetic figures in Russian history.

The Grand Duchess Natalia Aleksyeevna was, reckoning by years, still a child, for she was not yet thirteen. But although only twelve months older than her brother, as regards wisdom and prudence, she might well have been twelve years his senior. Personal beauty she did not possess, though she had a good figure, but, by way of compensation, Nature had endowed her with all imaginable gifts of heart and mind. All the Ambassadors at St. Petersburg unite in a chorus of praise whenever they allude to this charming Princess. Her sweet temper and gentle courtesy endeared her to everyone who had the privilege of approaching her, while her studious habits, cultivated tastes, and precocious common-sense, made all lovers of Russia augur the best from the influence she possessed over the somewhat unstable mind of her brother. To Ostermann she was an invaluable coadjutor in his pedagogic labours. As the Prussian Minister, Mardefeldt, put it, the "wise Grand Duchess" and the Vice-Chancellor seemed to have entered on an amiable plot together, to educate the young Tsar, in the most praiseworthy manner. Young, as she was, Natalia had already learnt to recognise the value of western civilization, and its immense importance to Russia. Unfortunately for her country, her life was to be a very brief one; but she lived long enough to merit the honourable title of "Protectress of Foreigners," at the very time when a reactionary cabal of grey-bearded intriguers was endeavouring to undo all the work of Peter the Great.

Another member of the Imperial Family, who was also to have a considerable, but, happily, only transient, influence over Peter II, whose acquaintance it now behoves us to make, was the Tsarevna Elizabeth, the young Emperor's youthful aunt. The future Tsaritsa, whose caprices, indolence and vindictiveness were, one day, to amuse or disgust all the courts of Europe, was at present a flighty, but very fascinating, girl of sixteen.[1] She was not quite so tall and stately as her sister Anne; her figure, perhaps, was less

[1] Compare the Despatches of Campredon, Mardefelt, and Lefort, and the *Diario* of the Duke of Liria.

absolutely perfect, her features were certainly not so classically correct. Yet there were many *connoisseurs* who preferred the laughing loveliness of the lively blonde, to the grace and majesty of the statuesque brunette. The Spanish Ambassador, who, by the way, disliked her personally, and is, therefore, quite an impartial witness, describes her as one of the most exquisite creatures he ever saw in his life. Her complexion, he says, was admirable, her mouth faultless, her neck most beautiful, her figure incomparable. The Saxon Minister Lefort praises her large and brilliant blue eyes, so like a merry bird's. But her salient, her most irresistible charm was her light-hearted, ravishing vivacity. She was one of the most delightful madcaps it is possible to imagine, bubbling over with fun and high-spirits,[1] never still for an instant, "always with one foot in the air," as Lefort expresses it. It was her vivacity quite as much as her beauty which made both Campredon and Menshikov fancy that she was born to shine at the gay Court of Versailles,[2] when the negotiations for her marriage with Louis XV were still progressing. From her parents she had inherited a robust and elastic physique, and in all sports requiring strength and skill, she excelled. She was a graceful and fearless rider, danced with fire and passion, and could, on occasion, handle a sword like a guardsman. For serious studies she had but little liking. Her early instructors were persons of mediocre talent, and her father lacked the leisure, her mother the learning, necessary to superintend her education. But her natural parts were by no means contemptible; her quick apprehension and retentive memory enabled her to learn French and

[1] "*Muy chula*," Liria calls her.

[2] Campredon says that she had "de l'esprit, de l'enjouement, et assez de vivacité pour s'accommoder parfaitement au génie françois." Compare Lefort; " Il semble qu'elle soit née pour la France, n'aimant que faux brillant."

German thoroughly, with scarcely an effort, and even those who shook their heads at her giddy frivolity, admitted that she possessed wit and understanding.[1] She was, moreover, infinitely good-natured, but loved pleasure above all things.

During the first four months of the new reign, the Government was entirely in the hands of Menshikov, who, despite frequent acts of tyranny, on the whole acquitted himself well of his enormous responsibilities. It is true that old enemies or troublesome rivals were removed to a safe distance, with little compunction. Thus, the ex-Vice-Chancellor Shafirov was despatched to Archangel, "to look after the whale fisheries"; Yaguzhinsky was sent away in a diametrically opposite direction, being given something difficult to do in the distant Ukraine, and Makarov received a lucrative post—in Siberia. But, on the other hand, his Serene Highness tried to attach to himself all able officials who were not over ambitious, and to win over such members of the old nobility as were not too exacting. Foreign affairs were left entirely in the hands of Ostermann, whose industry was indispensable, and whose meek obsequiousness made him appear the most inoffensive of mortals. The chair vacated in the Supreme Privy Council by the banishment of Tolstoy, was given to Prince Vasily Lukich Dolgoruki, and another Dolgoruki, Alexius Grigorevich, was appointed Hofmeister of the Court of the Grand Duchess Natalia. Nor were the Golitsuins, the influential rivals of the Dolgorukis, neglected. Apraksin and Golovkin, Menshikov's old colleagues, were not a little disgusted to discover that the Prince's new friend, Demetrius Golitsuin, had as much to say as themselves in the Supreme Privy Council, and the Lopukhins were conciliated by the release of the Emperor's grandmother, the Tsaritsa Eudoxia, from her prison at Schlusselburg.

[1] Liria.

And now Menshikov felt strong enough to rid himself of one who had long been a rock of offence to him. At the beginning of August the Duke of Holstein was requested to quit Russia, and take his Duchess along with him. Charles Frederick, much to the indignation of his partisans, obeyed without a murmur. But, in truth, resistance on his part would have been foolish. Nobody wanted him at St. Petersburg any longer. In Russia itself, he was regarded as an interloper, and, moreover, his departure disarmed the suspicions of Russia's neighbours, Sweden and Denmark. Nor did Menshikov, with all his roughness, treat the young Prince unhandsomely. He received a solemn assurance from the Supreme Privy Council, before he left, that all the secret articles on his behalf, contained in the treaties concluded by Russia, should be rigidly carried out at the proper time, and, until he was put into possession of Sleswig, he was to receive an annual pension of £50,000. The young Duchess, who detested Menshikov, was not sorry to exchange a doubtful position at a Court where she was less than nobody, for a comfortable country-house at Kiel, where everybody was kind to her [1] and she could do just as she liked. The happiness of this charming Princess was, however, of no very long duration. Six months after her arrival at her Holstein home, she was safely delivered of a son, and, after her recovery, a grand ball was given in honour of the glad event, followed by a display of fireworks. It was February, and the weather very cold and damp; but the joyful young mother (she was not yet twenty) insisted upon standing at an open window to look at the illuminations. Her ladies remonstrated with her, but she only laughed, and said: "I am a Russian, remember, and my rude health is used to a ruder climate than this." But she caught a chill, as might

[1] Letter to her sister Elizabeth, in Solovev.

have been expected, and ten days afterwards she was dead. In her will she expressed the wish to be buried in the same tomb as her father, whom she had tenderly loved, and a Russian frigate conveyed her remains from Kiel to St. Petersburg. The ill-fated babe whom she left behind her, was christened Peter Frederich Ulric. More than forty years after his mother's death, he was to ascend the throne of Russia as Peter III.

Tyrannous as it was, there can be little doubt that the administration of Menshikov was vigorous, capable and economical. Moreover, and this was undoubtedly its highest merit, despite its precautionary coquettings with the old Russian Party, it was mainly conducted on the lines laid down by Peter the Great. Writing to his Court in August 1727, Mardefeldt declared that the revenue of the State was no longer expended on unprofitable and unnecessary naval armaments, or dissipated in revelry and junketting, but judiciously employed to encourage trade, commerce and industry. He also notes a greater regularity and despatch in the conduct of affairs. Even the Saxon Minister Lefort, by no means well disposed towards Menshikov, praises highly his energetic initiative, courageous self-confidence, and irresistible power of command, and admits that were he to die, there was nobody who could take his place.[1] The humane, conciliatory, and economical policy of the last reign was continued. Peter I's export duty of 37 % on hemp and linen yarn,[2] which had practically ruined the trade, was reduced to 5 %; a commission for enquiring into the state of commerce was appointed by Ostermann, and the leading merchants were invited to send in memorials

[1] "Jamais le feu Tsar," he adds, "n'a été si fort craint ni si bien obéi, comme l'est Menshikov; tout plie sous lui ... et Dieu garde celui qui lui résiste." Lefort: Despatches. *Sb.* of *Ist. Rus. Imp. Ob.*, Tome VII, pp. 487—488.

[2] His object thereby was to encourage artificially his pet project of native manufactures.

as to the best method of reviving commerce generally. The trade in Siberian furs was also made absolutely free. A laudable first step towards softening the barbarous semi-Asiatic habits of the day was made by the Ukaz of 21st July, 1727, which ordered the immediate removal and utter destruction of the stone columns and iron hooks, on which the heads and limbs of executed criminals had hitherto been exposed to public view in the great square of St. Petersburg, till they rotted away. Still further concessions were made to the liberty-loving Cossacks. Peter the Great had treated them very roughly. He had looked upon these sons of the Steppe simply as so much extra cavalry, and had done his best to entirely incorporate them with the Russian army by abolishing their ancient privileges wholesale. The Government of Peter II smiled where the Government of Peter I had frowned. The Malo-Russian College, a new Public Office especially created to look after the Cossacks, was abolished by the Ukaz of Aug. 1st, 1727; the old Hetmanship was revived in the person of Apostol, a client of Menshikov, and the semi-independent Cossack Republic re-established on the basis of the conditions insisted upon by Bogdan Chmielnicki, when he threw himself into the arms of Russia. This great change not only mightily pleased the Cossacks, and bound them more closely to the parent State, but was far simpler, and less expensive, than the old tyrannous and inquisitorial system.

But salutary as the rule of Menshikov was, it was undeniable a usurpation. He had no right whatever to the position he held. The late Empress, by her last will, had, as we have seen, transferred all her authority to the Supreme Privy Council, and the Council was now treated as if it did not exist. Menshikov held sway simply because he was so much stronger than anyone else. Nevertheless, had he but shown reasonable moderation, he might still have retained his power, but it was not in his dictatorial nature to be moderate. "The despotism which prevailed formerly," wrote the Saxon Minister Lefort, on August 5th, 1727, "was a mere baby compared to the despotism which prevails now." One of Menshikov's first acts had been to appoint himself Commander-in-Chief, and only a week after Catherine's death, he literally kidnapped the young Emperor by carrying him off to his palace on the Vasily Island,[1] surrounding him by his creatures, and shutting out all the rest of the world. Shortly afterwards Ostermann announced in the Supreme Privy Council, that it was his Majesty's intention to wed Maria Aleksandrovna Menshikova, the eldest daughter of his Serene Highness, and the following day, the Foreign Ministers at St. Petersburg were duly informed of the fact, and invited in a body to Menshikov's palace, where the ceremony of betrothal took place with great pomp and splendour. Subsequently the Emperor and his betrothed entertained their guests at a banquet. Thus Menshikov meant to be the future father-in-law of his own Sovereign, and, from this time forth, his insolent elation knew no bounds. So long, however, as Peter submitted to the dictation of the strong man who had placed him on the throne, his Serene Highness was unassailable, for nobody durst attack him, but before long there were symptoms of rebellion on the part of the young Emperor himself, which filled all the enemies of Menshikov with the delightful expectation of a rupture. Peter II was a very affectionate youth, who would submit to much from those he loved; but he had a will of his own already,[2] and he very soon began to chafe beneath the constant,

[1] At this time the fashionable part of St. Petersburg, where the greater number of the nobility dwelt. See Liria: *Diario*, p. 106.

[2] "Le jeune Tsar semble déjà vouloir décider en maître... Il veut ce qu'il veut, il est ennemie des répliques." Lefort: *Despatches. Sb.* of *Imp. Rus. Ist. Ob.*, Vol. VII, pp. 474, 479.

and often petty, interference of Menshikov. No doubt he began to ask himself: By what right does this man keep me a prisoner in his house? Why does he dictate to me, and scold me? He is not my Governor, like Baron Ostermann, who is always kind and considerate; no relation of mine, like dear sister Natalia. Why should I obey him? Before long there were violent passages between the grim Dictator and the defiant young Tsar. Thus, on one occasion, the City of St. Petersburg had presented Peter with 9,000 ducats, which he at once sent to his beloved sister. Menshikov met the messenger on his way, and, discovering on what errand he was bent, exclaimed: "His Majesty is much too young to dispose of so large a sum of money, take and lock it up in my cabinet."—On hearing of this, Peter sent for Menshikov, and asked him, with a voice trembling with indignation, how he dared to countermand his orders. Taken aback by this unwonted display of temper in the hitherto docile young Prince, Menshikov pretended at first to have forgotten the incident, but, quickly recovering himself, declared that the Treasury was empty, and he could turn the money to better account than his Majesty. Then Peter stamped his foot with rage. "I will see," cried he, "whether you or I am the Emperor."—Another time the Tsar received a service of silver plate from the City of Yaroslav, which he also gave to his sister. Menshikov, with singular impudence, sent word to the Grand Duchess that she must give it up to him. "I know my duty better," replied Natalia, with spirit. "It is not likely that I shall surrender to a subject what I have received from my Sovereign."—At this juncture Menshikov was suddenly prostrated by the pulmonary complaint from which he had long been suffering. For the next six weeks he was seriously, dangerously ill. At one time his case seemed so desperate, that Extreme Unction was administered to him. But he rallied after all, and, towards the end of August, re-appeared at Court. Here, however, a series of disagreeable surprises awaited him. He found that the Tsar had flitted to a country château at Peterhof, about thirty miles from the Capital, where he amused himself all day long, with hunting and riding, and the Grand Duchess, and the Tsarevna Elizabeth had followed him thither, the former to look after, and the latter to play with, him. Ostermann and the Dolgorukis were also there. Things had gone on so smoothly and pleasantly during the Prince's absence, that people began to ask themselves why they had put up with his rough bullying ways so long? Indeed nobody had ever expected to see him again, and now this sinister spectre had risen from the dead, as it were, to trouble the mirth of the young Court once more. Everyone felt this fresh intrusion to be an intolerable nuisance. Yet even now a little tact and forbearance on Menshikov's part, might have put matters right; but, as usual, his ungovernable temper got the better of him, and his behaviour during the next few weeks was the behaviour of a madman. One of his first acts on reaching Peterhof, was to demand that the accounts of the imperial household should be submitted to him, and, discovering therein a small payment of extra pocket-money to the Tsar, instantly cashiered the *Kammerdiener* who had made the disbursement. This petty interference was more than Peter would tolerate. A stormy scene ensued. The offending Kammerdiener was reinstated, and when his Serene Highness continued to protest, he was rudely told to mind his own business. And now Menshikov committed the signal, the crowning imprudence of quarrelling with his best, or, rather, his only friend, the Vice-Chancellor. Ostermann had no wish to be on ill terms with Menshikov. During the great man's illness, he had been in constant communication with him, and kept

him informed of all that was going on at Court. His
language had been not merely courteous, but submissive;
he had even humbly expressed the wish that he might
long continue to enjoy his Highness's high and gracious
protection. But Menshikov had long been jealous of the
growing influence of Ostermann over the Tsar, and, unable
to brook a rival near the throne, had already marked
him out for destruction. Search as he would, however,
he could find no vulnerable point in the ever careful
Minister's public administration, for which he was responsible to the State, so he meanly resolved to attack him on
the side of his private opinions for which he was responsible to God alone. The religious views of the protestant
Ostermann had always been something of a puzzle to his
orthodox colleagues. So far as we can judge from his
writings (for he was one of those prudent or pusillanimous
persons who keep such matters to themselves) he seems
to have professed a coldly rational Deism, which, in the
eyes of contemporary Russians, would of course appear
tantamount to no religion at all. Ostermann's official chief,
the Grand Chancellor Golovkin, whose scrupulous observance
of all the ordinances of the Church did not in the least
interfere with his merciless rapacity and insatiable avarice,
once observed to his subordinate: "Does it not seem odd
that you, Ostermann, who are without any faith of your
own, should have the training of an orthodox Tsar?" All
this Menshikov knew, and therefore imagined himself to
be on safe ground in attacking Ostermann on the score
of his religion. He accordingly summoned him to his
presence at Peterhof, and roundly accused him of preventing the young Emperor from going to church, and of
bringing him up without any religious instruction.[1] The

[1] Yet Menshikov knew very well that Archbishop Theophanes had the
entire control of the Tsar's religious training.

Vice-Chancellor demanded an explanation. "An explanation!" roared Menshikov, infuriated that the mildest of men should presume to bandy words with him. "I owe no explanation to an atheist. Look to it, sir, lest I send you packing to Siberia."—"*You* have no power to send *me* to Siberia," replied Ostermann, himself waxing warm at this brutal treatment.—"Hold your tongue, sir," bellowed the other, "and if ever you dare to dispute with me so boldly another time, I'll have you broken on the wheel before my eyes."[1] To this tirade Ostermann never said a word, but he swore to be revenged, and from that moment the fate of Menshikov was sealed.

What first seems to have opened the eyes of the infatuated dictator to his peril, were two disagreeable little incidents which now befel him. On the 6th September, he had come out to Peterhof to pay his respects to his Majesty, but the young Tsar, instead of acknowledging his salute, ostentatiously turned his back upon him before the whole Court, and said, loudly enough for all in the room to hear: "You see I am learning at last how to keep him in order!" A week later, Menshikov, now seriously alarmed, made a great feast at his estate at Oranienbaum, on the occasion of the consecration of a church erected at his expense, and, in the humblest terms, begged the Tsar to honour the ceremony with his presence. Had Peter appeared at Oranienbaum, only for a moment, that would have been sufficient, in Menshikov's opinion, to dispel all the rumours of a rupture between them. But the Emperor sent a curt refusal, and the church had to be

---

[1] Dolgoruki. Compare the Despatches of Mardefeldt and of Lefort. The former says that Ostermann "ihm [Menshikov] viele *Duretis* gesagt," and even threatened to have him hanged and quartered. This, however, is extremely improbable. Ostermann always struck secretly, but never threatened. Dolgoruki, Mardefeldt, and Lefort all agree, however, that Menshikov's insane rupture with Ostermann was the cause of his fall.

consecrated without him. And now the unhappy man perceived at last that a storm was indeed about to burst upon him, and attempted to avert it. But it was too late. Hastening to Peterhof, he begged for an audience, and it was refused him. The next day he tried again, and again he was rejected. He succeeded, however, in seeing for a few moments the Tsarevna Elizabeth, to whom he poured forth his woes, bitterly exclaiming that all his services had been requited with ingratitude, and declaring passionately that he meant to throw up his appointments forthwith, and retire to his estate in the Ukraine. The Tsarevna listened to him in silence, and he quitted her with despair in his heart. He was certainly in a worse position than he had ever been in his life. Since the death of the Empress, he had no longer a kind protectress always ready to stand between him and his enemies. As a last resource, he wrote to Demetrius Golitsuin for assistance, but on the following day he received a visit from Major Saltuikov of the Guards, who demanded his sword, and placed him under arrest, whereupon Menshikov, knowing that all was over, fell fainting to the ground, and was only brought to again by copious bleeding. On recovering he wrote the Emperor a pathetic letter of remonstrance, pleading his innocence and past services, and exhorting him not to let the sun go down on his wrath. Of this letter no notice whatever was taken. On Sept. 19th, a Ukaz, issued in the name of the Tsar, forbade obedience to any orders coming from Menshikov, and on the 20th, the Supreme Privy Council met at the Palace, to decide the fate of the fallen Colossus. Its deliberations were expeditious. The same day Menshikov was deprived of all his charges and emoluments, for conspiracy against the Crown, fined 500,000 rubles,[1] and ordered to depart to the Steppes of Kazan within four-and-twenty

[1] £75,000.

hours. Meanwhile the young Tsar, who had nonchalantly signed the necessary Ukaz on his knee, went in state to church with the members of the Council, it being the feast of Our Lady's Nativity. On his return he found the Princess Menshikova, with her son and daughter, waiting for him at the Palace. This noble-minded woman, for whom even the enemies of her husband felt the deepest sympathy and respect, went down on her knees before the young monarch, and pleaded hard for him who had ever been dearer to her than life itself. But the Emperor, whose indignation was still hot against Menshikov,[1] escaped from the suppliants without uttering a word, leaving Ostermann behind to soothe and dismiss them. For three-quarters of an hour, it is said, the Princess Menshikova remained on her knees before the Vice-Chancellor, but the utmost concession she could obtain was that her husband might retire to his beautiful country house in the Ukraine instead of the desolate Steppes. On Sunday the 21st September, "the extirpated Matador," as Lefort calls him, quitted the Capital, with all his family, in four carriages, each drawn by six horses, and followed by a whole caravan of baggage wagons.[2] The streets through which the procession passed were lined by immense crowds of curious spectators, who looked on in absolute silence. There was a general feeling of relief at his departure. The betrothal of the Tsar with Maria Menshikova was of course put an end to. Indeed the ambitious elevation of this young lady, had been the head and front of her father's offending.

The overthrow of the tyrant Menshikov was undoubtedly an act of justice, but it might have been very injurious to Russia, as it brought to the helm a junto of narrow-

---

[1] He seems also to have been persuaded that Menshikov meant to treat him as he had treated his father, the Tsarevich Alexius. See *Lefort*.

[2] Some say 42, others 60.

minded, self-seeking Patricians, who had no regard for their country's true interests. The triumph of Menshikov's enemies proved in fact to be the triumph of the reactionary old Russian Nobility, who naturally regarded the ways and works of Peter the Great as altogether abominable, and who were chiefly represented at this time by the ancient princely families of the Golitsuins and the Dolgorukis. Not one of these magnates can be considered a great man, still less a great statesman; but the Golitsuins were not without a few patriarchal virtues, while the more modern and accommodating Dolgorukis had some fair pretensions to diplomatic talent. At the head of the Golitsuins stood Prince Demetrius Mikhailovich, a thoroughly honest, upright, and courageous man, whose many good qualities were ruined by an inflexible haughtiness, an incredible narrow-mindedness, and an insatiable ambition. He had always looked upon the Petrine reforms with hatred and suspicion. "What do we want with them?" he used to say. "Are we wiser than our fathers?"—He used to sneer at the fleet as a useless luxury for a country with so small a seaboard as Russia, and compared St. Petersburg to a gangrened limb, which must be lopped off to save the rest of the Empire from infection. He was the idol of the clergy, but his harsh, abrupt, masterful manner made him offensive to the gentry, while his pride was always more or less of a stumbling block to his ambition. At heart he was a brave and conscientious man, but had his conscientiousness been a little more enlightened, and his courage tempered with a dose of tact, it would have been better both for himself and for his country. In short, he was more like the chief of a clan, than the minister of a great empire.

A much more amiable and attractive character was Field Marshal Golitsuin. Michael Mikhailovich shared the views of his brother Demetrius; but he had seen more of the world, and, despite his prejudices against foreigners, was always ready to recognise merit wherever he found it. He had not spared Peter the Great with his tongue, but he had placed his sword at the Tsar's disposal, and rendered him notable services. It was he who first taught the Russians that the Swedes were not invincible, by defeating Charles XII's great lieutenant, Levenhaupt, at the Battle of Lesna,[1] yet it was characteristic of him that he valued the marshal's bâton he received for that great victory, far less than the love and devotion with which his grateful and admiring soldiers rewarded their brave and kindly captain. The Duke of Liria, who looked down upon most of the Russian nobles as semi-barbarians, considered Michael Golitsuin an excellent soldier, a high-minded gentleman, and the soul of honour.[2]

No men had a better right to the gratitude and favour of Peter II than the Golitsuins. They had ever been the friends of his unhappy father, and had all along regarded him and his sister Natalia as the only legitimate grandchildren of Peter the Great. But there was a stiffness and an imperiousness about most of the Golitsuins, which repelled the young Tsar, and, moreover, they had been suspected latterly of showing too much favour to Menshikov.[3] The affable and jovial Dolgorukis were much more to the lad's liking, and they also had suffered in the past for their attachment to his father.

The most conspicuous of the Dolgorukis was Prince Vasily Lukich, who had won a considerable reputation for diplomatic adroitness at half the Courts of Europe. He had failed at Stockholm, as we have seen, because there Eng-

[1] It is true that Levenhaupt was outnumbered five to one, besides being hampered by an immense convoy of waggons, still a victory it was. Peter the Great called it "the Mother of Pultawa."
[2] *Diario*. The English resident Rondeau also thought very highly of him.
[3] Solovev.

land threw all her gold into the scales against him; but at Paris, Copenhagen, Mittau, and Warsaw, he had shone magnificently. Vasily Dolgoruki was endowed with a handsome face, a majestic bearing, and most insinuating manners; but he was false to the core, and ready to sacrifice everything to attain his ends. The military celebrity of the Dolgoruki family was Prince Vasily Vladimirovich. His services had not been nearly so conspicuous as those of Michael Golitsuin, but, since Peter the Great's death, he had done some useful work in the Caspian Provinces, and added territory to the Empire, which had increased its revenue by several hundreds of thousands of rubles. He was, in the main, a rough, honourable soldier, whose worst fault was his excessive frankness. As much cannot be said for his brother Michael Vladimirovich, to whom the Spanish Ambassador attributes no merit whatever. He seems to have been a mere hanger-on at Court, vain, frivolous, and utterly unscrupulous, who lied with unblushing front, and loved nobody but himself.[1] Another Dolgoruki, very eminent in rank, but contemptible in character, was Alexius Grigorevich, who, as we shall see presently, appropriated the Tsar, as Menshikov had done before him. He was emphatically a poor creature, with little understanding, no knowledge of the world, and an almost insane hatred of western novelties. His one object was to keep possession of the power that accidentally fell into his hands, and to do so he did not shrink from the vilest expedients.

I have already hinted that the domination of these men *might have* proved highly injurious to Russia. That it did *not* prove so was due almost entirely to the counteracting influence of the Vice-Chancellor. To the Dolgorukis and the Golitsuins, Ostermann was detestable, both as a foreigner,

[1] Liria: *Diario*.

and also especially as the ablest pupil of Peter the Great. The Dolgorukis tried at first to poison the mind of the young Tsar against him, but they soon discovered that Peter's affection for his Governor was too strong to be easily overcome. He told the Dolgorukis plainly that he would not deliver Ostermann into their hands, but, on the other hand, he told Ostermann not to interfere with the Dolgorukis. It was not long, however, before the Vice-Chancellor perceived with consternation that he was losing his hold upon his pupil. His position was, indeed, extremely difficult. Officially responsible for the education of the young Tsar, he was well aware that he would one day be called to account if this precocious but naturally lazy lad should grow up in ignorance, and yet he could do nothing to keep Peter at his studies. For the Dolgorukis flattered the boy to the top of his bent, openly encouraged him to have his own way in all things, and one of their number, Ivan Aleksyeevich, a stupid, idle, and vicious youth of nineteen, who had been appointed Peter's Kammerherr, was always about him, even sleeping in his bedchamber. At first Ostermann tried remonstrances. "When you come of age," he said to the young Tsar, one day, "you will be ready to take my head if I do not now warn you of the precipice that lies right in your path. If things go on as they are now, I must resign my post of Governor, and leave you." On this occasion Peter burst into tears, and implored his dear Andrei Ivanovich not to desert him; but, as time went on, he became more callous; grew impatient of the continual reprimands of his Governor, and Ostermann, who knew well the youth's uncertain temper, shrank from provoking him too far. He appealed therefore to the Grand Duchess Natalia for help, and she did what she could, but the Dolgorukis, who hated her for her liberal ideas, soon succeeded in undermining her influence also.

Her brother now found her affectionate admonitions a little troublesome, and told her to her face that she was taking too much upon herself. Peter evidently was beginning to think that life, as he understood it, would be a much more pleasant thing without either tutors or mentors. "My dear Andrei Ivanovich," he said one day when his governor again ventured to warn him against bad companions, "my dear Andrei Ivanovich, I like you, and as my Minister of Foreign Affairs you are indispensable, but I must request you not to interfere in future with my pastimes," whereupon he threw himself upon his horse, and went off hunting. After this, Ostermann held his tongue for a time. He let the Tsar see, from his sour looks, that he did not approve of his conduct, and he took care to be at hand whenever he fancied he might be wanted; but his governorship had now practically become a sinecure, so he gave himself up almost entirely to public business, rarely emerging from his Chancellery for weeks at a time. He had learnt from experience that he had nothing to fear so long as his administration was without reproach.

The Dolgorukis had not been able to overthrow the Vice-Chancellor, but they were able to carry out their reactionary designs without any danger of interference on his part. Their first object was to remove the Tsar from St. Petersburg to Moscow, and this they readily contrived to do under the pretext of preparing for the coronation: in January 1728 the whole Court flitted to the old Capital. Another favourite idea of the Dolgorukis at this time, was to appoint the Tsar's grandmother, the long-neglected and half-forgotten Eudoxia Lopukhina, Regent during his minority. This unfortunate lady was escorted with great ceremony to Moscow; exhibited to the people, attired in the splendid old-fashioned robes of a Tsaritsa, and all the great ladies of the city flocked to her new residence, the Dyevitsky

Monastery, to pay their court to her. Ostermann and all the friends of the new system were, for a moment, seriously alarmed. The Vice-Chancellor even went so far as to address obsequiously respectful letters to Eudoxia, assuring her of his devotion, and warning her against the wicked libels of the Dolgorukis. But his apprehensions proved groundless. Thirty years of rigid seclusion had dulled the wits of the poor old Tsaritsa, and her best friends soon convinced themselves that a convent was a much more suitable place for her than a throne. The interview, too, with her grandson, from which so much had been expected, led to nothing. Peter, who now saw his grandmother for the first time, was sympathetic and respectful, and listened with a good grace to the little lecture the pious dowager thought it her duty to administer. But there was no warmth displayed, at least on his side, and both grandson and grandmother were visibly uncomfortable, although the presence of the Tsarevna Elizabeth throughout the interview prevented any awkward or embarrassing allusion to the past. Peter subsequently wrote to his grandmother two or three coldly courteous letters, and cheerfully agreed to the proposal made in the Supreme Privy Council, by Vasily Dolgoruki and Demetrius Golitsuin, that 60,000 rubles a year should be settled upon her for life.[1] After this the melancholy figure of the austere and aged Tsaritsa disappears within the shadow of a convent, where the brief remnant of her life was consumed in unceasing penance.

The Coronation, the ostensible object of the removal of the Court to Moscow, was celebrated on February 25th, 1728.[2] The Tsar prepared for the ceremony by a week of prayer

[1] £15,000.

[2] Compare Zmakin: *Koronatsui russkikh imperatorov*; Liria: *Diario*; and Solovev.

and fasting, as prescribed by ancient custom, at the village of Vsesvyatsk, near Moscow, and, a fortnight later, he made his triumphal entry into the city in a carriage drawn by eight horses, with his governor Ostermann by his side. The order of the ceremony itself was exactly the same as that observed at the coronation of Catherine I, down to the minutest particulars. The only observable difference was the change in the persons of some of the officiating dignitaries. With the exception of the Grand Chancellor Golovkin, who distributed the money among the people, and Yaguzhinsky,[1] who led the cortége at the head of the Guards, most of the chief functionaries were new. Michael Golitsuin, as Grand Marshal of the Empire, immediately preceded the Emperor in the procession, holding a gold wand garnished with diamonds, while young Ivan Dolgoruki walked at Peter's right hand. The ensuing festivities were very magnificent and joyous, but the illuminations and banquets given by the Spanish Ambassador, the Duke of Liria, in honour of the occasion, cast everything else into the shade. This nobleman, a son of the celebrated Duke of Berwick, and himself a person of considerable merit and distinction,[2] who had only recently arrived in Russia on an extraordinary mission,[3] now scattered his dubloons with a truly Castillian *grandeza* that delighted the Russian Court and people, but filled the hearts of his

[1] He had been re-called to the Capital immediately after the fall of his arch-enemy Menshikov, but now occupied a somewhat subordinate position.

[2] Born at St. Germaine in 1696, he was his father's adjutant in Spain in 1710, distinguished himself at the siege of Gerona, and received in 1714 the Golden Fleece for his services. He subsequently passed into Flanders, and accompanied Prince James Stuart to Scotland in 1715.

[3] He was sent, he says, "to establish a good correspondence with a Sovereign who could maintain the balance of power by making if necessary, in Germany, a useful diversion against those Sovereigns who had joined the Hanoverian Alliance."

less wealthy colleagues with all uncharitableness.[1] During the reign of Peter II, Liria occupied much the same position of superior influence as that enjoyed by the French Ambassador Campredon during the latter days of Peter I, and his diary, written in excellent Spanish, is one of our best authorities for the history of the period.

The lion's share of the coronation honours naturally fell to the dominant old Russian party. Another Dolgoruki, Alexius Grigorevich, took his seat in the Supreme Privy Council; and the one military celebrity of the family, Vasily Vladimirovich, was re-called from the Caspian, and made a Field Marshal together with Prince Trubetzkoi, an old friend of the Dolgorukis. This too was the time chosen by the reactionaries for altogether crushing an already fallen foe. We have seen that Menshikov had been allowed to retire to his estates in the Ukraine. It was felt that clemency might well be shown to a dying man, for his hemorrhage had burst forth again on his departure, and had been so severe, that nobody ever thought he would live to reach his journey's end. But the milder climate of the South having somewhat restored the invalid, his enemies began to tremble lest after all he might recover, and again become dangerous. But now Fortune placed in their hands the means of destroying him. Shortly after the coronation, anonymous letters were received by the Tsaritsa Eudoxia,[2] pleading the cause of Menshikov, and eulogising his capacity and past services. Eudoxia sent the documents to the Supreme Privy Council, which ordered a secret investigation; obtained, by the free application of torture, sufficient evidence to give the affair the dignity of a conspiracy, and Menshikov was held responsible and ultimately banished to the awful solitude of Berezov[3] in

[1] The English diplomatic agent, Claudius Rondeau, is especially bitter against him.
[2] Liria.
[3] The place lies on the Sowa, not far from its junction with the Obi, in

the Arctic Ocean, with his wife and family. Here, for the next two years, the fallen Satrap, who had been the friend and maker of monarchs, lived by the labour of his hands, weighed down by a mortal sickness, and glad of a sheepskin to protect him from the cold. It is said that he bore his terrible privations with noble fortitude and christian resignation, thinking less of his own sufferings and infirmities than of those of his devoted consort, whom he tried to cheer and sustain with something of that gaiety and good-humour which had first made his fortune. He died in her arms at the beginning of January, 1730.

The Dolgorukis meanwhile were gradually usurping an authority unattainable by Menshikov in the plenitude of his power. They had cunningly calculated that the equable climate, and the pleasant environs of Moscow, abounding as they did in all manner of game, would be a much more enjoyable residence for an active healthy lad with a perfect passion for field sports, than the cold, foggy, and humid St. Petersburg with its melancholy, and not very salubrious, surroundings of bog, fen and sand—and they were not mistaken. The young Tsar, who had learned to look upon the new capital as a prison, and to hate its ships,[1] its gloomy island-fortresses, its low barrack-like huts, its salt water, and in fact everything belonging to it,[2] was charmed by the superior attractions of the old

the midst of the frozen tundras, with a mean temperature of four degrees below zero.

[1] "El Czar no puede ver la mar ni los navios... aborrece la marina." *Liria.* Peter II's dislike of the sea, and all that sailed upon it, is indeed a salient feature of his character and recurs again and again.

[2] On the other hand the Duke of Liria, in 1729, praises highly the general situation of St. Petersburg, which, according to him, occupied more ground than any other European capital, and might, he says, be made one of the most beautiful. He was also delighted with the view of it from the Neva. Yet he much preferred the old capital. "Es imposible ver mas hermoso pais y clima que el de Moscow," he exclaimed enthusiastically.

capital. He soon became so enamoured of the Moscow district, that he forbade those about him to even mention the name of St. Petersburg. Henceforth there was not even the pretence of studying on his part. He gave himself up entirely to his horses and his dogs; frequently rose at dawn to go hawking or shooting, and spent weeks together at one or other of his numerous hunting-boxes, accompanied by half-a-dozen Dolgorukis. The effect of such an indolent, ill-regulated existence on the young Tsar's character, was soon discernible. Peter II, at this time, was an extraordinarily tall, strong, and handsome youth. He seemed to those about him to shoot up month by month, and had already the stature and the muscles of a full grown man. He was strikingly like his grandfather both in build and features, but rather resembled his father in disposition, being naturally reserved and inaccessible. His parts were excellent; he was not prone to any mean or base vice, and absolutely abhorred the national failing of drunkenness, seldom touching wine, and often up and about while his Kammerherr, young Ivan Dolgoruki, was still sleeping off the effects of an overnight debauch. Thus Nature had done her part by endowing the young Prince with many virtues and talents; but the best soil will produce little if no care be taken to cultivate it, and the Dolgorukis did not allow their young captive (for such he had already become) a moment to improve his mind,[1] or learn the rudiments of government, hurrying him on from one pastime to another, and brutalising him by an unlimited indulgence. Ostermann looked on with despair at the gradual demoralisation of his pupil, but he was powerless to prevent it.

[1] "His Majesty has no person about him, capable of instilling proper and regular notions of government, no part of his time is set aside for the improvement of his mind." Despatches of Claudius Rondeau, *Sb.* of *Imp. Rus. Ist. Ob.*, Vol. LXVI, p. 70; and compare Mardefeldt, Lefort, and Liria.

Now and then he would insinuate a timely remonstrance, and the Grand Duchess Natalia, so long as she was in health, followed her brother from place to place, and contrived to keep him from the worst excesses; but Peter became more difficult to manage day by day; pointers, setters and hunters seemed to be the only subjects that interested him, and on these subjects, unfortunately, the Vice-Chancellor had no opinion to give.

Under these circumstances, affairs were left to take care of themselves. Ostermann's apprehensions lest the removal of the Court to semi-Asiatic Moscow, might mean a relapse into barbarism, proved only too well founded. Confusion and apathy, the usual concomitants of barbarism, were already apparent everywhere. The Foreign Ministers at Moscow were growing alarmed at the anarchical state of things around them. "We are living here," wrote the Saxon Minister Lefort, "in an unparalleled indolence, and in so blind a security, that it is incomprehensible to a thinking mind, how the machinery of state still continues to go on,"[1] and he proceeds to compare the Russian Empire to a ship with a drunken crew, and a dozing pilot, drifting helplessly along on a tempest-tossed sea. The Supreme Privy Council never met for weeks at a time, and on the rare occasions when their "Sublimities"[2] came together, they did very little more than drink a dram, nod in their gilded arm-chairs, and refer all business details to the already overburdened Vice-Chancellor, whom alone they had to thank for the undeserved benefits of popularity at home, and tranquillity abroad. For the wise reforms inaugurated under Catherine I by Menshikov and Ostermann, had begun at last to bear good fruit.

[1] Lefort: *Despatches. Sb.* of *Imp. Russ. Ist. Ob.*, Tome III, pp. 314—346. Compare *Rondeau* and *Liria.*

[2] *Verkhovniki.*

Trade and commerce were reviving, money was beginning to flow steadily, if slowly, into the Treasury, the people, relieved of their more oppressive burdens, were happier, and the land was much more prosperous than it had been for many years. Abroad, too, such slight political changes as had taken place, were, on the whole, favourable to Russia. On the death of George I in 1727, the English Government, through its Minister at Paris, Walpole, had politely declared to the Russian Minister Kurakin, that the new King desired nothing so much as an oblivion of the past, and the re-establishment of friendly relations, and, shortly afterwards, an unofficial political agent, Claudius Rondeau, accompanied the English Consul, Ward, to Russia, to discover how the land lay, and expressed the opinion that, if England only took the first step, there was no reason why the two Courts should not be as good friends as ever.[1] The chief political event of the period was the attraction of Spain to the Hanoverian Alliance by the Treaty of Seville (1729), whereby England and France guaranteed to her her Italian possessions, and England received some important commercial concessions; but the only result of this defection was to draw Russia and Austria more closely together, and their growing influence in the East of Europe counterpoised the influence in the West of the "Allies of Seville", as the Hanoverian Alliance now began to be called. The two Powers agreed to maintain the integrity of Polish territory against the intrigues of Prussia; frustrated the dynastic schemes of Augustus II, by dissipating the Diet of Grodno, and succeeded in keeping Maurice of Saxony out of Courland. In Sweden, the state of parties remained pretty much

[1] Since the arrest of the Russian Minister Matvyeev in London for debt, in Queen Anne's reign, diplomatic relations between the two States had been interrupted.

as it was. England was, as usual, suspected at Moscow of intriguing at Stockholm to bring about a war with Russia; but a violent quarrel between Count Horn and King Frederick, told rather in favour of the latter Power, and was skilfully taken advantage of by the Russian Minister Golovkin.

But, according to all accounts, Russia's weak point, at this period, was her navy. "I give the Fleet another year," wrote the Saxon Minister Lefort, "and then it will no longer be able to put to sea." The Swedish Minister, Cedercreutz, too, reported from St. Petersburg that the galley-fleet was steadily diminishing; the grand fleet was rotting in the dockyards, and there was such disorder at the Russian Admiralty, that it would be quite impossible to place the navy in its former condition in less than three years. There can, indeed, be no doubt that the navy was purposely neglected. The Dolgorukis and the Golitsuins had always looked upon it as a useless luxury, and it seems to have been their deliberate intention to gradually reduce it to vanishing point. Soon after their accession to power, an order was issued that in future no more timber was to be cut than was just sufficient to build three ships a year. On the death of the Grand Admiral Apraksin, in 1729, no President of the Naval College or Admiralty was appointed to fill his place; and the earnest remonstrances of the Vice-President Münnich were treated with the most supine indifference, although it was well known that all the ships of the line built before 1721, were unfit for service, despite the brave show they made in dock.[1] Thus the navy of Peter the Great, that noble navy whereby he had intended to sustain Russia's maritime supremacy in the North, was in danger of disappear-

---

[1] Rondeau tells us that the Russian ships deteriorated more rapidly than the English, both because the timber of which they were built was too old, and also because of the injurious influence of a more rigorous climate.

ing, and with what feelings Peter's most faithful henchman, Ostermann, regarded the gradual destruction of his master's masterpiece, may be readily imagined. But though dismayed, he was not surprised. Well aware that the navy and the new capital were the twin pillars on which the Empire rested, and that they must stand and fall together, he understood that so long as the Court neglected St. Petersburg, there could be no hope of a better state of things. To induce the Tsar to return thither was the first step to be taken, but whenever he approached the subject, Peter II always replied: "What am I to do in a place where there's nothing but salt water?" The Grand Duchess Natalia, primed with Ostermann's arguments, had insisted all along upon the necessity of quitting Moscow as soon as possible; but unfortunately the Vice-Chancellor was now to lose this invaluable ally. All through the summer of 1728, the Princess, never very robust, had been ailing, and her pallor, her extreme thinness, and a hectic cough that never left her, began to seriously alarm her friends. In the late autumn, she was entirely confined to her rooms in the Kremlin, and the doctors prescribed opium to give her sleep, and human milk to sustain her rapidly ebbing strength. Consumption complicated by some gastric trouble, was the malady from which she was actually suffering; but it was generally believed that extreme anxiety on her brother's account hastened her end. On the 28th November, the illustrious patient had a prolonged fainting fit, from which she recovered with difficulty, and, a fortnight later, when the Duke of Liria called to enquire after her health, he was astonished to find the usually impassive Ostermann in the Princess's antechamber, bathed in tears. "If we lose the Grand Duchess, who still possesses a little influence with her brother," said he to Liria, "and we do not return to St. Petersburg, I shall demand my dismissal." At this time there was still a little hope, and on December 6th, Natalia had six hours of sound sleep; but on the 7th, fever supervened, and she was delirious till 10 o'clock at night, when she had a lucid interval, recognised those around her, and, joining her hands together, made an effort to pray. Almost immediately afterwards she was seized with violent convulsions, and expired in a few moments. No fewer than five couriers had been despatched to summon her brother to her death-bed, for on him her thoughts rested continually; but he was hunting, as usual, far from Moscow, and only arrived when all was over. Recognising too late the magnitude of his loss, he abandoned himself to a paroxysm of grief; shut himself up in the Kremlin, and for three days refused to see anybody.—"Thus died a Princess who was the idol of all good people, the pearl of Russia, a creature far too perfect to be left by God in the midst of barbarians who could not appreciate the value of real and solid virtue." [1]

After the death of Natalia, the Dolgorukis seemed to gain an absolute dominion over the mind of the young Tsar, especially after they had succeeded in removing from his path another very different, but, in their eyes, equally dangerous rival. This was Peter's lively young aunt, the Tsarevna Elizabeth, whose beauty, drollery, and exuberant high spirits, had so fascinated him, that it was generally supposed at one time that the young people would make a match of it. The Grand Duchess had always set her face against this intimacy, partly, no doubt, from jealousy, but partly also from moral and religious motives. The Dolgorukis were still more opposed to it from purely sordid considerations, for Alexius Dolgoruki had already resolved to make his second daughter Catherine the young Tsar's bride. As, however, personal beauty was *not* one of this nymph's attractions, whereas the Tsarevna was indisputably the

[1] Liria: *Diario*.

loveliest girl in Russia, the chances of Catherine Dolgoruki seemed at first very problematical. But now the Tsarevna herself played into the hands of her enemies, by her extraordinarily scandalous behaviour. The death of her mother had left her a degree of liberty which might have proved dangerous to the most modest and prudent girl in her situation, and the Tsarevna Elizabeth, unfortunately, was neither prudent nor modest. She seems to have inherited to the full, her father's ardent, impetuous, and voluptuous temperament, and never hesitated to gratify her desires the instant they arose. She had scarcely attained the age of puberty when she was convicted of an intrigue with her gentleman of the bedchamber, and, although not yet twenty, had already abandoned herself to the embraces of half-a-dozen ignoble paramours with a shameless publicity that revolted the most indulgent.[1] The Dolgorukis took good care that the amorous adventures of the Tsarevna (no doubt freely embellished by the ingenuity of malice) should reach the ears of the young Tsar. Peter, who seems to have really been enamoured of his aunt, was so disgusted at conduct which he perhaps regarded as infidelity to himself, that he flouted her before the whole Court, and from thenceforth would have nothing more to say to her. The Dolgorukis, however, were so fearful lest this too facile charmer should regain her ascendency, that they actually tried to persuade her to give her hand to young Ivan Dolgoruki, calculating that a *double* alliance with the Imperial Family would provide against every contingency, and make their position practically unassailable. But Elizabeth, who preferred variety to stability in her liaisons, refused to accept anyone as her

---

[1] "Isabel empezo a abandonarse con bastante publicidad á una vida muy indigna de su nacimiento, teniendo unos galantes publicos con gentes bajas y viles, como granaderos de guardias, y otros."—*Liria*. The other ministers frequently allude in more general terms to her bad conduct.

lord and master; whereupon the Dolgorukis attempted, in vain, to bring her to reason by cutting down her expenses to starvation point, even going so far as to mulct her household of such necessaries as table salt and small beer.

From Ostermann the Dolgorukis seem to have apprehended but little danger, and it is a significant fact that after the death of the Grand Duchess, they felt strong enough to transfer from St. Petersburg to Moscow, the Mint, and all the Colleges or Departments of State, a step which was rightly interpreted as a definitive and permanent transfer of the seat of Government from the new Capital to the old. But the patient, the ever patient Vice-Chancellor had now recovered from the shock of Natalia's death, and had already found two new allies, with whose help he was for secretly undermining the position of his opponents. These allies were the Austrian Ambassador, Count Wratislaw, and the Duke of Liria. The Court of Vienna had been not a little disturbed by the state of things in Russia, especially at the neglect and decay of her armaments, Russia was now the Kaiser's sole ally, and he was desirous of having in her as strong an ally as possible. Prince Eugene had repeatedly urged Wratislaw to counteract the policy of the Dolgorukis, and that Minister, aided by Ostermann and Liria, now composed an affectionate letter of remonstrance to the young Tsar, wherein he was earnestly implored, as well for his health's sake as for the greater glory of his Empire, to withdraw from Moscow for a season, and return to his "conquered provinces" and the place of his birth, so that he himself might have an eye upon that formidable navy, the fruit of the labours and the victories of his "heroic grandfather," and the terror of the North.[1] And now the question arose: how was this letter to be insinuated into his Majesty's hands? After

[1] See Liria: *Diario*, where the letter is given in full.

some debate, Liria undertook to gain over the Emperor's young Kammerherr, Ivan Dolgoruki, and succeeded in doing so chiefly by the aid of golden arguments. Ivan engaged to present the letter, if it were translated into Russian, the only language his young master would now condescend to read; but week after week passed away, and the weeks became months, and still the document was undelivered, for Alexius Dolgoruki had now begun to suspect his own son, and kept such strict watch upon the Tsar, that Ivan durst not give him the letter. Finally, the elder Dolgoruki, no doubt getting wind of this benevolent plot, determined to remove Peter altogether out of the reach of his rivals by organizing a grand hunt, more than a hundred miles off. In the beginning of September, the Tsar quitted Moscow with 620 pointers and setters, a splendid train of huntsmen, and an escort of watchfully attentive Dolgorukis of both sexes. He was away for two whole months, during which period he is said to have killed three bears, five wolves, fifty foxes, 4,000 hares, an innumerable quantity of feathered game,[2] and to have narrowly escaped death himself from the attack of a bear. On his return to the Capital in November, his betrothal with Catherine, the second daughter of Alexius Dolgoruki, was publicly announced in the presence of the Supreme Privy Council, the Senate and nobility specially summoned to the Palace for the occasion, whereupon everyone present first kissed the Tsar's hand, and then proceeded to the apartments of his betrothed, to do her the same honour. On the 11th December, being St. Andrew's Day, the ceremony of betrothal was celebrated with the greatest solemnity in the presence of all the Knights of St. Andrew, in full gala costume. The Dolgorukis took the most elaborate precautions on this occasion. Twelve hundred of the

[1] Lefort.

Guards were posted round the palace, instead of the usual one hundred and twenty, and Ivan Dolgoruki's company of grenadiers received secret orders to ascend the stairs of the palace, as soon as the Tsar had entered the grand saloon, and mount guard before all the doors and passages. Their muskets were to be loaded with ball, and they were to shoot down anybody who showed the slightest disposition to interrupt the ceremony.[1] Fortunately it was not necessary to resort to violence; but the apprehensions of the Dolgorukis were by no means unfounded. Not only was the prospect of having a Dolgoruki for their future Tsaritsa very offensive to all the other great families, especially the Golitsuins; but there were great searchings of heart among the Dolgorukis themselves. The wiser heads could scarce speak of the betrothal without fear and trembling. They felt that the path to such perilous heights was slippery at best, and that a single false step might mean Siberia. The Field Marshal warned his cousin Alexius, the bride's father, that he was treading perilously closely in the footsteps of Menshikov, while Vasily Lukich, the diplomatist of the family, took his niece aside and gave her some very sensible advice, which could not have been altogether palatable to that young lady. But the Alexius Grigorevich branch of the family, in the elation of its triumph, imagined that everything was permissible to the kinsfolk of the future Tsaritsa, and its rapacity now knew no bounds. They proceeded to lay their hands on all the good things within their reach, making a clean sweep, to begin with, of all the young Tsar's loose property which he was not immediately in want of, such as horses, carriages, plate, jewels, and even table-linen. This greed for gain led indeed to some pretty quarrels in the bosom of the bride-elect's own family. Thus, Alexius, the father, conceived

[1] Liria.

a jealous suspicion of Ivan, the son, and tried to remove him from Peter's person, lest he should injure the bride's prospects; the bride's own sisters, envious of her distinction, plagued and frightened her with allusions to monasteries, while the bride herself already regarded her brother with inextinguishable hatred, because he refused to surrender to her the jewels of the late Grand Duchess Natalia, which he said the Tsar had given him. As for Peter II, a complete change seemed to have come over him since his betrothal. He grew morose and melancholy; ceased to take pleasure in his favourite pastimes; gave away his dogs and horses, and altogether seemed very unhappy. He was evidently brooding over his position, and, now and then, his irritation overcoming his natural reserve, there were explosions of wrath which disturbed the Dolgorukis not a little. Thus, on the occasion of a great banquet, at which his satellites were, as usual, lauding to the skies his prowess at the chase, and congratulating him on having killed at least 4,000 hares, he haughtily replied: "That is all very well, but I have made a still bigger bag, for I have brought back with me four two-legged dogs"[1]—and with that he rose abruptly, and quitted the table, leaving the company open-mouthed with astonishment. Shortly after this, there was a party at the house of Alexius Dolgoruki, and a game of forfeits was proposed. Everything went on merrily enough till Peter drew a forfeit which condemned him to kiss one of the young Princesses Dolgoruki. No sooner, however, did he see what it was, than he left the room, mounted his horse, and galloped away. It was quite plain to everyone that he detested his betrothed. "If," writes the Saxon Minister Lefort, apropos of a state ball, "if the tenderness of the future spouses is not warmer in

[1] Lefort. The four two-legged dogs, it is supposed, were four of the Dolgorukis who were always in attendance.

private than I have seen it in public, I have no very great opinion of their mutual felicity in the future." The same authority says that Peter only visited his betrothed once in two months, and then had almost to be dragged to her by the hair of his head. Still he took no steps to break off the match, and continued to live on fairly friendly terms with Catherine's kinsfolk. This seems strange, for he was no fool, and quite capable, as we have seen, of resenting downright insolence with spirit. But there was much within him of that weak good-nature which cannot endure to break with friends once made, even when their unworthiness becomes manifest. The Dolgorukis, more cunning than Menshikov, had always flattered and caressed the poor youth, and he had not the heart to smite them in return.

So the wedding was fixed for the 30th January, 1730, and all went well till the 12th of the same month, when the Tsar was obliged to keep his bed in consequence of a slight chill which he had taken at the ceremony of the blessing of the waters. No alarm was felt at first. Peter's regular medical attendants, the Blumentrosts, pronounced his complaint to be a slight feverish cold, from which he would recover in a day or two, and they allowed him a liberal diet. On the third day, however, other symptoms supervened, which made them distrust their diagnosis, and a specialist, Dr. Bidlo, was summoned, who declared that his Majesty's complaint was smallpox. On the 21st there could no longer be any doubt that Peter II was suffering from that terrible malady in its most virulent form. The whole Court was filled with consternation. It was forbidden to call the Tsar's malady by its right name under pain of death. The Dolgorukis, perceiving their power ebbing away with the young monarch's life, did not shrink from the most revolting expedients for prolonging it if possible, even after his death. Alexius Dolgoruki was for privately solemnizing Peter's marriage forthwith, and so lost was he to all feeling, as to actually propose that his daughter should be secreted in the young Tsar's apartment, so that, in case he recovered consciousness, the marriage might be consummated, and an heir to the throne provided for. This abominable expedient was happily frustrated by the vigilance of the Vice-Chancellor. The moment Peter felt his illness coming upon him, he had sent for his Governor, and Ostermann, with rare devotion, never quitted him night or day, until he died. He would sit by his pupil's bedside for hours at a time, with the lad's hand in his own, and towards the last, when Peter could no longer see, he would enquire at intervals: "Dear Andrei Ivanovich, are you still there?" and—upon Ostermann replying "Yes!"—he would add, "That is right! I want nothing more." The boy's thoughts during his last illness seemed to go back to his earlier and happier days, and while delirious he exclaimed repeatedly: "Get my sledge ready, get my sledge ready! I want to go to my sister." On the 29th all hope was abandoned, and extreme unction was administered by the Archbishop of Novgorod and two assistant bishops, the only other persons present being the aged Tsaritsa Eudoxia, who had come all the way from her convent in order to pray by her grandson's bedside, and the Vice-Chancellor, but for whom the Dolgorukis would even now have forced their way in to the helpless Tsar, to obtain his signature to a will drawn up by them, whereby Peter was to have declared Catherine Dolgoruki his successor. But by this time he was too weak even to hold a pen, or raise his head, and at 25 minutes past 1, on the morning of the 30th January, 1730, the very day that had been fixed for his wedding, Peter II, after a long and painful agony, expired in the fourteenth year of his age, and the third of his reign.

What manner of ruler this young Prince might have become, had he attained to maturity, it is very difficult to conjecture. All who approached him, were much impressed by his precocious gifts both of mind and body. It was the opinion of Liria, that his sudden death cut short a career of rare promise. His face, figure, and outward bearing, as I have already said, strikingly recalled his grandfather's; but, it seems to me, that intellectually he was much closer akin to his unhappy father. Like Alexius, he was naturally serious, not readily familiar, unusually reserved. He had, too, the same distrust of his own powers, the same tendency to lean upon and be led, or rather misled, by those who flattered him. It is somewhat doubtful, therefore, despite his undeniable parts, whether he would have proved a great monarch; but he might well have made a good one, had he fallen into good hands.

# CHAPTER V.

### ACCESSION OF ANNE OF COURLAND.

### (1730—33).

FUTILE family council of the Dolgorukis—Apathy of the Tsarevna Elizabeth —Ascendency of Demetrius Golitsuin—His ambition and political views—Anne of Courland elected Empress—The Articles limiting the power of the Sovereign—Anne signs the Articles—Consternation at Moscow—Arrest of Yaguzhinsky—Arrival of the Empress—Her independent demeanour—The "Republican Gentlemen"—Anne under close surveillance—Preparations for a *coup d'état*—Cherkasky's petition to the Empress—Violent scenes at the Palace—Fall of the Oligarchs —The Empress declared Autocrat—Antecedents and character of the new Tsaritsa—Early marriage to the Duke of Courland—Liaison with Peter Bestuzhev—And with Ernest Johan Biren—Antecedents and character of the latter—First measures of Anne—Punishment of the Dolgorukis—Influence of Biren begins—The Löwenwoldes— Yaguzhinsky's elevation—Establishment of the Cabinet—Burkhard Münnich made Minister of War—His early career and character— Ascendency of the German Party—Insolence of Münnich—Unpopularity of Anne's Government—Causes of this unpopularity—Extravagant display at Anne's Court—Protest of Rumyantsev—Good points of Anne's character and government—Foreign affairs—French intrigues at the Russian Court—Münnich versus Ostermann—Triumph of the Austrian Faction—Polish affairs—Death of Augustus II.

THERE can be but little doubt that had the Dolgorukis, on the death of Peter II, only exhibited something of the spirit and resource displayed by Menshikov on the death of Catherine I, they might have placed another Catherine, the late Tsar's betrothed, and their own kinswoman, on the vacant throne. This was actually proposed in an agitated family council of all the chief Dolgorukis, hastily summoned to the bedside of the bride's sick father, Prince Alexius Grigorevich, at the very moment when Peter was expiring in an adjacent chamber of the Palace. "There is no hope of the Emperor's recovery," said Alexius to those about him, "so we must see about choosing his successor."— "Whom then do you propose?" enquired the diplomatist of the family, Prince Vasily Lukich.—By way of reply, Alexius pointed significantly to the ceiling, adding: "She is there!"[1]—"I think myself it would be safer if we had a will in her favour," suggested Alexius' brother, Sergius. "Is it too late for the Emperor to sign a will, if we draw it up at once?"—But here he was interrupted by the Field Marshal, who declared that the idea was preposterous. "Who would obey her? I should like to know," cried he. "Act energetically," replied the bride's father, "and the thing can soon be done. The Guards are with us."— "You chatter like children, I tell you," retorted the Field Marshal. "If I were even to hint at such a thing to the Guards, they would cut me down before the words were well out of my mouth!" and with that the outspoken old soldier quitted the meeting arm in arm with his brother, Prince Michael. Left to themselves, the subaltern conspirators attempted to filch by fraud what they could not ravish by force. By their united efforts, a letter, purporting to be the last will of the late Emperor, was, at last, drawn up, appointing Catherine Dolgoruki his successor, and to this crowning piece of roguery, young Ivan Dolgoruki, who had of late been wont to sign the young Tsar's letters for

[1] The bride's apartments were in the chamber above.

him, appended a creditable imitation of Peter's signature. Nevertheless, as things turned out, the Dolgorukis, on this occasion, debased themselves in vain, for when the moment arrived for using this precious document, not one of them had the face to produce it.[1]

The same night, possibly at the selfsame hour, Lestocq, the physician of the Tsarevna Elizabeth, made his way to that lady's bedchamber,[2] and, arousing her from her slumbers, informed her that the Tsar was already *in extremis*, and urged her to rise at once, place herself at the head of the Guards, and proclaim herself Empress, and, indeed, had the Tsarevna chosen to follow this audacious piece of advice, success was well-nigh certain. The confusion prevalent at the Palace, the discord among the leading dignitaries of the Empire, the absence, so far, of any serious competitor—all these things were so many chances in favour of the one surviving child of Peter the Great. Elizabeth hesitated, though not from fear. Her courage was indisputable, and eleven years later, under almost exactly similar circumstances, she was to show the world that she was just the woman to conduct a daring *coup-de-main*, at a moment's notice, to a triumphant conclusion. But in those early days, when she still rejoiced in the fulness of an exuberant youth, amusement was everything to her, ambition next to nothing, and though the imperial diadem was almost within her grasp, she would not take the trouble to stretch out her hand towards it. So she carelessly dismissed her medical adviser, and slept on till morning, by

[1] Manstein (Mémoires sur la Russie) relates as a fact, that on the death of Peter II, young Ivan Dolgoruki rushed out of the Palace, sword in hand, exclaiming: "Long live the Empress Catherine!" but retired dismayed when he saw that nobody took up the cry. It is true that, as Liria says, Ivan Dolgoruki was blockhead enough for anything, but this episode cannot be fitted into the chain of actual events.

[2] Manstein.

which time, even if she had changed her mind again, it was too late, for another Princess had already been elected Empress by the Supreme Privy Council.

From midnight till five o'clock the next morning, their Sublimities,[1] as the members of that august College were generally called, had been in anxious consultation behind closed doors. Death or misadventure had reduced their number to five persons, and the most sagacious of the five, Vice-Chancellor Ostermann, after closing the eyes of his dead pupil, had retired precipitately to his own apartments, where he was incontinently attacked by a peculiarly malignant form of chiragra, which prevented the unhappy gentleman from transacting any public business till the political crisis had been safely surmounted. Of the four remaining Supreme Privy Councillors, the aged Grand Chancellor Golovkin was practically a nonentity, while the two Dolgorukis were too diffident of themselves and of each other, to propose anything definite. All the more readily, therefore, did they listen to the one man of character among them, who now, for the first time in his life, saw fame and power within the reach of his ambition. Prince Demetrius Golitsuin, for he it was who, after patiently awaiting his opportunity for more than thirty years, was now to rule Russia for something less than thirty days, Demetrius Golitsuin owed his ascendency at this conjuncture, to the fact that he alone of all his colleagues, knew exactly what he wanted, and was fully determined to have it. This imperious, high-spirited magnate was essentially a *Grand Seigneur*, a type comparatively rare in Russia, though common enough in Poland. Proud of his talents, prouder still of his ancient lineage, he had always considered himself entitled to fill the highest offices in the State, yet, hitherto, his qualifications had been disregarded, and he

[1] *Verkhovniki*, lit. "those up above," *i.e.*, at Court.

was much too haughty to solicit as a favour what he claimed as a right. Frowned upon by Peter the Great, passed over by Catherine I, set aside by Peter II, he had had ample leisure to reflect upon the meaning of this singular and exasperating neglect. Why, he seems to have asked himself, should the Russian aristocracy remain absolutely useless to Russia? Why, for instance, should a great nobleman like himself have been ignored, while stable-boys, flunkeys, vendors of tarts, and the riff-raff of the Dutch Suburb were allowed to monopolize all the offices and dignities of the Empire? In his opinion there could only be one answer to this perplexing question. The scandal was due entirely to favouritism, that foul parasite which fed upon the very vitals of the monarchy, and sucked all the goodness out of it. He was firmly convinced that such a desperate evil could only be cured by a desperate remedy—the abolition of autocracy. Let the monarchy be made a limited monarchy, and favouritism must disappear, and then, and only then, could the national nobility take its proper place around the throne. What effect such a radical revolution might have upon the stubbornly conservative Russian people, whose patriotic veneration for their Tsars was almost an article of their religion, Golitsuin never took the trouble to consider. It was quite sufficient for this strong, if narrow-minded, man, that he had now, apparently, the opportunity of carrying out his long-cherished design. The only remaining question was: who should be chosen to fill the vacant throne? That Peter the Great's family must be excluded, was, to Golitsuin, a matter of course. He had never been able to regard Catherine I as Peter's lawful consort, and consequently, in his eyes, the children of Peter and Catherine were illegitimate. But, in any case, he had no danger to apprehend from that quarter. The levity of the Tsarevna Elizabeth made her an impossible candidate, while the adoption of the infant of her elder sister Anne would have exposed Russia to the dangers of a long minority, besides re-introducing the disturbing Holstein element. It was necessary, therefore, to go back to the elder line of the Romanovs, and seek a successor to the throne from among the three surviving daughters of Peter's elder brother, the weak-minded Ivan V. Of these, the eldest, Catherine, was undesirable because of her marriage with Charles Leopold, Duke of Mecklenburg, whose unspeakably brutal character, and offensive conduct, caused him to be generally detested, especially in Russia. The third daughter, Praskovia, was too sickly and too stupid to be seriously taken into consideration, but in the second daughter, Anne, the widowed Duchess of Courland, Golitsuin fancied he had discovered the very candidate he wanted. It is true that little was known of Anne in Russia, which she had quitted twenty years before as a girl of sixteen; but that little was rather in her favour. She had, moreover, a reputation for sobriety and common-sense, and her personal appearance was majestic and imposing. Golitsuin had little difficulty in bringing his four colleagues over to his opinion; the Vice-Chancellor, on being communicated with, joyfully acquiesced, and after the Supreme Privy Council had exercised its first act of sovereign power by inviting Field Marshals Golitsuin and Dolgoruki, and the latter's brother, Prince Michael, to occupy the chairs vacated by the death of Apraksin and the banishment of Tolstoy and Menshikov, it repaired in a body to the Council Chamber of the Palace, where the Synod, the Senate, the Officers of the Guard, and the representatives of the nobility were already gathered together. The Chancellor Golovkin being too hoarse to speak, Demetrius Golitsuin proceeded to address the Assembly in his stead. Inasmuch, he said, as it had pleased Almighty God to take to Himself their late Sovereign, Peter II, it had become necessary to choose a new head of the State, and, inasmuch as the Princess Anne, at present Duchess of Courland, was known to be adorned with many excellent virtues and talents, the Supreme Privy Council opined that no better candidate than her Imperial Highness could well be chosen. As, however, this was a matter for the nation itself to decide upon, he begged to submit the choice of the Council to the judgment of the assembled magnates, gentlemen and clergy, whom he regarded as the nation's representatives. A unanimous consent, accompanied by loud hurrahs, was immediately given, whereupon Golitsuin ordered that the election should be announced to the troops, and a deputation forthwith despatched to Mittau, the capital of Courland, to acquaint the Duchess with her election, and conduct her to the Capital.

The same evening the deputation set out for Mittau. It consisted of Prince Vasily Lukich Dolgoruki, on the part of the Council, Prince Michael Golitsuin, on the part of the Senate, and General Leontiev as the representative of the Army. Besides a letter signed by all the members of the Council, humbly begging Anne to accept the proffered crown, the deputation was provided with secret instructions, of which none but their Sublimities and one other person, presently to be mentioned, knew anything. They were to inform the Duchess that she could only be elected Tsaritsa conditionally upon her subscribing, in their presence, certain Articles which the Council had drawn up for her signature. By these Articles she was solemnly to engage herself (1) to govern solely through the Supreme Privy Council; (2) not to marry, or appoint her successor, without its consent; (3) to relinquish the right of declaring war and concluding peace, (4) the right of conferring any military appointment above the rank of a Colonel, (5) the right of bestowing gifts of land or money; (6) to surrender the command of the Army and the Guards to the Council; (7) not to confer any Court appointment without the consent of the Council; (8) not to degrade any member of the nobility without legitimate cause; (9) not to impose fresh taxes, and finally, to agree to everything which should be for the good of her subjects [1]—in a word, she was to sign away all her power in exchange for a high-sounding title, and a luxurious ease.

The Council awaited the return of its deputies with some anxiety. They knew that their demands were exorbitant, not to say revolutionary; but they seem to have hugged themselves with the comfortable belief that they had only a needy and easy-going woman to deal with. And yet they were not quite easy. Just before the deputation departed, an unpleasantly significant little incident had occurred—their most knowing colleague, the Vice-Chancellor declared himself physically incapable of signing the letter proposing to limit the power of the new Empress. Their Sublimities thereupon visited the sick man in his chamber, but he complained that his eyes were too weak even to decipher the document. Vasily Dolgoruki spared him the trouble by reading it aloud, and then insisted upon his signing it. Ostermann made an effort to comply, but in the very act of subscription, a fresh twinge of gout seized him, and the pen dropped from his hand.[2] Finally (how we know not) the Council *did* obtain the Vice-Chancellor's signature also, but they rightly interpreted his sudden chiragric paroxysm as a very ominous *political* symptom.

[1] See *Liria*, where the Articles are given in full. The last clause had in view the new Constitution which the Council was bent upon framing.

[2] Dolgoruki: Baron Ostermann. On the other hand, Solovev states expressly that when the letter did depart, Ostermann's signature was among the others.

On the 10th February the Council was relieved of much of its anxiety, by the arrival of a courier from Mittau, with the Articles *signed* by the new Tsaritsa, and accompanied by a letter from her Majesty. She was well aware, she wrote, that the charge of governing so great and glorious an Empire, must needs be a heavy burden, yet since it was the desire of her subjects that she should take such burden upon herself, she was ready, with God's assistance, to comply with their desires. Moreover, beneath her signature to the Articles, she had written with her own hands: "I hereby promise to observe everything herein contained, unreservedly."[1] Fortified by the Empress's sworn declaration Golitsuin (it is characteristic of the simplicity of this old-fashioned man of honour, that he believed in the inviolability of an oath, even when extorted by presumptuous subjects from an ambitious Princess)—Golitsuin, I say, now proceeded to make public his audacious political innovation at another assembly of nobility and gentry, convened at the Kremlin Palace for that purpose. There, with many rhetorical flourishes and devout ejaculations, he proclaimed and applauded the gracious and magnanimous condescension of her Majesty, and invited all present to lend him and his colleagues their assistance in framing a new Constitution. The Assembly received his announcement with an obstinate silence that was almost appalling. Amazement and consternation were written on every face. In the background some timid remonstrances were audible. To use the quaint language of Archbishop Theophanes, a much perturbed eye-witness of the scene, "All who had heard these words, drooped their ears like so many poor asses." Even their Sublimities were fluttered, and looked "amazed and open-eyed, like men surprised by something unforeseen." Then Demetrius Golitsuin hastily consulted

[1] Solovev.

his colleagues in a whisper, and, turning to his dumb and expectant audience, exclaimed: "Why does nobody open his mouth? Speak, someone, if only to express his gratitude to her Most Gracious Majesty!"—At this there was a still longer pause, but, at last, Prince Alexius Mikhailovich Cherkasky,[1] the wealthiest nobleman in Russia, and connected by marriage with the Imperial Family itself, stepped forward, and asked permission to submit in writing his views as to the new Constitution. Golitsuin, anxious to meet half-way all who seemed only to differ from him in detail, readily assented; but the evident consternation of the Assembly had profoundly impressed him, and he now attempted to overawe the waverers by an audacious act of authority. Close to the council board at which their Sublimities were sitting, stood Yaguzhinsky, an attentive spectator of the proceedings. Excepting Ostermann and Golovkin, Yaguzhinsky was the one surviving statesman of the great Petrine period, and no man understood his countrymen better than he did. During the last two reigns he had been suffered to remain in the background; but he had not forgotten the days when he, Paul, as Procurator-General (an inquisitorial office unknown to any other State, save perhaps mediæval Venice) had been "Peter's eye," which nothing could deceive or elude, and, in his usual impetuous fashion, he had expressed his resentment, with a characteristic disregard of the consequences. On the death of Peter II, Yaguzhinsky had diplomatically approached the Dolgorukis, in the hope of obtaining one of the vacant chairs in the Supreme Privy Council; but disappointed in this direction, and being at the same time informed by his father-in-law, Chancellor Golovkin, of the secret machinations of their Sublimities, he at once

---

[1] There had been intermarriages between the Cherkaskys and the Narishkins. Peter the Great's mother, it will be recollected, was a Narishkin.

despatched a courier to Mittau, warning the Duchess of what was in store for her, and advising her not to submit to the dictation of a handful of aristocrats, as her friends in the Capital would take care that she got her full rights at the proper time. This courier was so skilfully disguised that he eluded all the vigilance of the Council's spies, and succeeded in delivering his message to the Duchess, but was captured on his return journey[1] by Vasily Dolgoruki's satellites, and confessed, under torture, that he was the emissary of Yaguzhinsky. Now as Yaguzhinsky was, without doubt, the most energetic opponent the Council had to deal with, and equally dangerous whether drunk or sober, Golitsuin had resolved beforehand to secure his person. The capture of the courier was, however, kept a profound secret, and the ex-Procurator suspected nothing wrong, till Golitsuin, suddenly arising, confronted him with the letter that he, Yaguzhinsky, had written to the Duchess, at the same time asking him whether he recognised the handwriting. For the moment Yaguzhinsky was so taken aback, that he could not utter a word; but, immediately recovering himself, he defiantly owned to the letter, and declared that he was proud of having written it, whereupon he was deprived of his sword, and committed to the custody of a file of fusiliers, who conveyed him to the dungeons of the Kremlin: on the following day he was deprived of all his offices and dignities, including the blue ribbon of St. Andrew, with which Peter the Great had decorated him personally. The same day, thirty other persons were arrested, by order of the Council, on various pretexts; domiciliary visits were made

---

[1] Compare Liria: *Diario*; Manstein: *Mémoires*; Solovev and Kostomarov. There is some doubt as to whether Sumarakov, for that was the courier's name, was captured before or after his departure from Mittau, and also as to whether he or the deputation arrived there first. The discrepancies are, however, immaterial; one thing is quite clear, the Duchess, somehow or other, was acquainted with his mission.

daily upon suspected individuals, and all the approaches to the Palace where their Sublimities held their sessions, were guarded by troops. These prompt measures effectually prevented the outbreak of a rebellion of which the Council was seriously apprehensive at one time, and not without good reason. For the boyars, the lesser gentry, and the clergy, were alike horrified by the godless acts of the Verkhovniki who would fain have substituted a monstrous eight-headed despotism, unknown in Russia before, for the time-honoured and divinely sanctioned government of a single absolute monarch. But the malcontents, though numerous and mutinous, lacked a leader, and had perforce to keep quiet while the "Republican Gentlemen,"[1] as the English Resident Rondeau calls the members of the Supreme Privy Council, amused themselves every day, till the Empress's arrival, by endeavouring to frame a new Constitution. As, however, they had been in the habit all their lives, of blindly bowing before the will of a despot, they had but a vague notion of what a limited government should be, and were still in the midst of their Sisyphean labours, when the new Sovereign arrived at Vsevsyatskoe, a small place about six miles from the capital.

At first Anne appeared very desirous of complying with the wishes of the Council, in accordance with the solemn Convention she had sworn to at Mittau. When the Council and the Senate waited upon her to thank her for signing the Articles, and assure her of their "fidelity to her sacred person and to the Empire," on which occasion Golitsuin was the spokesman, Anne declared that she had only subscribed the Convention because she had been assured

[1] Despatches of Claudius Rondeau, *Sb.* of *Imp. Ist. Ob.*, Tome LXVI. Although a friend of the Dolgorukis, and of the old Russian Party generally, Rondeau feels bound to admit that "the plan of the Council was imperfect, and not well digested, and no doubt would have caused some confusion in the execution of it."

that such was the will of the nation, adding that to promote the welfare of her subjects was her sole ambition, and that she looked for the loyal co-operation of her counsellors to assist her in doing justice to all.

But the independence of the Tsaritsa's conduct belied the humility of her language. Their Sublimities, after again thanking their Sovereign for her condescension, begged her to deign to accept the ribbon and cross of St. Andrew, and the Chancellor Golovkin, as senior chevalier, was about to take it from the golden bowl in which it lay, and formally invest her with it, when Anne interrupted him by exclaiming: "Why, of course! I forgot to wear it!"—and, snatching it out of his hand, gave it to one of her ladies to put on for her. It was evident that she disdained to accept as a gift from the hands of subjects, what she regarded as hers by right divine, and not even Demetrius Golitsuin had the moral courage to protest against this manifest infringement of the compact of Mittau. Nor was this all. The Empress had not been four-and-twenty hours at Vsevsyatskoe, when she took an unexpected step which seriously alarmed their Sublimities. A battalion of the Preobrazensky Guards, and a detachment of the Imperial Horse Guards, had been despatched from the Capital to congratulate her upon her accession.[1] On their arrival, Anne, without waiting for the officers to be introduced, came forth to meet them, and, after graciously complimenting them on their courage and fidelity, declared that inasmuch as God had called her to the throne, it was her dearest wish to be their Colonel, as her predecessors had been. The officers, beside themselves for joy at the condescension of their Sovereign, forthwith threw themselves at her feet, and proclaimed her their Colonel with enthusiasm, whereupon Anne regaled each one of them with a glass of liqueur,

[1] Compare Liria: *Diario*, and Leport's *Despatches*.

which she filled and presented to them with her own hand. This still more flagrant breach of the Articles of Mittau, mortified Vasily Dolgoruki and his satellites exceedingly, but the suddenness even more than the audacity of the act paralysed all opposition, and unable to prevent, they pretended to applaud it. And there were other unpleasantly significant symptoms of a coming change. Thus, when the Tsarevna Elizabeth came out to Vsevsyatskoe, to pay her respects to her cousin, Anne is said to have taken her aside, and whispered: "My sister, we have very few of the Princesses of the Imperial House remaining,[1] and it therefore behoves us to live together in the strictest union and harmony, whereto I mean to contribute with all my power."—Elizabeth then complained that all her troubles had proceeded from her refusal to marry Ivan Dolgoruki.— "My dear," replied the Empress, "we'll soon put all that to rights."

In Moscow itself, too, the new Lycurguses no longer felt secure. Their repressive measures had indeed gagged and fettered the nobility and gentry, but the clergy, secretly instigated by the adroit and experienced Theophanes, Archbishop of Novgorod, who, as one of Peter the Great's disciples and fellow-workers, was particularly obnoxious to the Golitsuins and the Dolgorukis,—the clergy, I say, opposed to the measures of the Government a tenacious but intangible resistance which it was equally impossible to mistake or chastise. It was mainly due to Theophanes that the new oath of allegiance, whereby fealty was to have been sworn to the Empress *and the Supreme Privy Council*, was abandoned, the words "to the Empress and the Fatherland" being substituted for the original formula.

The one thing that still sustained the hopes of their

[1] Alluding to the recent deaths of the Duchess of Holstein, and the Grand Duchess Natalia. The incident is related by Lefort.

Sublimities, was the vigilance with which Prince Vasily Dolgoruki mounted guard over the new Empress. Anne herself subsequently complained, with great bitterness, that a dragon could not have been more watchful than his Highness. From February 26th, when she made her public entry into Moscow, till the 8th March, she was kept under such strict surveillance, that none but the emissaries of the Council could gain access to her person. She was not even allowed to speak in private to her own sister, the Duchess of Mecklenburg, except in the presence of witnesses. Their Sublimities seem to have argued that if this system of surveillance could only be kept up *until* the Coronation, it would be unnecessary afterwards, as then her Majesty, who was known to be religious, would have bound herself, in the sight of God and all the people, to observe the new Constitution, by oaths too solemn for an orthodox Princess to break. But her partisans, who had fully determined that things should not come to such a pass as this, were already working energetically on her behalf. There can be little doubt that the Tsaritsa's secret adviser during this anxious fortnight, was Ostermann, whose keen political instinct had told him from the first that a limited monarchy was impossible in Russia. As usual, his hand was hidden, but it was certainly in his cabinet that the cunning scheme was devised which upset all the calculations of the "republican gentlemen." His only possible intermediaries were the ladies of the Court, notably his own Countess, the Countess Saltuikov, and the Princess Cherkasky, whose ingenious contrivances baffled even the precautions of so subtle an intriguer as Prince Vasily Dolgoruki. The usual means of conveying letters to the Empress was by tucking them beneath the bib of her godchild, Count Biren's baby, Carl, who was taken up to her bedroom by his nurse every morning, and it is said that Archbishop

Theophanes, who was also in the plot, succeeded in letting her Majesty know that her friends outside were ready for action, by dextrously insinuating the message inside the case of a handsome clock which the clergy of Moscow had just presented to their new Sovereign. To Prince Cherkasky was entrusted the practical management of the impending *coup d'état*. Cherkasky was by no means a brilliant person, but his immense wealth, high position, and sturdy conservatism, entitled him to be the leader of the old Russian nobility, and he was universally esteemed for his courage and integrity. Nevertheless his lack of prudence and discretion nearly ruined the whole enterprise. It is even said that Demetrius Golitsuin discovered the plot, and had actually issued the order for his arrest and deportation to Siberia, when Cherkasky averted the blow by himself striking first. For a few hours, however, he was in extreme danger. On the evening of the 7th he narrowly escaped being kidnapped, and when, at midnight, he quitted his wife, in order to give his final directions to his subordinates, he never expected to see her again in this world.

The 8th March had been fixed for the *Coup d'État*, and early in the morning of that day,[1] some eight hundred noblemen and gentlemen assembled in the courtyard of the Kremlin. Presently they were joined by Prince Cherkasky, Prince Trubetskoy, and General Usupov; and Cherkasky, selecting one hundred and fifty of his adherents, all of whom were officers of the Guard, boldly ascended the staircase of the Palace, and demanded an audience of her Majesty. They were at once introduced, and found the Empress seated on her throne, surrounded by her Court. On the appearance of the deputation, she summoned to her

[1] Compare Solovev; Rondeau: *Despatches;* Liria: *Diario;* Leport: *Despatches;* Manstein: *Mémoires.* These five accounts agree in all essential particulars, and from them I have compiled the ensuing narrative.

presence the members of the Supreme Privy Council, who, much surprised at so early a summons, hastened to the Council Chamber, in a body. Their Sublimities having taken their places, General Usupov, on behalf of the noble deputies, thanked the Empress for her "unspeakable goodness" in signing the Articles of Mittau, but, at the same time, expressed the apprehensions of himself and his colleagues lest these same Articles should contain aught that was injurious to her Majesty's true interests, and he thereupon delivered to her a petition in writing, begging of her "clemency and benignity" permission to reconsider the whole question. This petition the Empress took, and delivering it to Prince Cherkasky, requested him to read it aloud, an order he immediately obeyed. It was in substance an indictment of the Supreme Privy Council, for acting as they had done without the knowledge and consent of the nobility, and after reading it Cherkasky was proceeding to comment in no measured language on the conduct of their Sublimities, when he was interrupted by the stately and dignified Vasily Dolgoruki, who, thinking to browbeat the fat little man, insolently enquired by what right he constituted himself a legislator. But Cherkasky, who had the heart of a lion in the body of a hog, was not to be silenced. "I have as much right to advise her Majesty," retorted he," as you had to impose conditions upon her by the Articles of Mittau, without consulting us."—Ignoring the taunt, Dolgoruki, shrewdly suspecting that the whole demonstration had been preconcerted, and fully understanding that unless the Tsaritsa were forthwith separated from the conspirators, all was lost, Dolgoruki approached her Majesty with his most courtly air, and respectfully suggested that she should retire to her cabinet, in order to discuss with her Council, such a weighty constitutional document with all due calmness. It was a dextrous move, and all but successful.

The Empress hesitated, her supporters, taken by surprise, were speechless, and the courage of their Sublimities revived, when the situation was saved by the promptitude of Anne's sister, the irrepressible Duchess of Mecklenburg, who at that moment drew nigh to the Tsaritsa, with a pen and ink-horn, and, smoothing out Usupov's petition before her, exclaimed: "What need for your Majesty to deliberate about so simple a matter? Surely 'tis better to sign at once."—The spell was broken. The Empress, recovering her sang-froid, immediately signed the document, and taking advantage of the loud murmur of approbation which thereupon arose from all parts of the Hall, pretended to be anxious for her personal safety, and commanded that henceforth no orders issued in her name should be obeyed unless they were delivered through her kinsman, General Saltuikov of the Guards. Usupov's petition was then handed to the nobility, who thereupon begged her Majesty's consent to retire into an adjoining chamber to deliberate, and to wait upon her again with the decision in the afternoon. Anne graciously granted their request, and dextrously prevented the members of the Supreme Privy Council from consulting together in the meantime, by inviting them all to dine with her. At four o'clock, the nobility returned with a fresh petition in which they implored her Majesty, in the most obsequiously respectful manner, to deign to accept the absolute authority which had always been possessed heretofore by her glorious and illustrious predecessors; to cancel the Articles imposed upon her by the Supreme Privy Council; to abolish that Council itself, and to reconstitute the Senate as it had been in the days of Peter the Great. On hearing the terms of the second petition, the Empress turned towards the deputies with well-feigned astonishment. "What!" she exclaimed, "do you mean to tell me that the Articles submitted to me for signature, at Mittau, were not framed with the consent of my people?"—"They were not, Gosudaruinya!"[1] was the unanimous reply. "Then you have lied to me, Prince Vasily Lukich Dolgoruki!" cried Anne, regarding the discomfited diplomatist, with that awful scowl[2] which, in later days, was to make the boldest tremble. Thereupon Anne directed Chancellor Golovkin to fetch the document from the archives, and, taking it from him, tore it in pieces in the presence of the assembly, amidst loud hurrahs, and indescribable enthusiasm. But the Dolgorukis' cup of humiliation was not yet full. An act of public reparation had yet to be made, which was more galling to them than anything that had gone before. Immediately after destroying the Mittau Convention, the Empress commanded General Chernuishev to release Yaguzhinsky, and conduct him with all honour to the Palace. On his arrival, his sword, by her Majesty's express command, was restored to him in the antechamber, by Field Marshal Dolgoruki, the selfsame dignatory who had deprived him of it a fortnight before, whereupon he was introduced into the presence of her Majesty, who raised him from the ground (for, in the effusion of his gratitude, he had prostrated himself at her feet) and treated this martyr for the cause of monarchy with extraordinary favour and distinction. The same evening, the accession of the new autocrat was proclaimed in the streets of Moscow, amidst the roll of drums and the firing of salvos; a new oath of allegiance was administered, and couriers were despatched to the provinces, to announce the glad tidings. Nowhere was there the slightest symptom of opposition. The "republican gentlemen" hid their heads, glad enough

---

[1] "Your Sovereign Majesty."
[2] Lady Rondeau, who knew the Empress personally, and liked her, was struck by "that awfulness in her countenance which impresses you so much at first sight."

not to lose them. Only one member of the late Government showed an unabashed front, and that was Demetrius Golitsuin. "The banquet was ready," he bitterly remarked to the little band that still believed in his impossible views, "but they that were bidden were not worthy. I know I shall be the victim of this miserable business. Be it so! I am ready to suffer for my country. My time is short, but those who make me weep now, will one day shed far more bitter tears than I shall."

The evening after this successful *coup d'état*, the inhabitants of Moscow were startled and dismayed by a singular spectacle. The whole horizon was dyed blood-red by an extraordinarily vivid display of the Northern Lights. The superstitious interpreted this phenomenon as a heavenly portent, foreboding bloodshed and all manner of evil; and the subsequent cruel severities of the new reign, seemed to many to justify these prognostications.

For the government of Anne, prudent, beneficial, and even glorious, as it proved to be, was undoubtedly severe, and became at last universally unpopular. This was no doubt due in a great measure to the injurious constraint of peculiar circumstances; but, as in all absolute monarchies, the personal character of the sovereign was also a determining factor in the evolution of events, it behoves us to examine the new Tsaritsa a little more closely.

Anne Ivanovna, when she ascended the Russian throne, was in her seven-and-thirtieth year, and therefore considerably past her prime. Her natural parts, if not brilliant, were at least sound, and she was capable of deep and lasting attachments; but a worse than indifferent education, and a life-long series of petty vexations and humiliations had dwarfed her intelligence, and soured her disposition. Her girlhood[1] had been passed at Ismailovo, the favourite

[1] The only accounts of Anne's earlier career I am aware of, are (1) Kos-

palace of her grandfather, Tsar Alexius, delightfully situated close to Moscow, where she had resided with her widowed mother, Praskovia, a typical old-fashioned Tsaritsa of the better sort, infinitely good-natured, indiscriminately benevolent, and very pious, according to her lights, although her piety was not without a strong dose of superstition, and Christian priests and pagan sorcerers found an equal welcome at her hospitable table. Indeed, so long as she lived there, Ismailovo resembled a hospital rather than a palace. The lame, the halt, the blind, and the weak-witted flocked to it from all quarters, and fared sumptuously at Praskovia's expense. Only on the rare occasions when Peter the Great visited his kinswoman, did this mob of mendicant pensioners vanish, for a time, from before the face of the stern and saturnine Tsar, who would never allow anyone to eat his bread unless he worked for it. Praskovia was terribly afraid of her brother-in-law, but as she, very prudently, made it the rule of her life never to contradict him, and to obey his commands, however inconvenient and unintelligible, without a murmur, Peter smiled indulgently upon her many absurdities, and even acted as a second father to the Ivanovs,[1] as she and her daughters were generally called at Moscow. That he should have treated them as the mere instruments of his political schemes, was only what might have been expected. Thus, he compelled them, in 1709, to move from their pleasant quarters near Moscow, to the damp and dreary palace he had erected for them amidst the fens and marshes of his newly founded St. Petersburg, and, in 1710, he made his niece Anne, in her seventeenth year, give her hand to the first suitor who presented

tomarov: *Anna Ivanovna;* (2) Semevsky: *Tsaritsa Praskovia;* (3) Shcherbatov: *O povreshdeny nravov v Rossy*, and (4) Solovev: *Istoria Rossy.*

[1] *I.e.*, Ivan's people, the Ivan here mentioned being Peter's elder brother, Ivan V.

himself, Frederick William, Duke of Courland. The bride was scarcely prepossessing. It is true that she had fine hair and eyes, and, for one of her massive dimensions, by no means a bad figure. Her carriage, too, was dignified and majestic. But her features were coarse, swarthy, and masculine; she had no manners to speak of, and her temper was sullen, sulky, and extremely vindictive. Many were of opinion that the Duke would have done better had his choice fallen upon the elder sister Catherine,[1] a lively, good-humoured, outspoken, pretty little woman, whose incessant and irrepressible bursts of laughter were always audible above the din and racket of Peter the Great's rough-and-tumble dancing assemblies, at which the Russian ladies, freshly emancipated from the seclusion of their *terems*, amused themselves, by order, in an atmosphere redolent of hollands and stale tobacco smoke. But the Duke, who only courted his bride for what he could get by her, was not over nice, and the marriage was celebrated, with barbaric splendour, at Menshikov's palace. Peter entertained his guests in his own peculiar fashion. At the wedding feast, for instance, two gigantic pies were placed before the bride and bridegroom, and when the Tsar cut them open, a couple of richly attired dwarfs leaped out upon the table, and diverted the company by dancing a minuet. Peter's favourite dwarf, Euphemius Volkov, moreover, was compelled to take unto himself a spouse at the same time, and seventy-two other little pigmies were collected from all parts of the Empire, to march in the bridal procession, and entertain the Court after the nuptials. Of junketings and drinking bouts there was no end, and the unhappy bridegroom partook so excessively of the hospitality of his

---

[1] For Anne's personal appearance, compare Liria: *Diario;* Lady Rondeau: *Letters from a Lady;* Semevsky: *Tsaritsa Praskovia;* Solovev: *Istoria Rossy*, and Kostomarov: *Anna Ivanovna.*

too lavish host, that he died of surfeit on his return journey, at the village of Duderhof, when only thirty miles from St. Petersburg. This *contretemps*, however, was not allowed to interfere with the Tsar's far-reaching plans. The reluctant young widow was ordered to proceed on her way to Mittau, to take over the government of Courland; but the real ruler of the Duchy, for some time to come, was the Russian resident, Count Peter Bestuzhev, whom Peter placed by his niece's side as general adviser. The relations between the young Duchess and the indispensable diplomatist soon became more tender than innocent, but the *liaison*, long kept secret, was betrayed at last by Vasily Fedorovich Saltuikov, the Duchess's maternal uncle, not from any regard for his niece's morals, as he hypocritically pretended, but from sheer vindictiveness at her chivalrous interference between him and his wife, whom he was in the habit of brutally ill treating. Praskovia, who had always been a model spouse herself, was horrified at this lapse from virtue on the part of the sagest of her daughters, and moved heaven and earth to have the seducer removed. But as Peter refused to interfere in the matter, the Tsaritsa had to be content with cursing the impenitent young sinner, as Anne obstinately refused to sever the disreputable connexion. Presently, however, Bestuzhev was supplanted by a *protégé* of his own, who owed everything to his past favour. This upstart, Ernst Johann Biren by name,[1] was the grandson of a groom in the service of Duke James III of Courland, who bestowed upon him a small estate, which Biren's father inherited, and where Biren himself was born. The little we know of Ernst Johann's early career is not very creditable to him. He received what education he had at the Academy of Königs-

---

[1] I am acquainted with no biography of Biren. I have gleaned the above particulars from passing notices in Solovev: *Istoria Rossy*, Vol. XVIII; Manstein: *Mémoires*; Dolgoruki: *Graf A. I. Ostermann*; Kostomarov: *Anna Ivanovna*.

berg, but was expelled from that institution for brawling in the streets with the civic guard, and, being unable to pay the fine of 700 thalers imposed upon him, was kept for a time in gaol. In 1714, he set out to seek his fortune in Russia, (his family being too miserably poor to support him at home) and solicited a place at the Court of the Princess Sophia, the consort of the Tsarevich Alexius. The request of the needy adventurer was rejected as an impertinence, and, dismissed with contempt, he returned to Mittau, where he succeeded in gaining a footing at Court, through the influence of one of his sisters, who had in the meantime become Peter Bestuzhev's mistress. From all accounts, Biren was a very handsome insinuating fellow,[1] who had sense enough (for he was no fool) to conceal his want of education and manners behind a bluff *bonhommie*. One thing he understood thoroughly, and that was horse-flesh. At a subsequent date, the Empress Catherine I sent him to purchase a steed for her at Breslau, and he acquitted himself of the commission to her entire satisfaction. Even those who disliked him most used to consult him about their mounts, and the Austrian Minister, Ostein, is reported to have said of him on one occasion, "When Monsieur de Biren speaks of horses, he talks like a man; but when he speaks of men, he talks like a horse." Biren soon attracted the attention of the young Duchess, and succeeded, during the temporary absence of his patron, Bestuzhev, not only in completely supplanting him, but in poisoning Anne's mind against her former favourite, and procuring the disgrace and banishment of himself and his family. From henceforward, Biren's influence over the Duchess, if not quite so absolute as some Russian writers[2] have supposed, was at least

---

[1] Lady Rondeau, however, who frequently saw him, describes him as having "a forbidding look."

[2] Kostomarov and Dolgoruki, for instance.

paramount. Only once, when that irresistible paladin, Maurice of Saxony, conquered her Highness's heart, almost in despite of herself, was Biren's position seriously imperilled. Anne felt deeply the refusal of the Court of St. Petersburg to consent to her marriage with Maurice; but disappointed affection and domestic meddling were not her only troubles. During the whole time of her residence at Mittau, she was very badly off from a pecuniary point of view, and felt the pinch of poverty most keenly. Most of the revenues of Courland flowed into the Russian treasury, and the allowance meted out to the Duchess was so scanty and irregular, that she was often hard put to it how to pay her servants and keep a decent table. Piteous are some of the letters she wrote to Catherine I, Peter II, and even to the Grand Duchess Natalia, humbly throwing herself on their protection, and begging for relief, yet, in almost every instance, her complaints were disregarded. It will thus be seen that Anne's lot hitherto, had not been a very happy one. Ever since girlhood, she had been forced to drink to the dregs the cup of humiliation; made to feel her dependence on tyrannous and unsympathetic kinsfolk; compelled to keep a sharp look-out for spies and informers—in a word, she had been brought up in an atmosphere of anxiety and suspicion, and constant anxiety and suspicion do not tend to soften the heart of a naturally hard, proud, sensitive and ambitious woman like Anne of Courland. And if she was indignant with the past, she was also uneasy as to the future. Her first experience of the Russian nobility and gentry had been anything but agreeable. They had shown a dangerous disposition to limit, or at any rate to define, her prerogatives, and it was only the energetic intervention of the Guards that had saved the monarchy. Suspicious and resentful as she was, Anne felt that she could never trust the Russian gentry with power after what they had done or attempted to do. She must henceforth surround her throne with persons entirely devoted to her interests, and these persons, from the nature of the case, could only be foreigners—Germans, Livonians, and Courlanders. Yet, being as shrewd and sensible as she was distrustful, Anne recognised the necessity of proceeding with the utmost caution. A Russian herself, she perfectly understood that the domination of foreigners would be an abomination to all true Muscovites, and she was much too prudent to take a single step without carefully weighing all the consequences beforehand. She had made up her mind to eliminate from her government all dangerous or disturbing elements; but she clearly perceived that the process of elimination must be as tentative and gradual as possible. The men she feared or hated, should all be removed in time, if not at once, and those who were suffered to remain should not have the opportunity of doing much mischief. But justice should be done, and some concessions should also be made to national prejudices. Then too, not all the offenders had been equally offensive, and a few, a very few, of the Russian magnates had never swerved from their loyalty, and these should be rewarded.

Such, judging from the proceedings of her government, were the intentions of the new Sovereign. Her earliest measures seemed to breathe a spirit of clemency and indulgence. She appeared bent rather upon compensating the disappointed, than upon chastising the froward. The Supreme Privy Council was of course abolished; but among the twenty-one members of the reorganized Administrative Senate, which superseded it, Demetrius Golitsuin, Vasily Dolgoruki, and their respective kinsmen, the two Field Marshals, much to their own surprise, were commanded to take their places by the side of Ostermann, Golovkin,

Yaguzhinsky, and Cherkasky. The Empress also appointed the wife of Marshal Golitsuin her first lady-in-waiting, and his son one of her gentlemen, while the Marshal himself was presently nominated President of the College of War, or War Minister. He died, however, at the end of the year, much to the relief of the Government, who then gave the post to his colleague, Marshal Dolgoruki. Demetrius Golitsuin was presented with a rich estate, a welcome gift, for he was honest and had a large family. Yet the day of reckoning was but postponed. Only five weeks after Anne's accession, the first blow fell, and the Dolgorukis were the victims. The Ukazes of the 8th and 24th April pronounced sentence of banishment against Alexius Dolgoruki and his family, for causing, if not actually compassing, the death of the late Emperor, and against Vasily Dolgoruki "for forgetting the duty of an honest and faithful servant, and deceiving us with vain imaginings, godlessly devised by himself."[1] The sentences were carried out with merciless haste and rigour. Alexius was sent to Yakutsk in Siberia; his family, including his daughter Catherine, the late Emperor's bride-elect, to the still more terrible Berezov, whither the Dolgorukis themselves had banished Menshikov two years before. Vasily Dolgoruki, after being pronounced infamous, and having his sword broken before his eyes, was imprisoned in the Monastery of Solovets, on the White Sea. His cousin, Prince George, was so cruelly knouted before his departure, that he died on his way to exile.[2] For the Alexian branch of the family, little sympathy was felt. Their offences had been notorious, and their punishment was held to be just. But Vasily Dolgoruki's crime, as set forth in his indictment, was so mysteriously worded as to be absolutely unintelligible. Indeed he was looked upon

[1] Solovev.
[2] Liria: *Diario;* and Lefort: *Despatches.* Compare also Solovev.

as a scapegoat, and it was generally believed that the illustrious diplomatist would not have been treated so savagely but for the vindictiveness of the favourite Biren, who had never forgiven him for stipulating that he, Biren, should not be allowed to accompany his mistress to Russia. That upstart had now arrived at Moscow with his wife—formerly a Fräulein von Treiden, who had accepted him despite the protests of her parents and the indignation of the Courland gentry, who would never recognise Biren as one of themselves—and honours and riches were heaped upon him. On the occasion of the Empress's coronation, which was celebrated on the 19th May, with unexampled magnificence,[1] Anne having a veritable passion for pageants, the handsome Courlander, besides being made Grand Chamberlain and a Count of the Empire, was presented with an estate at Wenden worth 50,000 crowns a year. Another foreigner, Carl Gustaf Löwenwolde,[2] the scion of an old Livonian baronial family, whose elder brother, Reinhold Löwenwolde (much esteemed both by Catherine I and Anne), had quitted the Swedish for the Russian service, after being captured at Pultawa,—Carl Gustaf Löwenwolde, I say, was, at the same time, created a Count, and made Grand Marshal of her Majesty's household, while his brother Reinhold, a few months later, was nominated Colonel of the newly

[1] A new crown on the model of Catherine I's, but much more splendid, was specially made for the occasion. It contained 28 large brilliants, and 2,579 other gems. It was placed on her head by Archbishop Theophanes. A liturgical novelty at Anne's coronation was the introduction of the touching prayer in which the Sovereign was made to thank "the Tsar of Tsars" for his graciousness in giving her the "grandest vocation on earth."—Zhmakin: *Koronatsy, etc.*

[2] The Duke of Liria, who gives him a very bad character, says, "he would have sacrificed his best friend to his ambition or his vanity." The English Minister Rondeau and Prince Dolgoruki, however, speak much more favourably of him, and he seems to have been good-natured on the whole, if somewhat greedy and stupid.

raised (Sept. 1730) regiment of foot-guards, consisting of 2,000 gentlemen, mostly Livonians, henceforth known as the Ismailovsky Regiment.[1] No wonder, then, if the old Russians began to murmur loudly that her Majesty had too many Germans and Courlanders about her person. Nevertheless, the process of eliminating the national element from the Government continued, although, to superficial observers, the Russian party appeared for a time to be actually in the ascendant. This was especially the case so long as the impetuous and energetic Yaguzhinsky took a leading part in affairs. The Empress had at first been very gracious to him. At her coronation, he too had been created a Count, and five months later (Oct. 1730) was reappointed to his old inquisitorial post of Procurator-General, with jurisdiction over the Senate itself, and as the Chancellor, Golovkin, was his father-in-law, and the wealthy and influential Cherkasky his friend, there seemed no limit to his authority, and many persons fancied that both Ostermann, whom he hated, and Biren, whom he despised, must bow before him. But the sharp-sighted English resident, Claudius Rondeau, was not so easily deceived. "Cherkasky and Yaguzhinsky," he reported to his Government, "are working to pare Ostermann's nails... but if they don't take a great deal of care, the Count will ruin them as he has done several others."[2] The event showed that Rondeau was right in his prognostications. In November, 1731, Ostermann persuaded the Tsaritsa to establish an inner Council, or Cabinet, ostensibly for the prompter despatch of business, but really in order to shake off his

[1] So called after the Emperor's favourite summer residence near Moscow, Ismailovo. The institution of this new regiment gave great offence to the two older regiments of the Guard, the Preobrazhensky, and the Semenovsky, each of which consisted of 7,000 men, mostly Russians. See Rondeau: *Despatches. Sb. of Imp. Ist. Ob.* Tome Vol. LXVI, p. 228.

[2] Rondeau: *Despatches*, Vol. LXVI, p. 228.

rivals, who were becoming troublesome to him even in his own special department of Foreign Affairs. This Cabinet was to consist of three persons only, presided over by the Empress, and the Senate, the Synod, and all the Departments of State were only to communicate with her Majesty by means of it. It was, in fact, the Supreme Privy Council over again, in miniature. The three members of this Cabinet were Golovkin, Cherkasky, and Ostermann himself. "It must be confessed," writes Rondeau admiringly, "that Ostermann has played his game very cunningly, for he has found means, without appearing to do so, to set aside all the great men who could have done him harm." Yaguzhinsky was naturally furious at being passed over. He pretended, not without reason, that nobody had a better right to a seat in it than himself, considering that when her Majesty first came to the throne, he had hazarded his life and fortune to procure her the sovereignty. He therefore inveighed bitterly against the Cabinet, and as no consideration in the world was ever capable of restraining him when in wrath or in liquor, he took advantage of the first public banquet to make the Vice-Chancellor the butt of his ribald jests, in the presence of the Empress. Anne, whose sardonic humour delighted to observe the vagaries of drunken men, though she never drank herself, rather enjoyed the scene, and laughingly excused the bibulous Procurator-General, when Ostermann warmly protested; but when Yaguzhinsky, shortly afterwards, insulted the favourite Biren at his own table, cast his lowly origin in his teeth, and fiercely drew upon him in the presence of his guests, the Tsaritsa felt that this was an outrage she could not overlook, and Yaguzhinsky was accordingly banished to Berlin, in the honourable capacity of Minister Extraordinary (10th Dec. 1731); while his post of Grand Equerry of the Empire was conferred upon the younger Löwenwolde. Three weeks later, the War Minister, Prince Vladimir Dolgoruki, was also safely got rid of. Biren had long been lying in wait to ruin this blunt, outspoken old soldier, but the Field Marshal had of late been so extraordinarily discreet, that even his enemies could find no fault with him. At length, however, on New Year's Day, 1732, in a circle of friends, as he thought, he permitted himself to make some harmless joke at the new oath which the Empress had thought necessary to have administered. His words, grossly misrepresented and exaggerated,[1] were at once reported to Biren, and, a few days later, the old warrior was arrested, accused of "outraging her Majesty's imperial person by using offensive words," and shut up for the rest of his days in the fortress of Schlüsselburg. As now one of the two Russian Field Marshals was in his grave, and the other in prison, and there was no other native officer who could be considered capable of filling the all-important post of Commander-in-Chief, the Cabinet gladly gave this appointment also to a foreigner, who was, however, in every respect worthy of their choice, I mean the eminent engineer Münnich, whose past services to his adopted country had never yet been adequately rewarded, and whose future exploits were to shed such a lustre on the Russian arms.

Burkhard Christoph Münnich,[2] the future creator of the Ladoga Canal, and conqueror of the Crimea, sprang from a sturdy stock of Oldenburg squires renowned for generations for their engineering talent. His father and his grandfather before him, both officers in the Danish service, had done

---

[1] By the Prince of Hesse-Homburg it is said, who had lately entered the Russian service and was eager to make his way in the world.—*Manstein.*

[2] See G. A. Halem: *Lebensbeschreibung des Feldmarschalls B. C. Graf von Münnich,* an adequate and interesting, if somewhat fulsomely eulogistic biography. Compare also Dolgoruki: *Graf A. I. Ostermann;* and for personalia, Lady Rondeau's *Letters from a Lady;* Manstein: *Mémoires*; Lefort: *Despatches.*

much towards improving and maintaining the elaborate system of dikes in the low-lying Delmenhorst district between the Weser and the North Sea, and young Burkhard, when only in his sixteenth year (he was born in 1683), used regularly to accompany his father on his tours of inspection. In 1701 he received a commission in the Hesse-Darmstadt army, and had almost immediately afterwards the privilege of learning the rudiments of the science of war under no less a captain than Prince Eugene. He served with distinction throughout the War of the Spanish Succession, took part in the siege of Landau and the invasion of Provence; was present at the battle of Oudenarde, was made a Colonel for his valour at Malplaquet, and was left for dead on the bloody field of Denain. Fortunately, the life of the young officer was saved by the kindness of his captors. He was taken to Paris, courteously treated there, and took away with him a life-long admiration of French manners, and a vivid recollection of the saintly Fenelon. On his release he returned to his native land where he assisted in the construction of the Carlshaven Canal; but a humdrum existence among the dull Delmenhorst marshes, and the still duller Oldenburg *junkers*, soon became intolerable to the ambitious and enterprising engineer, and in 1716 he entered the Polish service, which he was compelled to leave three years later in consequence of an unlucky duel. He was hesitating whether he should next offer his sword to Charles XII or Peter the Great, when the sudden death of the Swedish hero determined him in favour of the Russian Tsar. Accordingly he submitted to Peter, through Prince Vasily Dolgoruki, a new and elaborate system of fortification for the recently acquired Baltic Provinces, with which the Tsar was so satisfied that he offered Münnich the post of Lieutenant-General of Engineers, which the latter at once accepted, arriving at St. Petersburg in 1721. Peter, however, did not take to Münnich at first sight. He was surprised by his extremely juvenile appearance, and somewhat disgusted by his affectation of French *esprit* and *finesse*. The Tsar evidently considered his latest acquisition somewhat more of a fop than a good soldier ought to be.[1] For months, therefore, Münnich remained neglected, when a lucky accident again drew Peter's attention to him. The young officer had been much struck by the handsome spire of the newly built church of St. Peter and St. Paul, and, in a leisure moment, amused himself by taking a sketch of it. A few days later, the spire was struck by lightning and utterly destroyed. Peter ordered it to be rebuilt at once, on exactly the same lines as before; but no plan of the steeple could anywhere be found. At last the ever watchful Yaguzhinsky recollected having seen Münnich's sketch, and, pouncing upon it, forthwith conveyed it to his Master. The very next day Münnich received his patent of Lieutenant-General. The first work entrusted to him was the construction of the Ladoga Canal. It was the object of Peter the Great to make Petersburg the commercial, as well as the political, capital of his Empire, and, in order to accomplish that purpose, he had formed a gigantic plan of connecting the Baltic with the Caspian, by means of a canal, starting from Schlüsselberg on the Neva, proceeding along the shores of Lake Ladoga, to the town of the same name, and thence to the little river Volchovka, a tributary of a confluent of the Volga. The work was begun in 1717 by a Russian engineer, Gregory Pesarev, who had received an expensive technical education at Berlin, at the cost of the State, but proceeded so slowly that Peter began to have his doubts about the competence of his pupil, so Münnich was sent to superintend Pesarev's work. Pesarev, bitterly

[1] Charles XII thought the same of the Duke of Marlborough.

resenting this interference, threw every possible obstacle in the way of his coadjutor; refused to listen to any of his suggestions, and insisted upon constructing the canal on the old lines, till Münnich, driven at last to despair, begged the Tsar to come and inspect Pesarev's work for himself. Peter, himself no mean engineer, at once complied; rode in silence along the whole route, and, though suffering severely from rheumatism at the time, frequently dismounted to throw himself prone on the wet earth, and take measurements. By the time he had finished his tour of inspection, he had quite convinced himself not only of the justice of Münnich's criticisms, but also of the utter incompetence of Pesarev, and, turning fiercely on the latter, asked him why the course of the canal was so sinuous and uneven, and why its shores were not properly banked up.—"It is because of the hillocks all about," replied the trembling Pesarev.—"Hillocks, eh?" cried the Tsar, looking around him in every direction. "Where are they, man? I don't see any."—"Gregory," he continued, approaching the speechless wretch, "Gregory, there are two kinds of faults. The first kind is from ignorance, and may be excused; but the second and worst is when a man won't use his five senses." Everyone expected that Peter would have felled Pesarev to the ground, but, for a wonder, he restrained himself, simply ordering that henceforth Münnich should have the entire control of the work, and, for the next twelve years, the great engineer laboured at it incessantly. Peter the Great only lived to see the first four versts completed; but he was so delighted with what he did see, that he ordered spades to be given to him and Münnich, and forthwith they both set vigorously to work to pierce the last dam which prevented the flow of water into the first section of the canal. After Peter's death, Münnich's promotion was slow. Menshikov frowned upon, the Dolgorukis slighted, the intelligent foreigner. Yet Catherine I gave him the ribbon of St. Alexander Nevsky, while Peter II created him a Count and Governor of Ingria. Not till the reign of Anne, however, can he be said to have become world-renowned. The new Empress made him, in rapid succession, War Minister, Field Marshal, Governor of St. Petersburg, and Chief of the newly organized Corps of Cadets; and when, in 1732, the Court returned to St. Petersburg, after an absence of nearly six years, an event which marked the culmination of the ascendency of the German Party, Münnich enjoyed what was perhaps the sweetest triumph of his career. After twelve years of strenuous labour against all manner of difficulties, the Ladoga Canal was completed and opened for navigation, and Münnich had the honour of escorting the Empress and her Court in state barges, along the whole course of the great water-way, which to this day is a standing monument of his engineering skill.[1]

And now with Münnich at the head of the army, the Löwenwoldes over the Court, Cherkasky in the Cabinet—as a concession to popular pride, Biren at her side to amuse her frequent leisure, and Ostermann half concealed behind the rest, to rule the Empire, the new Tsaritsa could at last feel tolerably secure. It took some little time, indeed, for the new men to fall into their proper places. Münnich, in particular, whose hitherto latent but altogether extravagant vanity now began to come to light, (he was one of those men who make a better figure in adversity than in success) Münnich now threatened to become dangerous to all his colleagues. His most intimate friends protested that since the Marshal's baton had been placed in his hands, his character had completely changed. He grew distant

[1] It was 104 versts in length, 70 feet wide, and 16 feet deep, and was provided with 24 sluices.

towards his equals, supercilious towards his inferiors, and used his cane even more freely than his tongue when his orders were not instantly obeyed. Not content with his numerous offices and dignities, he began to meddle with the departments of finance and commerce, nay, at last he even aspired to a place in the Cabinet, and aimed at ousting Ostermann from the control of Foreign Affairs in favour of his own brother Councillor Münnich. But the wily Vice-Chancellor was more than a match for this political tyro. Without appearing to move in the matter, he secretly insinuated to Biren that Münnich was bent upon supplanting him in the Empress's favour. The Courlander at once took alarm. In his eyes Münnich was just the sort of rival he had every reason to fear. Unlike the general run of contemporary Russian officers, whose grim uncouthness seemed out of place in a drawing-room, the new Field Marshal was handsome, elegant, graceful, witty, very young-looking for his years, and dangerously sentimental when ladies [1] were in the way. What if her Majesty should really take a fancy to this fascinating soldier? Such a fatality Biren determined to prevent at all hazards, and therefore in his capacity of Grand Chamberlain, he ordered Münnich to quit the apartments he had hitherto occupied in the Palace, under the pretext that they were wanted for the Duchess of Mecklenburg, within twenty-four hours, and move over to the other side of the Neva. Münnich took the hint and departed, but, as we shall see, this meddlesome soldier was again and again to come into collision with Ostermann.

There was all the more reason for the Empress's Ministers

[1] That is to say from the standpoint of the Russian ladies, to whom gallantry of the western order was then a novelty. On the other hand, Lady Rondeau, an *habituée* of Courts, was rather amused than otherwise by Münnich's affectation. "To see a man of that cast," says she, "attempt the prettinesses of a *petit-maître* is like seeing a cow frolicsome."

to live together in peace and harmony, as it was plain that their sway was becoming more and more unpopular every day. This unpopularity was due to several causes. In the first place, Anne's government was undoubtedly severe. Now the policy of the two preceding reigns had been purposely and consistently easy-going, and although such laxity had been injurious to the State in many ways, it had made Catherine I and Peter II extremely popular. Under Anne, things were necessarily very different. The reins of government that had hung so slackly before, were now drawn tightly, and the nation felt, and winced beneath, the change. The overdue contributions from the small proprietors and peasantry were exacted to the very last copeck; the soldiery were compelled to labour again at the many arduous public and military works; discipline was more sternly enforced, breaches of discipline more severely chastised; the dread *Preobrazhensky Prikaz*, or Torture Chamber, (the very name inspired terror) which had been abolished during the reign of Peter II, was now revived under the new high-sounding title of "The Chancellery of Secret Investigations." It was also an additional grievance that the Court had removed to St. Petersburg, where the Russian magnates, far away from their estates, found life extraordinarily costly and inconvenient.

And if the severity of Anne's government alienated the people, the extravagance of her Court scandalized the clergy and gentry. Until her reign, indeed, there can scarcely be said to have been a Court at all in Russia, at least in the modern sense of the term. Life in old Russia had been of an almost patriarchal simplicity; anything like luxury had been practically absent. The rooms of the richest magnates had been roughly, not to say poorly, furnished. Arm-chairs, carpets, pictures and mirrors, had been unknown, except in the palace of the

Tsar.[1] It was considered wicked wastefulness to burn wax candles except in the churches, and a room lit by more than ten tallow dips was considered extravagantly lighted. What pomp and magnificence there was, was dedicated to the service of the Church; the only ornaments in private houses were of a religious character,[2] and the only room where there was any pretence of display was where the votive lamp burnt perpetually before the holy ikons. It is true that the banquets in the ancient days were grand affairs, for hospitality is the national virtue of Russia; but the fare, though plentiful, was plain, and till Peter the Great introduced his countrymen to Tokay, Hermitage, and Hollands, they were well content with their native beer, kvass, mead and vodka. The old Russians possessed indeed some garments, the oriental magnificence of which amazed the curious foreigner, but as such gorgeous vestments were only assumed on rare and solemn occasions, they lasted for generations, sons and grandsons thinking it no shame to wear the garments in which their fathers and grandfathers before them, had made so brave a show. It should also be borne in mind that these show robes being, for the most part, made at home, were more splendid than costly. But with the advent of Anne, all this was changed. The new Empress was passionately fond of the pomp and circumstance of power, and her court soon had the reputation of being one of the most expensive in Europe. "Your Excellency cannot imagine how magnificent this Court is since the present reign," wrote the English resident, Rondeau, to Lord Harrington, at the beginning of 1731, "though," he adds, "there is not a shilling in the

[1] Of course I am speaking of pre-Petrine times.

[2] See Shcherbatov: *O povrezhdeny nravov v Rossy*, a delightful little book by one of the most amiable and intelligent of the old-fashioned Russians.

treasury, and nobody is paid."[1] And again, only twelve months later; "I cannot well express how magnificent this Court is in clothes. Though I have seen several Courts, I never saw such heaps of gold and silver lace laid upon cloth, and even gold and silver stuffs, as are seen here... I cannot imagine that this magnificence will last many years, for if it should, it must ruin most part of the Russian nobility, for several families are obliged to sell their estates to buy fine clothes."[2] Elsewhere he assures the Ministry at home, that £150 or £200 for a suit of clothes is not considered anything out of the way at St. Petersburg, and begs for an increase of his allowance to enable him to meet his extraordinary expenses. Then there was an endless succession of balls, masquerades, and banquets, and, inasmuch as a new dress was required for every fresh feast, the nobility and gentry had much difficulty to keep pace with the ever increasing gorgeousness of the Tsaritsa's Court. Old men and wise men began to shake their heads. It was not right, they whispered, that a poor country should spend so much money in pure ostentation. Even Peter I had known better than that. He had indeed extorted millions from his subjects, but every penny of those millions had been used to develop the resources of his country, and promote civilization. In his private life, Peter had always been simplicity itself, expending far less upon his own person than his niece threw away upon her liveries and her equipages. And there was one Russian nobleman who had the courage to tell the Empress to her face what his compeers thought, but durst not say, of these new-fangled fashions. Amongst the victims of the Dolgorukis, during the last reign,

---

[1] Rondeau: *Despatches. Sb.* of *I. R. I. Ob.*, Tome LXXVI.

[2] Ibid. p. 410. As to the bad effect of this luxury and extravagance upon manners and morals, see Chap. VIII.

had been Count Aleksander Ivanovich Rumyantsev, one of Peter the Great's most zealous adherents, whom they had banished after confiscating his estates. On her accession, Anne had summoned him to Moscow, and made him a Senator, Lieutenant-Colonel of the Guard, and given him 20,000 rubles by way of compensation for his losses. But Rumyantsev, a rugged, simple, economical soldier of the Petrine stamp, could not reconcile himself to the luxury of Anne's court, while the outrageous insolence of the foreign favourites revolted alike his pride and his patriotism. At last he quarrelled with one of Biren's disreputable brothers, and was reported to the Empress as a spy and a traitor. Anne, who saw through the plot, would have removed Rumyantsev out of harm's way by making him President of the College of Finance, or Finance Minister; but the sturdy old noble, with more honesty than tact, declined the proffered honour, bluntly declaring that while the people were so poor, he could not in conscience undertake to find money for the luxuries of the Court. Nay, he was even proceeding to give his Sovereign a lecture in economy, when the Empress, livid with rage, cut him short, drove him out of the room, and ordered him to be arrested immediately, and his case submitted to the Senate. He was ultimately condemned to death, and though Anne commuted the capital sentence to banishment to Kazan, she deprived him of the Order of St. Alexander, and took back the 20,000 rubles she had previously given him. Rumyantsev was naturally regarded as a martyr, but nobody had the hardihood to imitate his example.

But the cardinal offence of the new Government in the eyes of the Russian nation, was its partiality for foreigners. Peter the Great, even in the hottest fervour of his reforming zeal, had been very jealous of the national honour.

He had employed intelligent foreigners freely, but he had never entrusted to them the foremost places in the realm, which, he maintained, belonged of right to natives alone. Even when on his death-bed, he had confided the destiny of Russia to the care of Russians. Unfortunately, when the all-controlling hand of the Master had been withdrawn, his pupils began to quarrel amongst themselves, and their mutual jealousies and hatreds had, as we have seen, ended in the extermination of the Russian Party. Menshikov had ruined Tolstoy, the Dolgorukis and the Golitsuins had ruined Menshikov, Cherkasky had ruined the Dolgorukis and the Golitsuins. Yaguzhinsky was the sole survivor of the little band of capable native statesmen whom Peter the Great had left behind him, and Yaguzhinsky had been banished to Berlin. The government, the army, and the navy were now almost entirely in the hands of foreigners. With Ostermann and Münnich, indeed, it was easy for the most stubborn patriots to be reconciled. They kept alive in Russia the memory of the great monarch who had given them to her. Both of them were men of extraordinary talent, and they devoted all their energy to promote the honour and glory of their adopted country. But it was impossible to become reconciled to such mere parasites as the Birens,[1] and the Löwenwoldes, who fed lazily and luxuriously on the very blood and sweat of the people. The favourite, Johann Ernst Biren, was held in peculiar detestation, nor can we very much wonder at it. He was not, indeed, a monster of iniquity delighting in evil for its own sake, as he is popularly supposed to have been. As a matter of fact his vices were

[1] Biren had two brothers who came in for their share of court favour. The elder, Carl, was a mere rowdy, whose features were notched and scarred with sword and rapier cuts, received in various drunken brawls. This brutal bully was made a general. The younger brother, Gustav, was a dull honest man without any education. He became a major in the Guards.

## ACCESSION OF ANNE OF COURLAND.

rather of the sordid than of the satanic order. But his insatiable greed was never restrained by any higher consideration; he used his exalted position simply as a means of accumulating wealth, and, well knowing that he was generally detested, the instinct of self-preservation made him prosecute to the death everyone who threatened in any way to become dangerous to himself personally. He had insinuating manners, indeed, and could make himself very agreeable if he chose; but he was mean, treacherous, rapacious, suspicious, and horribly vindictive, visiting the slightest offence with the most merciless severity. But perhaps the most unamiable feature of this low-born upstart's character was the ostentatious contempt for all Russians, high and low, which he exhibited on every occasion in the most public manner. One can imagine the feelings of the gentry towards this ungrateful adventurer, who owed everything to Russia, and gave her nothing in return, when they saw the scions of the noblest houses, a Golitsuin, a Volkonsky, an Apraksin, turned into buffoons for his good pleasure, and compelled to play the fool before him and his satellites.[1] No wonder then if the memory of the Empress, who protected such favourites and tolerated such outrages, has fared somewhat hardly at the hands of Russian historians.[2]

And yet, in justice, it must be admitted that the reign of Anne was on the whole, as we shall see, most beneficial to Russia. If she was severe, extravagant, and partial to foreigners, she was also just, prudent, careful and conscientious. She really does seem to have tried to do her

---

[1] For an account of the grotesque buffooneries, and semi-oriental splendour of Anne's Court, see Chap. VIII.

[2] Kostomarov, in particular, is, I opine, unduly severe towards her. Prince Shcherbatov, uncompromising *laudator temporis acti* as he was, is much fairer. But then Shcherbatov is *always* fair.

duty towards her people. Her intellect was not brilliant perhaps, but she had sound common-sense, which is a much better quality in a ruler than mere brilliance. For a woman, too, she had a natural turn for affairs; loved order and decency; never acted hastily; took pains to get at the truth of matters; always took the advice of people more experienced in affairs than herself, especially in the Cabinet, where she invited debate, and tolerated contradiction, and hence most of her measures were sound, well matured, and stable. Under Catherine I and Peter II, Russia had stood still, as it were; but under Anne, her advance in every direction was unmistakable. Vigorous measures were taken to arrest the decay and repair the damage done to the state during the haphazard sway of the Dolgorukis, especially after the return of the Court to St. Petersburg, in the beginning of 1732, when the Empress applied herself to business with commendable assiduity. Particular attention was paid to the national armaments. A College of Cadets was instituted as a sort of nursery for the army, where over two hundred young gentlemen were instructed in geometry, fortification, drawing, fencing, technical arts, and modern languages, at a cost of 30,000 rubles [1] per annum, by foreign professors. Special Commissioners were appointed to enquire into the condition of the army and the fleet, both of which did excellent work under the watchful eyes of Ostermann and Münnich. The state of the navy was found to be downright alarming. It was reported that scarce twelve liners were in a fit condition to put to sea, and the question arose whether it would not be better, for reasons of economy, to give up the grand fleet altogether, and preserve only the galleys.[2] But all the naval

---

[1] £7,500.

[2] The galleys were for cruising among the skerries, and defending the rocky coasts of the Gulf of Finland and the Baltic; the grand fleet, as the

## ACCESSION OF ANNE OF COURLAND.

authorities protested against such a measure as suicidal, inasmuch as the galleys could not go out alone at any time, and never in stormy weather, and without a grand fleet the Baltic Provinces would be constantly exposed to the risk of invasion from Sweden. It was resolved therefore by the Cabinet to reconstruct both the grand and the galley fleets, but gradually, so as to lighten the expense as much as possible.

The decision of the Cabinet on this occasion was mainly determined by the critical condition of foreign affairs and the necessity for Russia to be ready for war on the first emergency. The unwillingness of the Kaiser to accede to the guarantee-treaty of Seville, whereby the Spanish Princes were to be put into possession of the fortresses of Parma and Tuscany, was the primary disturbing element in the European situation. In the course of 1730, war between Austria and the Allies of Seville seemed inevitable, and in that case, Russia was bound by a special treaty to aid the Emperor with 30,000 men. Great Britain, whose interests were not likely to be materially affected any way, looked on with comparative indifference; but France, through her *Chargé d'Affaires*, Magnan, protested energetically against the despatch of this Russian Army Corps, and he was supported at the Russian Court itself by a strong peace party, headed by Yaguzhinsky, whose strongest argument against engaging in such distant enterprises, was the wretched state of the finances. Ostermann, on the other hand, was prepared to make heavy sacrifices for Austria in view of the impending difficulties in Poland, and a fierce struggle ensued between the Vice-Chancellor supported by the Löwenwoldes, and the Procurator-General encouraged by the French Chargé d'Affaires. Biren remained neutral till he was

liners and frigates were called, was for the open sea. The distinction also obtained in Sweden.

bought by a present of 200,000 thalers from the Austrian Minister, Wratislaw, with which he purchased a fine estate at Wartenburg in Silesia, whereupon he threw the whole weight of his influence into the scales against France. Magnan, however, persisted in his intrigues at the Russian Court, and his insolent behaviour led to a sharp exchange of incivilities between the Russian Minister at Paris, Golovkin, and the French Ministry; but as the Emperor ultimately acceded to all the terms of the Treaty of Seville, in consideration of the Allies guaranteeing the Pragmatic Sanction, there was no war after all, and shortly afterwards Ostermann disembarrassed himself of Yaguzhinsky by causing him to be sent as Ambassador to Berlin, as already mentioned. But now a dynastic question was coming to the front which was to absorb all other questions and lead to a still fiercer diplomatic struggle and still more dangerous complications—the question of the Polish Succession.

Augustus II, Charles XII's former perfidious opponent, who, for the last five-and-thirty years, had misruled Poland, and well-nigh ruined his Saxon Electorate[1] by his follies and extravagances, both private and political,—Augustus II, whose physical strength had been the talk of Europe for three generations, was now a visibly failing old man, and the principal Potentates of Europe, himself included, were busily speculating as to who should be his successor on the Polish throne. France, reinvigorated by a repose of twenty years, and eager to recover her lost political ascendency, had her candidate ready in the person of Stanislaus Leszczynski, whom Charles XII had crowned King of Poland a quarter of a century before, and who had subsequently found some slight compensation for the speedy loss of his slippery crown by becoming the father-in-law of

[1] His wars alone cost Saxony 80,000 men, and 90 millions of thalers.

Louis XV. With Stanislaus as King of Poland, both Austria and Prussia would, it was hoped, be kept in check, and French influence become dominant in Eastern Europe, especially as the Court of Versailles reckoned upon the friendship of Sweden and the Ottoman Porte. Both Austria and Great Britain, as the hereditary foes of the House of Bourbon, were strongly opposed to the elevation of Leszczynski, although the latter, having little to lose in Poland, was content with aiding the Kaiser by purely diplomatic methods. But the Court of Vienna, extremely alarmed at the prospect of the elevation to the throne of Poland of the French King's father-in-law, naturally looked for assistance to Russia who was even more deeply interested in Polish affairs than herself, and a fierce diplomatic struggle began at the Russian Court between the Ministers of the two antagonistic Powers. Ostermann was the chief champion of Austria at St. Petersburg, but he found a troublesome opponent in Münnich, whose insatiable ambition and restless vanity readily induced him to lend an ear to the artful insinuations of the French Chargé d'Affaires, Magnan. Münnich, delighted at this opportunity of meddling with the department of the Vice-Chancellor, went as far as to offer France, on his own responsibility, 50,000 men and 15 ships of the line in return for ample subsidies. He even informed Magnan that the Empress was ready to free herself from the onerous obligations of the Treaty of Vienna, but, to make assurance doubly sure, advised that her favourite, the Grand Chamberlain Biren, should be bought over by a present of 100,000 crowns. When, however, Magnan was pressed to say what France would give in return, the reply he gave was altogether ambiguous and unsatisfactory. The King (Louis XV), he said, was willing to support the Russian interest in Poland, but he must first of all place on the Polish throne a man devoted to himself. But, indeed, from the very nature of things, a league between France and Russia was out of the question, and it was therefore no difficult task for a statesman of Ostermann's experience and perspicacity to expose the fallacies of such a political dabbler as the meddlesome Münnich. Was it conceivable, he asked, that France would subordinate the interests of a King of Poland chosen by herself, to the interests of Russia in that country? "France," he exclaimed, "requires Russia to break with her allies, and neglect her true interests, for the sake of uncertain subsidies and a useless alliance." It would be far better, he urged, to bring about a league between the three Black Eagles.[1] Ostermann's arguments were irrefragable, and the Cabinet rejected the notion of the French alliance once for all. The result of these deliberations was to strengthen still further the Austro-Russian Alliance, and on the 26th May, 1732, Denmark also acceded to it by a treaty of mutual guarantee, on condition that the Duke of Holstein should be made to abandon his claims upon Schleswig in return for a compensation of 1,000,000 ducats. Sweden, too, much to the relief of Russia, Austria and Great Britain, finally decided to remain neutral, although Castege, the French Minister at Stockholm, not content with promising her rich subsidies, held out the prospect of recovering her lost Baltic Provinces, if only she would take the part of Stanislaus.

But now urgent solicitations reached St. Petersburg from another quarter. Augustus of Poland was anxious to secure the succession to his own son Augustus, the electoral Prince of Saxony, and offered Biren half a million ducats, and the Duchy of Courland, if he would gain the Empress over to this project. Biren, who, under pressure from the English and Austrian Ministers, had steadfastly resisted the

[1] Russia, Austria and Prussia.

golden arguments of France, was quite dazzled by the magnificence of this new offer, and, for a moment, he actually wavered. But as Russia, Austria and Prussia were, at this time, almost as much opposed to the Saxon as to the French candidate, the Grand Chamberlain had not the courage to listen to the allurements of the King of Poland. Unable to move Russia, Augustus next attempted to bribe Prussia. In the beginning of 1733, he came to Warsaw, where an extraordinary Diet was being held, and from thence communicated with Frederick William, offering him, as the price of his friendship, Polish Prussia, Courland, and even part of Great Poland, the shameless schemer being quite ready to dismember the State he had sworn to defend, if only he could secure the bulk of the carcase for his son. Now, as Courland was the utmost that Russia and Austria could offer Prussia, the temptation to close with the more liberal offers of Augustus was well-nigh overwhelming. But fear of Russia and Austria prevailed in the end, and the Court of Berlin said no. But Augustus, now grown desperate, offered to satisfy Russia and Austria as well as Prussia, and actually proposed that "the four[1] Eagles should divide the banquet between them," in other words, the actual King of Poland formally proposed a definite partition of the Polish Republic! He died, however, (1st Feb. 1733) before he could give effect to his nefarious design. His death was the signal for the outbreak of a general European war.

[1] The fourth eagle was the White Eagle, *i.e.* Poland.

# CHAPTER VI.

## THE WAR OF THE POLISH SUCCESSION.

(1733—1735.)

THE Polish Primate Theodore Potocki—France declares in favour of Stanislaus Leszczynski—The Convocation-Diet—Dissensions among the Poles—Protests of Russia—The Elective Diet—Russia and Austria support Augustus of Saxony—The Polish Diet elects Stanislaus King—Protest of the Minority—Flight of Stanislaus to Dantzic—Fruitless negotiations—Attitude of Prussia—And of Great Britain—A Russian army under Peter Lacy invades Poland—Antecedents of Lacy—He begins the siege of Dantzic—Arrival of Münnich—Unsuccessful attack on the Hagelberg—Arrival of a French force to aid Dantzic—It is captured and sent to Russia—Anne's courtesy to her captives—Fall of Dantzic—State of Europe—Victories of the French over the Emperor—Lacy sent to his assistance—Anti-Russian intrigues of the French at Stockholm and Stambul—Lord Kinnoul—Negotiations of Russia with Kuli Khan—War declared against the Porte.

THE leading man in Poland on the death of Augustus II, was the Primate and Interrex,[1] Theodore Potocki, a devoted adherent of Stanislaus Leszczynski. This aged ecclesiastic possessed not a few excellent virtues. He was liberal-minded, upright, conscientious, large hearted, not without taste and culture, and so generous to the poor as to be popularly known as "the Orphans' Father." He was also

[1] During an interregnum, the Primate of Poland was, ex-officio, the ruler of the land until the election of a new King.

a true patriot (a rare quality in those corrupt days), and anxious above all to make Poland independent of her neighbours; but he was too old to fight effectually for freedom, and then, too, circumstances were against him. His first steps were to dissolve the *Sejm*, or Diet; dismiss the body-guard of the late King; order the 1,200 Saxon guards at Court to incontinently quit Poland, and post small corps of observation along the Austrian and Prussian frontiers. He found active supporters in the French Ambassador, Count Monti, in the great Lithuanian family of the Czartoryskis, and above all, in the Palatine of Mazovia, Stanislaus Poniatowski,[1] the one really capable statesman Poland then possessed, who had served Charles XII's *protégé*, King Stanislaus, with such zeal and ability thirty years before, and was now ready to sacrifice everything for him once more. It was to France that both Potocki and Poniatowski primarily looked for help, nor was France slow to champion a cause that, after all, was but her own. For the first time since her eclipse at the Peace of Utrecht, she saw before her an opportunity of recovering her hegemony on the Continent, and she seized the chance with characteristic vigour and *élan*. It had ever been her interest, as the arch-enemy of the House of Hapsburg, to environ the *Reich* with actual or possible foes. Her ideal political system, so far as it concerned Eastern Europe, was a hostile combination of Sweden, Poland, and Turkey, against the common foe, and although this ideal had not yet been realized (perhaps was unrealizable), she had never ceased striving after it. This had been the real motive of her interference in Polish affairs, on the death of Sobieski thirty-seven years before, this was the real motive of her interference now. With the father-in-law of the French King on the Polish throne, a first and very important step would

[1] He was the father of the last King and the last Primate of Poland.

have been taken towards the re-establishment of French influence in the East. As a preliminary measure, therefore, 4,000,000 livres of secret service money were despatched from Versailles to Warsaw for bribing purposes (the Kaiser had already sent a million ducats in support of the contrary interest), and Monti succeeded in gaining over to the cause of Stanislaus, the influential Palatine of Lublin, Adam Tarlo, by promising him the Grand Hetmanship of Poland. Moreover, in a circular letter, addressed to all its representatives abroad, the French Government formally declared that as the Court of Vienna, by massing troops on the Silesian frontier, had sufficiently revealed its intention of destroying the liberties of Poland, by interfering with the free election of her Kings, his Most Christian Majesty could not look on with indifference at the political extinction of a Power to whom he was bound by all the ties of honour and friendship, but would do his utmost to protect her against her enemies. Encouraged by this demonstration, the Polish Primate proceeded to use, freely and fully, his by no means inconsiderable prerogatives. On April 27th (O.S.) he summoned a preliminary or "convocation" Diet to Warsaw. The temper of the assembly was unmistakably hostile to any foreign candidate. Indeed many of the members declared they would sooner see a gipsy on the throne than another German, and it was finally resolved that none but a native Pole, who was a Catholic and married to a Catholic, should be elected King, and that whoever should dare to proclaim a King without the previous consent of the Diet, should be declared a traitor to his country. So far then, the *Sejm* had acted with dignity and decision, but when the Senators and Deputies were called upon by the Primate to solemnly swear to observe their own resolutions, many of them drew back, and, most ugly sign of all, the Primate could only overcome their scruples by striking out the clause forbidding the reception of bribes from the future candidates. Even this did not satisfy everyone, for on the following day, when Potocki, with the crucifix in his hand, took the oath himself first of all, not a few deputies began to raise objections, or make reservations, while others departed from the Diet altogether, with the fixed determination of protesting against all its proceedings, on the very first opportunity. Thus the chronic and incurable divisions of the Republic encouraged the Powers opposed to the election of Stanislaus to plausibly come forward as the champions of a *free* election, with the certainty of finding partisans among the Poles themselves.

The chief of these Powers was Russia.

When the tidings of the death of Augustus II reached St. Petersburg, a general assembly of the Ministry, the Senate, and the nobility, was held in the Cabinet, when it was unanimously agreed that the interests of Russia would not permit her to recognise Stanislaus Leszczynski, or any other person dependent directly on France (and therefore indirectly on Turkey and Sweden also), as a candidate for the Polish throne. Again, Stanislaus's antecedents were distinctly dangerous, from a Muscovite point of view. As the henchman of Charles XII, he had done Russia some mischief in the past, and had all the will to do her still more mischief in the future, if only he had the power, and by his side, as chief counsellor, stood that same Stanislaus Poniatowski, who was directly responsible for the humiliation of Peter the Great at the Peace of the Pruth.[1] Anne therefore felt justified in addressing to the Polish Primate a menacing letter, demanding that the name of Stanislaus should be struck out from the list of candidates, and Count Carl Gustaf Löwenwolde was sent to Warsaw, to reinforce

---

[1] It was owing mainly to his diplomatic ability at Stambul in 1709—10 that the Sultan declared war against Russia. *See* Nisbet Bain: "Charles XII," Chap. VIII.

his brother, Frederick Casimir, the actual Russian resident at the Polish Capital. The two Ministers, accompanied by the envoys of Austria and Prussia, lost no time in waiting upon the Archbishop, but their interference only led to a sharp altercation. The Primate hotly declared that the intervention of the opposing Powers was a diplomatic blunder, only tending to facilitate the election of Stanislaus, inasmuch as the Poles would never submit to any interference with their liberties. Löwenwolde then declared that if reasonable representations proved fruitless, the Empress possessed other means of chastising her enemies and preserving the general peace. "If God be with us, who shall be against us?" returned Potocki, and with that he arose and dismissed his guests. The Primate spoke with all the greater boldness because he well knew that the vast majority of his countrymen was with him, and much as he feared Russia, he never imagined that even that Power would dare to question the decision of almost the entire Polish nation, the number of the malcontents being comparatively insignificant.[1] He therefore summoned an elective Diet, and took measures for securing an absolutely free election by reviving, for that purpose, a long obsolete statute which forbade the foreign Ministers to remain at Warsaw during the session of that Assembly. This step immediately led to a collision with the Russian and Austrian Ministers. Löwenwolde absolutely refused to leave the Polish Capital without the Empress's express command, while his Austrian colleague, Count Welczek, declared that he must first await instructions from Vienna, adding significantly: "As long as I remain at Warsaw, a guard of 30 men is sufficient for me, but should I be forced to leave it, I should require his Imperial Majesty to increase my escort to 30,000."

[1] Manstein: *Mémoires*, etc. Compare Solovev, who is very fair on the whole.

Yet for all their bold language and resolute bearing, Russia and Austria were hampered at the outset by a peculiar difficulty: they had no alternative candidate of their own to offer. No other native Pole but Stanislaus Leszczynski had the slightest chance of being elected King. To have designated any other nobleman as a candidate, would have been sufficient to have united all the other great families against him. It was necessary, therefore, to look abroad for a candidate. The Infant Emanuel of Portugal, who had visited Russia in 1731, as a suitor for the hand of the new Empress, was at first proposed by the Court of Vienna; but his father would not consent to his nomination, and ultimately both Russia and Austria agreed to support the pretensions of the late King's son, Augustus of Saxony. Hitherto, indeed, he had been regarded at Vienna with no very friendly eye. He was suspected of leaning too much upon France, as his father had done before him, and he had always steadily opposed the Pragmatic Sanction; but when it became evident that none other but the Saxon faction was strong enough to oppose Stanislaus, all objections on the part of the two Courts ceased, and Löwenwolde concluded a compact with the Elector, on Aug. 14th, 1733, whereby Augustus acceded to the Pragmatic Sanction, contracted a treaty of mutual defence and guarantee with both Prussia and Austria, and promised to relinquish Poland's claims to Livonia, leave Courland her ancient liberties, and keep inviolate [1] the constitution of the Polish Republic. And now Russia took vigorous measures to support her candidate. Eighteen regiments of infantry and ten of cavalry were sent to the frontier, in order to be ready, at a moment's notice, to enter Poland,

---

[1] In other words, to introduce none of the indispensable reforms for the want of which that State was perishing.

while 10,000 Cossacks were, at the same time, ordered up from the Ukraine.

And indeed the march of events had been so rapid, that it had now become necessary not merely to direct, but to reverse, the decision of the Polish nation. On the 26th August, 1733, the Elective Diet met at Praga, a suburb of Warsaw; but the Lithuanians, most of them already in the pay of Russia, led by Prince Radziwill, remained at the village of Wengrowa, some few miles off, from whence they sent a deputation to the Primate, demanding the enforcement of the decree of banishment pronounced against Leszczynski fifteen years before. The Primate paid no heed to this insolent demand, whereupon the malcontents formed a confederation protesting against all the acts of the Elective Diet, and they were presently joined by two other powerful dissentients, Prince Wiesniewicki, and the Palatine of Cracow, Prince Lubomirski, who brought away with them no fewer than 3,000 deputies. But the vast majority of the Polish electors remained faithful to the Primate, and Count Radziewsky, an ardent partisan of Stanislaus, was duly elected Marshal of the Diet. Even the rumoured approach of a Russian army did not damp the enthusiasm of the electors. On the contrary, the Diet issued (Sept. 4) a manifesto solemnly cursing all those of their countrymen who should assist or welcome the Muscovites, and on the 9th, Stanislaus himself arrived at Warsaw, having travelled night and day through central Europe, disguised as a coachman. On the following day, 60,000 armed and mounted noblemen assembled on the field of election near Warsaw, and when the malcontents, who, all this time, were observing the proceedings from the opposite side of the Vistula, sent in a protest against the election of Stanislaus, the Primate rejected it as irregular, inasmuch as, contrary to ancient custom, it had not been presented with the usual formalities, on the field of election. The election itself then proceeded. For eight hours the aged Interrex proceeded on horseback, through the drenching rain, from group to group, asking all the deputies in turn whom they would have for their King, and greeted everywhere with cries of "Long live King Stanislaus." The malcontents maintained, after the event, that Potocki had acted unfairly by ignoring forty groups of deputies opposed to Stanislaus; but it is quite certain that not a single deputy on the field of election pronounced for Augustus. Finally, after making another vain appeal to the patriotism of the malcontent minority, the Primate, in the name of the Holy Trinity, solemnly proclaimed Stanislaus the duly elected King of Poland and Grand Duke of Lithuania, and he was escorted in state to the church of St. John, where a Te Deum was sung in his honour, while the minority returned to Wengrowa, and issued a counter-manifesto, declaring the election null and void.

Thus Stanislaus had been elected King of Poland for the second time, but his tenure of that perilous office was to be even briefer than it had been before. Immediately after his election, he issued a proclamation ordering a *levée en masse* of the gentry; but having no forces ready at hand to support him (the Polish regular army existing only on paper), he was obliged, only twelve days after his election, to leave the defenceless Capital, and shut himself up in Dantzic, with the Primate, Poniatowsky, Czartoryski, and the French and Swedish Envoys. His departure was the signal for an outbreak of fanaticism against the philo-Russian foreign Ministers. Löwenwolde's house was plundered and he himself was forced to take refuge in the house of the Imperial Ambassador; while the Saxon Minister's residence was stormed and looted, after a bloody resistance, his Excellency flying precipitately from the city. Order was not fully restored till the 30th September, when General Lacy, at the head of a Russian army, appeared on the right bank of the Vistula.

The tardy arrival of the Russians on the scene of action, was mainly due to diplomatic embarrassments. Immediately after the dissolution of the first or Convocation Diet, the Polish Primate had sent to St. Petersburg an extraordinary Envoy, Rudamina, to pacify the Russian Court, and persuade the Empress, as became such "a mirror of justice," not to interfere with the elections. Nor did he come empty-handed. Prompted by the French *Chargé d'Affaires*, Magnan, he offered Anne, in the name of Stanislaus, as much as, and even more than, she could expect from anyone else. The new King would be ready to concede the Imperial title;[1] induce Turkey and Sweden to contract definite alliances with Russia; allow the Courlanders to elect a new Duke after the death of the reigning Duke, relinquish the claims of the Republic on Livonia, and lay waste the frontiers between Russia and Poland, for the space of thirty or forty miles, according to ancient treaties.[2] But Russia was too far engaged already to the Elector of Saxony, to listen to these very liberal proposals. Besides, Anne not only had no confidence in the French candidate, but conceived it to be in her own power to obtain whatever terms she liked from Poland. The Empress therefore informed Rudamina that Stanislaus, as being the inveterate enemy of Russia, was the only candidate she disapproved of; and him she would oppose with all the power that God had given her. Her intentions, she added, were perfectly honest and disinterested. She wanted none of

[1] The Polish Republic had hitherto always refused to allow the Imperial title to the Russian Tsars.

[2] There was also the offer of a large sum of money to Biren. See Rondeau: *Despatches. Sb. Imp. Rus. Ist. Ob.*, Tome LXXVI.

the territory of the Republic for herself, nor would she allow anyone else to take so much as a foot of it. Then Rudamina requested that at least the offensive Löwenwolde should be withdrawn from Warsaw, to which Anne haughtily replied that she would consult none but herself in the choice of her ambassadors.

Nevertheless, Russia was at first considerably embarrassed by the backwardness of the two Powers to whom she most naturally looked for assistance—England and Prussia. The mysterious and uncertain conduct of the King of Prussia was particularly unsatisfactory. Frederick William I had already decided to observe the strictest neutrality in the Polish quarrel, partly for fear of his Rhenish provinces being attacked by France, and partly because he expected to get more from Stanislaus than from Augustus. Nay, on hearing of the election of the former, the King of Prussia had gone so far as to express his profound satisfaction, and declare that he was ready to spend a million to keep Stanislaus on his throne. Neither the indignant remonstrances of Yaguzhinsky, nor the frequent promises of fresh batches of gigantic grenadiers from Russia, could move his Prussian Majesty from this resolution, and we shall see that during the war he was looked upon more as a foe than a friend by the Court of St. Petersburg.

Nor was the Empress's Government altogether satisfied with the attitude of Great Britain. At the end of 1731, regular diplomatic relations had been resumed between the two countries after an interval of nearly twenty years. The former Secretary of Legation, Claudius Rondeau, was appointed English Resident at St. Petersburg,[1] and a distinguished

[1] He had as his colleague and superior, for a short time, Lord George Forbes, but that nobleman was very unhappy in Russia, and exchanged the diplomatic for the naval service.

Moldavian, young Prince Antiochus Cantemir, was sent to
London to represent Russia. Henceforward the relations
between the two countries continued to be cordial, it is
true, but not nearly so intimate as the Russian court desired
them to be. It was the constant ambition of Ostermann
to form an offensive and defensive alliance with Great
Britain to counteract the Franco-Swedish influence in the
North; but the English Government resolutely refused to
be drawn into any such alliance. "It is absolutely impossible," wrote the English Foreign Secretary, Lord Harrington, to Rondeau, "it is absolutely impossible for us, on
any consideration whatever, to charge ourselves with the
guaranty [1] of such distant and extensive dominions [as the
Tsaritsa's]. It is a burden we have determined *never* to
take upon ourselves." [2] On the outbreak of the War of
the Polish Succession, when there were rumours of the
despatch of a French squadron to the Baltic to assist
Stanislaus, Ostermann duly informed Rondeau of the fact,
and suggested that England should also send a squadron
to the Baltic, to observe the French squadron. [3] Cantemir,
too, was urged, again and again, to press the English
Ministry on this point. But Lord Harrington declared that
he saw no occasion to disturb the Peace of the North by
such a hostile demonstration, while Horace Walpole expressed
his astonishment to Cantemir that Russia should decline to
sign a simple commercial treaty so advantageous to both
countries unless England first took upon herself the responsibility of the defence of all Russia's possessions. Nevertheless the
Court of St. Petersburg, during the course of 1734 and 1735,

[1] A mutual guarantee of each other's possessions was of the very essence
of any such treaty.

[2] Rondeau: *Despatches*.

[3] Compare Rondeau: *Despatches*, and Solovev: *Istoria Rossy*. Vol. XX,
Chap. 1.

repeatedly returned to the charge, and the unhappy Cantemir was scolded and bullied because he could not succeed in convincing the English Ministry of the expediency of sending a fleet to the Baltic. "I am not unmindful of my duty," he wrote at last, when blamed for his tardiness, "but I would spare her Majesty the humiliation of so many rebuffs."[1] The English Ministry, in fact, was definitely committed to the peace-at-any-price policy of their chief, Robert Walpole, and although they wished well to the cause of Augustus, as being the enemy of France, they declined to lend him any active assistance, and even hesitated to give him the royal title. Mr. Woodward, the English Minister at Warsaw, was instructed indeed to act in concert with the Russian, Austrian, and Saxon Ministers there, but the Russian Government frequently complained of his want of co-operation, and Cantemir seems to have deeply resented the amused indifference of the British Government. "What is our Saxon Elector doing so long at Leipsic?" enquired Harrington of Cantemir one day, with a smile. "Methinks 'tis a pity he is not a little more lively!"—"The reason is," replied Cantemir, "that, except Russia, none of the Powers who profess to befriend him, render him the slightest assistance."[2] To this unanswerable answer, Harrington discreetly made no reply. At last Ostermann informed Rondeau that as nobody would help Russia, she must help herself.[3] And indeed she was now provided with a respectable pretext for direct interference in Polish affairs. Shortly after the election of Stanislaus, a declaration from the dissentient minority of the Diet reached St. Petersburg, in which they appealed to the Empress for

[1] Cantemir's Despatches cited by Solovev.
[2] Ibid.
[3] Rondeau: *Despatches*.

assistance, and placed themselves under her august protection. This treasonable document was anonymous, not one of the traitors who composed it having the manliness to sign it; but their names were well known at St. Petersburg, and, before the year was out, they were known [1] in Poland also, for the estates of these gentlemen were the only ones spared by the invading Russian forces. For by this time (June 30) a Russian army of 20,000 men was already on its way to Warsaw, under the command of Peter Lacy, one of the most able and popular of the foreign officers in the Tsaritsa's service. This gallant officer was born at Killedy, County Limerick, in 1678, and adopted the military profession while still a lad. His first taste of war was at the siege of Limerick, and, on the capitulation of that town, he fled with Sarsfield to France. His military training had been in a different school to Münnich's. While the former had learnt the art of war under Marlborough and Eugene, Lacy had had the equally illustrious Catinat for his master. He had served under that great Captain during the Piedmont campaigns; brilliantly distinguished himself at the Battle of Marsiglia, 1693, and, at the conclusion of the war, entered first the Polish, and then the Russian, service, being first introduced to Peter the Great by the Duke de Croy, that unfortunate officer whom the panic-stricken Tsar left to bear the brunt of the Swedish attack at the Battle of Narva. He had been one of the hundred foreign officers whom Peter selected to train his raw levies during the Great Northern War; was wounded at Pultawa; had the honour of being the first to mount into the breach at the murderous siege of Riga, in 1710, and took an active part in all the principal operations of the campaigns of 1710, 1711, 1712, 1713 and 1719,

[1] The chief of them were Mniszek, Grand Marshal of Poland, Lipski, Bishop of Cracow, Sanguszko, Grand Marshal of Lithuania, the Radziwills, the Sapiehas, the Szembeks, and the Branickis.

finally emerging from the struggle with the rank of Lieutenant-General. Catherine I decorated him with the ribbon and cross of St. Alexander, and made him Governor of the Baltic Provinces and Commandant of St. Petersburg, but it was not till the reign of Anne that he had an opportunity of fully displaying his military talents. Lacy had a quick, not to say hot, temper, and was a little too apt to take offence at trifles, but he was generous to a fault, as brave as a lion, and incapable of committing a mean action. He is said to have been beloved and esteemed by everyone who knew him,[1] and his soldiers were always ready to go through fire and water for him. Unlike his meddlesome colleague, Münnich, Lacy had the good sense to abstain altogether from political intrigues, and thus contrived to escape the dreadful fate which ultimately overwhelmed the former officer.

In October, 1733, Lacy reached the right bank of the Vistula, opposite Warsaw, and was joined by the Polish malcontents, who at once placed themselves beneath his protection, and formed a confederation. On the 6th, this phantom of a Diet (it consisted of but 15 Senators and 500 gentlemen)[2] proclaimed the Elector of Saxony King of Poland, amidst loud vivas, and the election was confirmed at a solemn service held in the Church of the Bernadines, hard by. Not till the end of the year, however, did the newly elected King venture to show his face in Poland, and he returned to Leipsic with a precipitation which seriously embarrassed his partisans.

The Empress had hoped to terminate the Polish difficulty in a single campaign, but this hope had soon to be

[1] *See* Bantuish-Kamensky: Biografy rossyskykh generalissimusov. Vol. I, Chap. 12. The biographical sketch of this officer in the Dictionary of National Biography, Vol. XXXI, p. 385—88, is very slovenly, and full of mistakes. Compare also Liria: *Diario*.

[2] Liria.

abandoned. Almost the whole of Poland was in favour of Stanislaus, the country swarmed with his partisans, and he himself lay in the strong city of Dantzic, awaiting the arrival of the promised succour from France. He knew his countrymen much too well to expect any material help from their guerilla bands, which, despite numbers and valour, were powerless against regular troops, and his past experience had taught him that the invasion of Saxony was the only way to make Augustus relinquish Poland. So he looked to Louis XV to do for him now what Charles XII had done twenty-five years before. Failing this, he felt that all was lost. "I shall be compelled to return to France if the King does not occupy Saxony," he wrote to his daughter, Queen Mary. It was therefore of paramount importance to Russia that Stanislaus should be driven from Dantzic, whither help could so readily be conveyed to him by sea, and accordingly at the end of 1733, Lacy was ordered to proceed thither, and besiege the city without delay. The gallant Irishman obeyed with alacrity, but it very soon became evident that he had underrated the difficulties of the enterprise. After leaving garrisons at Warsaw, Thorn (which he captured on his way) and other places, he found, on sitting down before Dantzic, that his army had dwindled to 12,000 men. In order to properly invest the fortress from the land side, he was obliged to distribute his inadequate forces over an area of two leagues, swarming with more than fifty thousand hostile guerillas, thus exposing himself to the imminent risk of being attacked and cut off in detail. The Dantzicers, moreover, encouraged by the presence within their walls of the King, the Primate, and the French and Swedish Ministers, were determined to resist to the uttermost. Their garrison was numerous, their ramparts were strong, their magazines full of provisions and muniments of war, and their numerous artillery, well served by French and Swedish gunners, did great execution. Fortunately for Lacy, the partisans of Stanislaus outside the walls, thought far more of plundering their private enemies than of succouring their beleaguered King; while the garrison took care to keep well behind its ramparts. On the 17th March, 1734, he was relieved of all responsibility by the arrival in camp, with reinforcements, of Marshal Münnich, who now took the supreme command, and resolved, in a council of war held immediately after his arrival, to press the siege vigorously. Two days later, a strongly fortified redoubt, called "Scotland," was assaulted at night and captured after two hours' hard fighting, the Russian soldiers advancing to the attack in the teeth of a driving tempest, with the most dogged courage. The following day the bombardment of the city itself commenced, and for the next fortnight the siege languished, as the Marshal had no field-pieces with him but 8-pounders, and the King of Prussia refused to allow any artillery to be conveyed through his domains to the besiegers. The unfriendly attitude of Frederick William I bitterly incensed Münnich, and he is said to have threatened that when he had done with Dantzic, he would proceed a little further, and pay a visit to Berlin likewise. At one time an actual rupture with Prussia was feared, and Münnich actually wrote to the Empress that [1] Stanislaus had bought over Frederick William, who was reported to have said that he could not regard with indifference the destruction of Dantzic, and would send an army "to mediate." Had such an intervention taken place, it would have gone hard with the Russians, who were already suffering so severely from want of forage, boots, and sheepskins, that nearly half of them lay in the hospital. They were also harassed incessantly by the Polish guerillas, although such attacks were more troublesome than

[1] Solovev.

dangerous, three thousand Polish horsemen being easily put to flight by three hundred Russian grenadiers.[1] Finally, some mortars from Saxony arrived *by post* (an event hitherto unique in the history of warfare) to the address of Weissenfeld, the Commander of the Saxon contingent, and on the last day of April, the first bombs were thrown into the town. On the 6—7th May, an important advantage was gained by the capture of Fort Sommerschanz, which cut Dantzic off from its port at the mouth of the Vistula,[2] and, encouraged by this success, Münnich resolved to end the siege at a blow, by capturing the Hagelberg likewise. This strong redoubt, the key of the whole position, was built on and around a hill lying south of the city, and abutting on the river. The right side of the Hagelberg, looking towards Oliva, was so steep as to be practically inaccessible, but the left side, looking towards Scheidlitz, was only defended by a simple earthwork without either a covered way or glacis, against this side therefore, the attack was to be directed. At ten o'clock on the night of the 9th May, the besiegers, 8,000 strong, advanced to the assault in three columns, the attention of the enemy being diverted by a simultaneous false attack made by 1,500 of the best troops. The assaulting columns advanced, in absolute silence and perfect order, to the foot of the hill, and at midnight the ascent began. A small battery of seven guns was captured with a dash, but, by a strange and unlucky fatality, nearly all the Russian officers where shot dead at the very first onset, so that, instead of keeping their distances properly, and acting separately, the three columns intermingled, were afraid to profit by their first success, and yet, while hesitating to go on, doggedly refused to turn back, but remained for three hours on the

[1] Manstein.
[2] Hence called Weichselmünde.

brow of the hill, exposed all that time to the murderous fire of the enemy's batteries higher up. Münnich perceiving that the enemy was on the alert, and the attack had failed, sent adjutant after adjutant to his men, ordering them to retreat at once, but they refused to budge from the position they had won, till their favourite commander, Lacy, went to them in person, and persuaded them to return to camp, though only with the utmost difficulty. This abortive attack cost Münnich no fewer than 120 officers and 2,000 men, but he attempted to console the indignant Empress by extolling the valour of her troops, and expatiating philosophically on the unavoidable chances of warfare.[1] By this time 1,500 bombs had been thrown into the town, yet still the besieged betrayed not the slightest disposition to surrender, and, on May 20th, the long-expected French fleet appeared in the roads, and disembarked three regiments, consisting of 2,400 men, under the command of Brigadier La Motte Perouse. A week after their arrival, this little army gallantly attempted to force the Russian intrenchments, but were beaten back with the loss of 160 men, and retired to an island called La Platte, lying beneath the cannon of Weichselmünde, and here they remained unmolested for the next four weeks. Hitherto Münnich had been much hampered in his operations by the want of siege artillery, but, at last, on June 10th, he was cheered by the sight of the Russian fleet under Admiral Gordon, who brought him eighteen large mortars, and eight-and-forty battering cannon, ranging from eighteen to thirty-six pounders.[2] Gordon had orders to attack the enemy's fleet wherever he found it, but as the Frenchmen had deemed

[1] Compare Manstein, an eye-witness of the events described, and Solovev.
[2] Rondeau: *Despatches*. Rondeau, by the way, had not the very highest opinion of the Russian navy at this time. He calls their fleet "a grimace," and says that Gordon's men were not of the best, and his officers very indifferent.

it prudent not to await his arrival, he had to content himself with blockading Weichselmünde, while Münnich, who had now been joined by the Saxon contingent, vigorously bombarded La Motte's little army corps on the isle of La Platte, till it was forced to surrender, and conveyed on board the Russian fleet to St. Petersburg. It was the first time in history that the French and Russians had crossed swords with each other in the open field, and the Empress was not a little proud of her novel triumph, although somewhat indignant with the French for provoking a quarrel which had not been of her seeking. La Motte and his staff, shortly after their arrival in the Russian Capital, were somewhat cruelly compelled to be present at a grand fête, given at the Winter Palace, in commemoration of their defeat, and much curiosity was felt at Court as to how they would demean themselves on such a delicate occasion. The grave and manly deportment of La Motte, "who looked as if he had a soul that felt his disgrace and despised the insult,"[1] excited universal sympathy and respect. Anne commanded him to approach her, and, after allowing him to kiss her hand, remarked severely that she now had it in her power to avenge the injury which the King, his master, had done her, but that the infliction of the present mortification was the only reprisal she intended to take, and as the French were noted for their politeness, she hoped some of the ladies present might have charms sufficient to lessen even this rebuff. She then beckoned to several ladies who, she knew, spoke French, of whom Lady Rondeau was one, and bade them do all in their power to make the French gentlemen forget that they were prisoners, at least for that evening, allowing them, moreover, to wear their swords on parole, so long as they remained in her presence. "Your Majesty,"

[1] *Letters by a Lady*, by Lady Rondeau, a sympathetic witness of the scene.

replied La Motte, with a deep bow, "has found a double way of subduing us, and while I hope that Mons. de Münnich will do us the justice to admit that we submitted our persons unwillingly to his valour, I feel sure that we shall now most willingly submit our hearts to our fair conquerors."—And Anne's consideration for her captives went even further than this. "It must be confessed," wrote Mr. Rondeau some time later, "that her Majesty has been very kind to the three French regiments, most of which would have perished here of cold if the Tsaritsa had not been so good as to give every common soldier a greatcoat lined with sheepskin, and to every officer one lined with fine foxskin."[1]

Two days after the capture of the French army, the fortress of Weichselmünde also surrendered, and the loss of its port speedily decided the fate of Dantzic, which was now entirely cut off from the sea. On June 30th the city capitulated unconditionally, after sustaining a siege of 135 days, which cost the Russians 8,000 men. The Polish Primate, the French Ambassador, Monti, and Poniatowsky were arrested, and sent prisoners to Thorn. King Stanislaus, disguised as a peasant, had contrived to escape a day or two before. A deputation of the principal citizens proceeded to St. Petersburg, to beg the Empress's pardon, and promise never in future to harbour any of her enemies, and the town was condemned to pay one million ducats for the expenses of the war, another million for allowing Stanislaus to escape, and 80,000 more for ringing the church-bells during the siege, contrary to ancient custom. The Dantzicers in their extremity appealed to the British Government to use its good offices in their behalf, and Mr. Rondeau was instructed to represent their miserable position to the Tsaritsa's Ministers, in "a modest and

[1] Rondeau: *Despatches*.

friendly sort of way," at the same time informing them how agreeable it would be to the King if her Majesty would generously ease them, as much as possible, of the great burden laid upon them. But Ostermann replied that he thought her Majesty had been very generous in laying so moderate a tax upon them, considering what they had done.[1] Ultimately, however, a remission *was* made, and the port of Weichselmünde restored to the City.

The flames of war in Poland were all but extinguished by the fall of Dantzic, though the embers still continued to smoulder till nearly twelve months afterwards. The fugitive Stanislaus was first heard of again at Königsberg, whence, in August, 1734, he issued a manifesto to his partisans, urging them to form a confederation on his behalf, and a confederation was formed accordingly, at Dzikowa, under the presidency of Adam Tarlo, which sent an envoy, Ozarousky, to Paris to urge France to invade Saxony with at least 40,000 men, the confederates promising to co-operate simultaneously on the side of Silesia. In the Ukraine, too, Count Nicholas Potocki, the Primate's kinsman, kept on foot a motley host of 50,000 men, and entered into negotiations with the pretender to the throne of Transylvania, Francis Rakoczy, with the avowed object of shaking off the yoke of their common oppressor, Austria; but nothing came of these isolated, and therefore impotent, efforts. France was ill disposed to waste any more men and money on a patently unserviceable ally, more particularly as she had found ample compensation for her reverses on the Vistula in the triumphs of herself and her allies in Lombardy and on the Rhine. In the course of 1733 and 1734, the Spaniards had conquered Naples and Sicily; the combined forces of France and Savoy had occupied Sardinia, and nearly the whole of the Milanese;

[1] Ibid.

while on the Rhine, Prince Eugene, now a mere shadow of his former self, was unable to save Culm, Phillipsburg, and Lorraine, or prevent two French armies from penetrating into the heart of the *Reich*, where they were received with open arms by many of the German Princes. In her extremity Austria applied to Russia for assistance, in accordance with the terms of the Treaty of Vienna, and this assistance Russia was now able to give, she herself having in the meantime completed the pacification of Poland by scattering Tarlo's Confederation, and routing the Cup-bearer of Lithuania at Grodno. Lacy therefore received orders to march to the assistance of the Kaiser, with 20,000 men, and after a tedious two months' journey through Silesia and Thuringia, united with the Imperial forces on the banks of the Neckar. It was the first time that a Russian army had ever been seen in Central Europe, and the strict discipline and perfect order of the northern barbarians excited some surprise, and not a little admiration. Lacy, however, came too late to render the Emperor any active assistance. A month after he had gone into winter quarters at Pforzheim, peace negotiations were opened between Austria and France, and at the end of November, Lacy and his army were summoned eastwards again to meet a new enemy—the Turk.

Ever since the Peace of the Pruth, indeed, a fresh war between Russia and the Porte had been inevitable. Both the honour and the interests of Russia imperatively demanded that that humiliating treaty, which had thrown her back into the steppes of the Don, should be annulled, and that she should recover her former frontier on the shores of the Sea of Azov. But, though she was bent upon war, she desired a war in her own time, and under favourable conditions, and was therefore disinclined to break with Turkey until the Polish trouble had been happily terminated. France, on the other hand, equally anxious to prevent the

Tsaritsa from aiding the Kaiser, and the Kaiser from aiding the Tsaritsa, skilfully used the Polish question as a weapon against them both. From the beginning of 1733 onwards, the Court of Versailles put forth all the resources of its diplomacy to bring about a simultaneous rupture between Russia and her northern and southern neighbours, Sweden and Turkey. Sweden, it must be borne in mind, although no longer a great, was still a considerable Power, indeed it is not too much to say that, up to the middle of the 18th century, she was of much more account in Europe than the young and still barely tolerated Kingdom of Prussia.[1] Now Sweden nourished many old grudges against Russia, she had not even yet abandoned the hope of recovering her Baltic Provinces from that Power, and the re-appearance in the political arena of Stanislaus Leszczynski, the former comrade of the still idolized Charles XII, recalled the most splendid triumphs of the blue and golden banner[2] a quarter of a century before, and sent a thrill of martial enthusiasm through the country. Sweden, moreover, was the only Power to which Stanislaus had applied directly for assistance, and the tidings of his re-election caused unspeakable enthusiasm at Stockholm, especially among the younger officers of the army, forty of whom at once departed for Dantzic as volunteers, accompanied by eighty soldiers disguised as their lacqueys. The Marquis de Castège, the French Envoy in Sweden, did his utmost to fan this fervour into a blaze, and for the moment the Russian Government was seriously alarmed. Ostermann desired Rondeau, very earnestly, to inform Lord Harrington that advices had been received from Stockholm that the Swedes were in a great ferment, and seemed inclined to

---

[1] So late as 1735, the Elector of Saxony refused the royal title to Frederick William I of Prussia. Saxony at that time was considered at least the equal of Prussia.

[2] The Swedish colours are blue and yellow.

favour the French proposals, one of which was to engage the Swedes to send 10,000 men to Poland to aid King Stanislaus,[1] in return for ample subsidies from Versailles. Fortunately, Russia's alarm proved premature. The aging Swedish Chancellor, Count Horn, was as much opposed to war as the British Premier, Walpole, himself, and despite the virulent invectives of the hot-headed minority in the extraordinary Riksdag of 1734, who bitterly complained that the honour and glory of Sweden were being sacrificed by the pusillanimity of a peace-loving dotard, he more than held his own, and steadily refused to embark his country in fresh perils. On the fall of Dantzic, too, the martial enthusiasm of the Swedish gentry began to evaporate, and with the assistance of the English Minister at Stockholm, Mr. Finch, the defensive alliance between Russia and Sweden, which was only for twelve years, and had just expired, was, towards the end of 1735, renewed, to the great satisfaction of the Russian Cabinet.[2] Thus, for the first time since the death of Peter the Great, Great Britain and Russia were acting together in Sweden.

But it was at Stambul that the diplomatic contest between France and Russia was keenest and most persistent. There the energetic French Ambassador, the Marquis de Villeneuve, used all his efforts to induce the Sultan to declare war against the Tsaritsa, but his intrigues were no secret to the Russian envoy, Ivan Ivanovich Nepluyev, who, by the judicious employment of rubles and rare furs, bought the most private information, bit by bit, from the dragomans of the Porte. There were many grounds for a quarrel between the two Powers. First, for instance, came the chronic

---

[1] Rondeau: *Despatches*.

[2] Ibid. This, however, did not prevent Sweden from contracting a new treaty of amity with France also, whereby the Court of Versailles undertook to pay Sweden 450,000 crowns a year.—*Rondeau*.

dispute about the doubtful ownership of the Kabardine district, lying south of the Government of Astrachan, between Georgia and the territories of the Kuban Tartars, and divided among some thirty petty sovereignties or khanates, nine of which were of the Greek religion. The Khan of the Crimea pretended that this district was beneath his jurisdiction, but this the Russian Court stoutly denied. Then there was the repeated violation of undisputed Russian territory by the Tartar hordes, on their way to fight against the Persians, with whom Turkey had been waging an exhausting and unprofitable warfare for some years; and finally came the Polish question in which Turkey was very deeply interested. Again and again Villeneuve reminded the Porte that Russia was bound by a whole catena of treaties not to send troops into Poland unless directly threatened by that Power, and that she had no right whatever to interfere in such purely domestic affairs as the election of a new King. On the election of Stanislaus and the outbreak of the Franco-Austrian war, Villeneuve became still more urgent, representing that now or never was the time for Turkey to fall upon Russia, while Stanislaus still had partisans in Poland, while the Emperor was embroiled with France, and the Maritime Powers remained neutral. To wait till Poland was converted into an actual enemy by Russia's candidate, Augustus III, were folly. The Porte was profoundly impressed by these representations, and at a Divan held in November, 1733, it was resolved to make peace with Persia, and fall upon Russia forthwith. The Grand Vizier, Ali Pasha, informed Nepluyev that an ultimatum was about to be despatched to the Empress, requiring the immediate withdrawal of her troops from Poland. The presence of a Russian army-corps in that country was, he added, not only a breach of Russia's treaties with Turkey, but an unbearable insult to the latter, who had not even been previously consulted, and he asked Nepluyev what he had to say on this head. "We must first consult the Court of Vienna," replied Nepluyev.—"Oh!" replied the Vizier, with a sneer, "how long is it since you became dependent on the Court of Vienna? We always took the Russian Empire to be quite independent of the Roman Empire!"[1] On another occasion when Nepluyev was expatiating, somewhat rashly perhaps, on "the inviolable liberty of the Polish Republic," the Vizier sarcastically observed: "How can you talk of the inviolable liberty of the Poles when you compel them by force to do what they have the strongest inclination *not* to do." Nepluyev's pride and patriotism were revolted by the sinister pleasantry and the contemptuous tone of the too well-informed Ali. He rightly attributed the arrogance of the Turks to the poor opinion they had begun to entertain of Russia ever since the Peace of the Pruth, and certainly, had the Porte been able to attack Russia in 1733, the latter Power would have been placed in a very critical position. Fortunately for Russia, however, the effects of Villeneuve's intrigues were counterpoised by the crushing defeats inflicted upon the Turks at this time by the great Persian General, Kuli Khan, at Erivan and Kars, which indisposed the Porte to rashly take upon itself an additional war. On the other hand, Nepluyev himself now began to urge his Government "to fall upon these barbarians" while they were still suffering from the effects of their reverses, and represented the whole Ottoman Empire as weak to the last degree, and even tottering to its fall. The situation was still further complicated by the British Ambassador at Stambul, Lord Kinnoul. This nobleman was under strict instructions to act in unison with the Russian and Austrian Ministers, but, for all that, he constantly consorted with Villeneuve, and allowed himself to be guided in all things by his dragoman, Luke Kirik,

[1] Nepluyev: *Despatches*, cited by Solovev.

"a great rascal"[1] who was in the pay of France and very malevolently disposed towards Russia. As early as 1733 Nepluyev had begun to regard Kinnoul as a wolf in sheep's clothing, and both from Cantemir in London, and from Rondeau at St. Petersburg, the British Government received, in the course of 1734, frequent complaints of the conduct of their Ambassador. Kinnoul was warned to behave better, and Ostermann declared at first that he would be quite satisfied if the dragoman Kirik, "our great enemy," were dismissed; but as the offending Ambassador, so far from amending his ways, continued to do the Russian Government all the ill offices he could, and make representations to the Porte very detrimental to the Tsaritsa, it was found necessary at last to recall him altogether, and he was superseded at the end of 1735 by Sir Everard Faulkener, to the great satisfaction of Ostermann and his colleagues.[2] Another piece of good luck for Russia was the fall of the able and enlightened Grand Vizier Ali, which Nepluyev piously regarded as a providential interposition. His disappearance from the scene left the Turkish Government weaker than ever. His successor was Ismail, a low-born, ignorant upstart with no knowledge of affairs, who owed his elevation to a Palace intrigue conducted by his kinswoman, the Sultan's mother, a Georgian. As for the Reis-Effendi, or Minister of Foreign Affairs, he was described by Nepluyev as a political chameleon who always took his cue from the Vizier of the moment, while his chief colleague, the Mufti, was old and stupid.[3] Now, therefore, was Russia's opportunity persisted Nepluyev, and his representations at last prevailed—the Empress resolved upon war. What seems to have ultimately

[1] Rondeau.

[2] For an account of Kinnoul's strange behaviour, see Rondeau: *Despatches*, and Nepluyev: *Despatches*, cited by Solovev.

[3] Nepluyev: *Despatches*, cited by Solovev.

decided her was the persuasion that she had gained a valuable confederate in the victorious Persian, Kuli Khan.

In the beginning of 1733, the Court of St. Petersburg sent an Extraordinary Envoy, Prince Sergius Dmitrevich Golitsuin, to Ispahan, to bring about an alliance with Persia. At first, however, Golitsuin's reports were very unsatisfactory. He described Kuli Khan as a haughty imperious man who disliked being dictated to, and had therefore to be treated with extreme caution. Nay, the Khan was not merely haughty, he was contemptuous and even menacing. He did not see how Russia could help him in his war with Turkey. Her offer of friendship was a mere matter of words. He doubted whether she could even lend him 10,000 men if he wanted them, and he savagely inveighed against the Russian Government for retaining Baku and Derbend, which had been conquered from Persia by Peter the Great. "Thank Allah!" he exclaimed, "I need not your friendship. I solemnly declare that if it be needful I will unite all Mussulmans beneath my banner, and invade Russia from all quarters, advancing even to the walls of Moscow." Nevertheless he declared that if these places were surrendered to him, he would enter into a solemn compact never to make peace with the Porte without the consent of Russia, but march straight upon Constantinople through Anatolia, while the Russians advanced upon the other side. These half-promises induced the Russian Government to restore Daghestan to Persia, whereupon Kuli, in an access of gratitude, called himself "the least of the Empress's slaves," and turning towards the town of Gandscha, which he was besieging when the Russian envoys met him, exclaimed: "Woe to you, ye inhabitants of Gandscha! If Allah doth lengthen my days, I swear that not only you, but all the subjects of the Padishah shall perish beneath the sabres of the

Persians."[1] The definitive treaty between Russia and Persia was then signed, and the Russian troops evacuated the fortresses of Derbend, Baku, and Svyestoi Krest.

Now, although these provinces, so far from proving profitable to Russia, had been little else than a cemetery for thousands of her troops, it was somewhat humiliating for the Empress to begin her reign by surrendering conquests made by her illustrious uncle after a great expenditure of blood and treasure. Honour demanded therefore that she should seek compensation from the Turks for her concessions to the Persians, and, at the same time, wipe out the disgrace which had clung to the Russian arms ever since the Peace of the Pruth. Münnich, too, was eager to draw his sword once more. He longed for glory, he longed still more for the power that always waits upon glory. Moreover, his Dantzic laurels had been somewhat tarnished by the reverse on the Hagelberg, and that ominous word was constantly in the mouth of his detractors. And for once the wishes of Russia's greatest captain coincided with the plans of her greatest statesman. Ostermann also advised war, and at once. Conjunctures were favourable, and everything promised success. The treasury was full, the army in an excellent condition, and no interference was to be anticipated from any foreign power. Accordingly a formal declaration of war[2] was drawn up by the Russian Vice-Chancellor and despatched to the Grand Vizier, and on the 23rd July, 1735, Münnich received orders to proceed at once from the Vistula to the Don, to make the necessary preparations for opening the campaign.

[1] Golitsuin: *Despatches*, cited by Solovev. It was after this that Kuli advanced into Anatolia and defeated the Turks in two bloody battles as already described.

[2] Characteristically enough it was almost apologetic in tone, and reads as if Ostermann were trying to persuade the Turks that Russia was about to wage war upon them for their own good.

# CHAPTER VII.

## THE FIRST CRIMEAN WAR.

### (1736—1739).

THEATRE of the War—The Crimea—The Lines of the Ukraine—Campaign of 1735—Campaign of 1736—Quarrel between Münnich and Lacy—Münnich's march across the Steppes—Skirmishes with the Tartars—Münnich's tactics—The Lines of Perekop—Münnich carries them by assault—Advance upon Koslov—Sufferings of the army—Advance on Bagchaserai—Insubordination in the army—Return to the Ukraine—Lacy captures Azov—Terrible mortality in the Russian army—Indignation of the Empress—Her correspondence with Münnich—Vishnyakov—Campaign of 1737—General James Francis Keith—The siege of Ochakov—Münnich's blunders—Lacy ravages the Crimea—Peace Congress at Nemirov—Complaints against Münnich—Campaign of 1738—Sufferings of the army—Coolness between the Austrian and Russian Courts—France mediates between the belligerents—Campaign of 1739—Battle of Stavuchanakh—Fall of Chocim—Surrender of Jassy—Münnich's progress arrested by the news of the Peace of Belgrade—His indignant remonstrance—End of the War—Rejoicings—Reflections.

THE Turkish War of 1736—1739 marks the beginning of that systematic struggle on the part of Russia to recover her natural and legitimate southern boundaries, which was to last throughout the eighteenth century, finally succeeding only after the expenditure of millions of lives and an incalculable quantity of treasure. During the whole of this bloody struggle, everyone to whom Christianity is something more than a name, everyone who prefers civilization to barbarism, must needs rejoice at the victories, and deplore the defeats, of the Russian arms. In following the contest of Russia with her northern and her western neighbours, we are not always quite so sure that our hearts are with her. During the war with Sweden, for instance, a generous mind will naturally sympathize with the weaker but manlier power which, though bound, from the very nature of the circumstances, to succumb ultimately, yet fought the unequal fight with such incomparable gallantry, and performed prodigies with such pitiful resources. It was unfortunate, too, for the reputation of the Tsar that he should have been pitted against such an ideal hero as Charles XII. The contrast between the nobility and chivalry of the latter and the grossness and chicanery of the former, is so glaring that again and again we are tempted to doubt whether Peter I was really Peter the Great. During the contest with Poland our sympathies are again divided. All along we are disturbed by doubts as to whether Poland or Russia has the better right to the eastern Slavonic lands, and even in the darkest days of Polish degradation, when the decrepit and moribund Republic seems but to cumber the earth, we can never forget that the splendid extravagance of Polish valour was, for generations, the bulwark of Christendom, and the salvation of Europe. But as regards Russia's southern confines, there can be no room for two opinions. The possession of the shores of the Euxine and the circumjacent tracts was even more indispensable to the complete and normal development of the Russian Empire than the recently acquired shores of the Baltic, and ever since the unspeakable desolation of the great Tartar invasion, these regions had been infested rather than inhabited by the predatory tribes dependent on the Porte. Originally, in the golden days of the Tartar domination, these barbarians had held sway over the best part of central as well as of southern Russia, but, on the collapse of the great Kipchak horde, they had split up into half a dozen fiercely antagonistic and mutually destructive Khanates, and the natural consequence was a gradual recession of the Tartar element before the gradual but constant pressure of the persevering Muscovite Tsars. But though the dimensions of European Tartary had, by the beginning of the eighteenth century, shrunk considerably, its territories still embraced the whole of that vast plain extending from the Danube to the Don, and from the Don to the Caucasus, including Moldavia, the Dobrudja, the Crimea, and the steppes on both sides of the sea of Azov. A glance at the map of Europe will show that Turkey had thus the entire control of the five great rivers[1] that drain southern Russia, and consequently could control and even suspend, at will, no inconsiderable portion of her rival's commerce. The most powerful vassal of the Sultan in these parts was the Khan of the Crimea, who, from his Capital at Bagchaserai, ruled over all the scattered Tartar hordes from the Dnieper to the Don. The wealth of the Crimea at this time was very great. The Steppes poured the inexhaustible wealth of their flocks and herds into it, and the trade between the peninsula and Turkey was enormous. Koslov, the chief port on its western side, exported 200,000 head of cattle, and an incalculable quantity of grain to Stambul every year, while the still wealthier Kaffa, on the east coast, was perhaps the largest slave mart in the world. Münnich[2] estimated the annual income of the Khan at 1,000 purses of 500 crowns each, exclusive of his private possessions. The peninsula was divided into forty cantons, each consist-

[1] The Dniester, the Bug, the Dnieper, the Don and the Kuban.

[2] *Tagebuch des Grafen von Münnich* [descriptive of the campaign of 1736]. Pt. III of Hermann's: Beiträge zur Geschichte des russischen Reiches.

ing of from 30 to 40 villages governed by their own cadis, and the approaches to it were very strongly guarded. As the Turks had the absolute command of the sea, no danger was apprehended from that quarter; on the land side the Lines of Perekop protected the narrow isthmus which united the peninsula to the mainland, while the fortress of Azov, at the head of the sea of the same name, commanded the Delta of the Don, and was thought sufficient to prevent an indirect attack coming from the north-east. Additional outlying defences towards the north-west were the fortresses of Kinburn and Ochakov, at the confluence of the Bug and the Dnieper. The steppes between the Danube and the Dniester were defended by the Tartars of Budjak, the steppes between the Don and the Kuban by the Kuban Tartars, while the more distant hordes of the Nogai in the steppes of the Volga formed an almost unlimited reserve for the Khan to draw upon. In order to keep out the Tartars from central Russia, and at the same time to form a base of future operations against them, Peter the Great, while still smarting beneath the humiliation of the Peace of the Pruth, had characteristically conceived the gigantic project of connecting the rivers Dnieper and Donetz by a chain of fortifications a hundred leagues in length, to which he proposed to give the name of the Lines of the Ukraine. The plan, which was begun in 1731, six years after the Tsar's death, and completed in 1738, only partially fulfilled its double purpose. The ground covered was too extensive to be adequately guarded, and the forts were placed so far apart that the Tartars were able to pass and repass the Lines continually, despite all the efforts of the Russians.[1] Nevertheless, this system of fortification was to prove an invaluable *point d'appui* for armies operating against the Turks, and hither, in the early autumn of 1735, arrived

Marshal Münnich, intent on perfecting his arrangements for the ensuing compaign. The Cabinet had given Münnich the choice between investing Azov at once, or postponing the siege till the following spring. He chose the latter alternative, and wisely, for an epidemic raging at that time in those parts had placed most of his principal officers *hors de combat*, and neither his artillery nor his commissariat was in a satisfactory condition. He himself was laid up for three weeks with malaria at Pultawa (it was while he was on his way to that place that he received from the Empress the rescript appointing him Commander-in-Chief of the armies of the Dnieper and the Don), and consequently was obliged to limit his operations that year to despatching General Leontiev southwards with 28,000 men to ravage the Crimea, and destroy if possible, all the Tartars dwelling between that peninsula and the Ukraine. Leontiev, who could not take the field till October, did succeed in severely chastising the Tartars with very little loss to himself, and capturing 3,300 head of cattle; but the season was too advanced for active operations, and an unusually fierce north wind began to blow as early as the middle of October, bringing with it snowstorms and severe cold. In one night Leontiev's dragoons lost a thousand horses, whereupon he fell back behind the Lines of the Ukraine, and went into winter quarters. Still Münnich could congratulate himself on having struck the first blow, and it was a satisfaction to him that the old Tartar Khan had suffered more severely than himself. On hearing of Leontiev's advance, the Khan, who was marching against Persia, hastily retraced his steps, but winter overtook him, and, in less than a week, he lost ten thousand men and 50,000 horses, whereupon the rest of his forces dispersed, and sought refuge in the Crimea.

Münnich employed the winter in diligently inspecting and strengthening the Lines, marshalling his troops, and providing all things necessary for the ensuing campaign. Every regiment was ordered to provide itself with a score of *chevaux de frise* to be used for the defence of the camp against night attacks; the old-fashioned halberds and spontoons or demi-pikes, were superseded by bayonets; while, to keep off the Tartar cavalry, the Marshal invented a new sort of lance, 18 feet long. This heavy and cumbersome novelty did not, however, stand the test of experience, and seriously impeded the soldiers while on the march; but, on the other hand, it proved unexpectedly useful for escalading walls, and took, to some extent, the place of scaling ladders, in which the army was very deficient. Early in February Münnich quitted his head-quarters at Isum, on the extreme left of the Lines, and paid a flying visit to the little fortress of St. Anne, at the confluence of the Donetz and Don, a few miles above Azov, to make preparations for the siege of the latter place, and before he left, succeeded in surprising the outlying fort of Kabutschi, the Russians losing only the stern end of a canoe. By the end of March he was back again behind the Lines, and at Tsaritsinko on the Dnieper, the appointed place of *rendezvous* for the army, had a conference with his colleague Lacy, who had just arrived in the Ukraine from Vienna, to take part in the campaign. This interview, which was not a pleasant one, marked, according to Münnich,[1] the beginning of those unfortunate differences between the two commanders, which very nearly led to serious consequences. Since last they met, Lacy had also received his Marshal's bâton, and during his passage through Vienna, the court there, which detested Münnich, had ostentatiously fêted and flattered his rival, the gallant Irishman. The Kaiser presented him with his portrait set

---

[1] Münnich: *Tagebuch*. Manstein, however, as we shall presently see, gives another reason for their differences.

in brilliants, and a beautiful gold and scarlet casket containing 5,000 ducats,[1] and Lacy, proud of these distinctions as well as of his new dignity, had been given to understand by his own court that he was to hold a command independently of Münnich. Münnich, on the other hand, had been led to suppose that Lacy was to be his subordinate, and, at their first interview at Tsaritsinko, treated his fellow-marshal as if he had come to receive orders. Lacy hotly resented this offensive tone of superiority, whereupon Münnich produced his last rescript, which Lacy perceived to be manifestly contrary to his own written instructions.[2] A compromise was finally come to. It was agreed that Münnich should indeed take the initiative, but that at the same time he should invariably communicate his plans to Lacy beforehand, and treat him as an equal. They then amicably arranged between them the plan of campaign. The enemy was to be attacked on all sides simultaneously, Münnich invading the Crimea, Lacy besieging Azov, and Donduk-Ombo, the chief of the Kalmuck tribes dwelling in the steppes of Astrachan and the lower Volga, acting against the Tartars of the Kuban. As soon as Münnich had stormed the lines of Perekop, he was to detach 12,000 men against the fortress of Kinburn on Dnieper—whither the Crim Tartars had driven the greater part of their cattle—so as to prevent the Budjak Tartars from crossing the river, by way of Ochakov, to aid the Crimea; whilst Lacy, after capturing Azov, was to hasten to the relief of Münnich's army.[3] The two Marshals

[1] He had scarce departed from the Imperial presence, however, when the Austrian Exchequer *borrowed* from him the ducats he had just received.
[2] Münnich: *Tagebuch*.
[3] Ibid. We are fortunate in possessing two contemporary accounts of this interesting campaign, Münnich's contained in his *Tagebuch*, and Manstein's relation in his *Mémoires*. Manstein, by the way, was one of Münnich's adjutants throughout the war. See also the numerous letters and despatches cited by Solovev.

then parted. On his way to Azov, Lacy narrowly escaped falling into the hands of some thousands of Tartar freebooters, who massacred his escort of dragoons, and robbed him of his baggage to the value of 12,000 rubles. Hastily dismounting from his carriage, the Marshal threw himself on a cart-horse which he succeeded in cutting loose from its traces, just in time to elude his pursuers—another five minutes and the army of Azov would have had to mourn its commander.

On April 20th Münnich began his march across the steppes to Perekop. His army consisted of 57,000 men, including the Zaporogean and Don Cossacks, whose hardy little horses, that kept sleek and plump even on a grass diet, matched the long lean steeds of the Tartars for speed and endurance. General Leontiev commanded the vanguard, General Ismailov the rear, the Prince of Hesse-Homburg the centre. Prince Trubetskoy was left behind at Tsaritsinko to look after the commissariat, and Münnich, at parting, threatened to hang him up if he failed to supply the requisite quantity of stores and provender at the stipulated times. "Seemingly impossible things can be brought about in a very short time in this country, by such threats," explains Münnich apologetically ; and his Highness for the rest of the campaign certainly worked wonders. For 330 miles the march continued through the wilderness where nothing was to be seen but grass and sky, the army encamping every night on the banks of the Dnieper or one of its affluents. The first brush with the enemy occurred at Chernaya Dolina, or Black Valley, a small lake midway between the Dnieper and Perekop, where Colonel Witte and Major Spiegel, with less than 5,000 men, were assailed by 15,000 Tartars, whom they gallantly repulsed, after an engagement of several hours, during which the Marshal was very anxious about their safety. This success had an excellent effect on the *morale* of the troops, and opened their eyes to the fact that, by keeping a bold front and firing point-blank, they had little to fear from the onset of the hitherto much dreaded Tartars, however numerous. The howling of these savages, as they advanced to the attack, was now found to be the most terrible part of them. As for the thousands of darts with which they darkened the air, not one in a thousand took effect. Münnich rested for a day or two at Chernaya Dolina, and then, learning from his scouts that the whole Tartar host was approaching, formed his army into a vast hollow square, with the field artillery at the corners and in the centre, and the Cossacks inside, guarding the baggage with their long lances. This formation, now introduced into the Russian army for the first time, continued to be adopted throughout this and the ensuing campaigns, and was admirably suited to the character of the foe and the nature of the ground, the whole country between the Ukraine and the Crimea being perfectly flat, not a hillock or a ravine appearing once in ten leagues, while the enemy could be seen approaching almost from the horizon. The army now resembled an immense moving fortress, and its progress, naturally slow, was still further impeded by the enormous amount of *impedimenta* it was forced to take along with it. For as there was not a single town in the whole region, except the capital of the Zaporogean Cossacks, and that was little better than a good sized village, every necessary, even to fire-wood and water, had to be provided beforehand. It will be readily comprehended therefore that the equipment of such a host was necessarily enormous; and, incredible as it may seem, we are assured by an eye-witness[1] that Münnich never entered upon a campaign without dragging at least 80,000 wagons after him! Shortly after leaving Chernaya Dolina, the Russians came in sight of the Tartars, who formed,

[1] Manstein.

as it were, another square, enclosing the invaders on every side. The old Khan had called out all the male population from 17 to 70, and there were besides, among the combatants, hundreds of Tartar women armed with darts and sabres, who when captured, we are told, "did not make the most delightful of Amazons."[1] After some hours of hesitation, during which the Russians remained silent and immovable, the bolder of the Tartars attacked Münnich on all four sides, rushing impetuously up to the very mouths of the guns, armed only with their sabres. But the fire of the Russians was so steady and continuous that the assailants recoiled from the iron square again and again, and, at last, after a two hours' combat, fled hastily in all directions. Münnich, who during this encounter had not lost a single man, then ordered a general advance and on the evening of the same day, 15th May, sat down before the famous Lines of Perekop.

The Lines of Perekop[2] consisted, as the name implies, of a deep trench five-and-twenty fathoms broad,[3] drawn across the isthmus connecting the Crimea with Russia, and defended by an earthern wall eight fathoms high, and nearly five English miles long,[4] reaching from the sea of Azov to the Black Sea. In the centre of the Lines stood the fortress of Or-Kapi, possibly of Genoese origin, an oblong square, the walls and narrow bastions of which were made of square flagstones.[5] It was garrisoned, as were all the Crimean fortresses in those days, by Turkish regulars, Janissaris, and Spahis, some four thousand in number, while the bulk of the Tartars lay behind the Lines. On May 19th Münnich held a Council of War, at which it was resolved, unanimously, that as the enemy's positions were too extensive to be besieged in

[1] Münnich: *Tagebuch*.
[2] Perekop, in Russian, means a long ditch drawn across a road.
[3] Rondeau.
[4] Ibid.
[5] Münnich: *Tagebuch*.

form, an assault of the weakest part of the Lines should be attempted without delay. Accordingly, at eight o'clock the same evening, when it was quite dark, the Russians advanced towards the left wing of the hostile camp, in three columns, one behind the other, with the field artillery in the wings, the attention of the enemy being simultaneously distracted by a false attack made by Prince Ryepnin, and at break of day they safely reached the *rendezvous* at the foot of the glacis of the Lines, where they took up their position. The advance had been so swift and silent that the Turks had had no warning of Münnich's approach, and when the signal for the assault was given and the storming columns scaled the breastwork, hewing their way up the wall, step by step, with their axes and the butt-ends of their muskets, and even dragging their guns up after them with "incredible"[1] enthusiasm, they met with little or no resistance. The first to scale the breastwork, side by side, were a German ensign named Rechenberg, and a Russian priest, crucifix in hand, who called continually to the soldiers beneath him to mount boldly and fear nothing, as the cause was God's and the Empress's. The garrison, completely taken by surprise, was more intent on flight than on fighting. Most of the Tartars were asleep when the attack began, and the old Khan, who was absorbed in his morning's devotions, had only two minutes to escape from the claws of the Don Cossacks, leaving behind him his accumulated sacks of ducats, and an English telescope, presented to him by Peter the Great, which Münnich appropriated for the remainder of the campaign. In less than an hour the whole army had surmounted the ramparts, and cut to pieces all who ventured to oppose them. The town of Perekop itself, where was stored an enormous quantity of merchandise from Turkey, the Crimea and

[1] Ibid.

the Ukraine, was then abandoned to pillage, and Münnich's triumph was crowned by the surrender of the fortress of Or-Kapi, the Janissaries after the capture of the Lines, losing all stomach for further fighting.

The news of the storming of the Lines of Perekop produced the utmost consternation throughout the Crimea. Every man who was able, after driving his wife and children into the mountains, fled to the nearest haven, while the Khan himself and his harem sought refuge at Balaclava. But it was in the very hour of his triumph that Münnich's troubles now began, and he had the mortification of seeing his victorious army dwindle away even more rapidly than the scattered host of the vanquished. For five weary weeks his soldiers had been marching continually through a malarious country, without a morsel of fresh meat, or a drop of fresh water, and compelled to subsist for the most part on sweet wheaten bread or badly baked biscuits, instead of the sour rye bread to which they had always been accustomed. The consequence was that dysentery and other diseases began to ravage the camp, and the daily mortality grew alarming. The horses, too, were dying by hundreds for want of forage, the Tartars having burnt bare the whole district around Perekop, so, in order to find food and provender, Münnich determined to march on to Koslov, the chief port on the west coast of the Crimea, after leaving Dewitz at Or-Kapi to keep open his communications, and detaching 7,000 men, under Leontiev and Stoffel, against the fortress of Kinburn, as concerted with Lacy. Münnich then rode slowly along the ranks and addressed his men, with whom he was always very popular.[1] "Keep a stout heart, my

[1] Prince Dolgoruki says (*Graf A. I. Ostermann*) that the troops used to call Münnich: "Fenis, the bright falcon," the favourite hero of old Russian folk-lore.

children!" cried he. "We shall soon, I know, have good meat, and fresh water, and to spare!"—"God grant it, little father!" they shouted back, "for we want it badly enough!"

The march to Koslov only lasted a few days, but it was the severest trial the troops had yet encountered. More than once there was an absolute dearth of water and fodder, the Tartars having not only destroyed everything in their way, but contaminated the wells by filling them with all sorts of offal.[1] Only three potable streams were met within six-and-thirty leagues. However, on reaching Koslov, which was abandoned by the enemy as they approached, the Cossacks captured 20,000 head of cattle, which supplied the army with fresh meat till its return to the Dnieper, and thus greatly relieved its sufferings. Koslov, the oldest town and one of the best harbours in the Crimea, where the Grand Duke Vladimir, in 988, was baptized, and exchanged bridal rings with the daughter of the Byzantine Emperor, was entered on the 5th June; but Münnich finding the pasturage there very poor, resolved to proceed still further south, to Bagchaserai, the capital of the Khan. Accordingly, after stripping all the lead from the mosques, for the use of the army, he proceeded on his way towards the Crimean high lands. Nowhere did he encounter the least resistance. Not one of the numerous rivers and defiles of that mountain region was defended. On the 16th June the army passed through the narrow gorge leading into the amphitheatre of hills, not quite a German mile in circumference, in the midst of which lay the pleasant town of Bagchaserai. The valley well deserved the name of "Garden of Palaces".[2] The fair plain which now opened out before the gaze of Münnich and his staff, was studded, as far as the eye could

[1] Manstein: *Mémoires*.
[2] This is the literal meaning of the Turkish word Bagchaserai.

reach, with country houses embowered in fresh and fragrant groves. In the distance below, like a long street running between rocks and cliffs, lay Bagchaserai, consisting of about 3,000 well-built houses, conspicuous among which towered the snow-white marble palace of the Khan, and the cupolas and minarets of the mosques. A road, broad enough for a company of infantry to march along it abreast, led down into the valley. To the left rose the lofty eminence called by the Russians, Palatki Gor, or tent mountain, whence the whole peninsula could be surveyed. At the foot of it, a range of downs stretched right away towards Kaffa. On the approach of the army, all the inhabitants of the country fled to the mountains, and Münnich, advancing all night in pitch-black darkness, came, on the morning of the 17th, in sight of the town, and sent forward the Cossacks and hussars to plunder it. They were attacked unexpectedly, on the outskirts of the place, by an army of Tartars and Spahis, each of whom had a well-armed janissary astride behind him. The struggle was a sharp one, the Russians losing three hundred men before they succeeded in repulsing their assailants, but it proved to be the last skirmish of the campaign, and this was a very fortunate thing for Münnich, as he was now suddenly confronted by the spirit of insubordination in his own army.

Among the Marshal's leading officers was the Prince of Hesse-Homburg, a peculiarly mean-spirited specimen of that envious type which is quick to detect and resent any natural superiority in others. The vices of a man like Münnich, his boundless vanity and his fatuous self-assertion, for instance, are, after all, more ridiculous than offensive; but the vices of a man like Hesse-Homburg excite not laughter, but loathing. It was he who, while partaking of the hospitality of Marshal Dolgoruki, had carefully noted the incautious words that escaped his host while in liquor, in order to betray him next day to his deadliest enemies, and he hated Münnich because, although of lowlier birth, the Marshal held a higher rank than he did. Throughout the campaign he had been carping at and criticising all Münnich's arrangements, and, not content with ignoring or neglecting orders, did his utmost to excite dissensions, and never ceased speaking disparagingly of the Marshal, not only to his fellow-officers, but even to the common soldiers. He succeeded in gaining over the principal Russian generals, as well as Major Magnus Biren, the favourite's cousin, and his audacity went so far as to propose that if Münnich advanced any further, his orders should be disobeyed, and if he attempted to enforce them, he should be arrested, and the supreme command conferred on the senior general present—in other words Hesse-Homburg himself. But here the Russian officers drew back for fear of losing their heads,[1] whereupon the Prince addressed 28 Articles of remonstrance to the Marshal, protesting against the whole plan of campaign, and posing as the champion of the weary and distressed soldiers.[2] Münnich sent back the Articles to the Prince unread, by his adjutant, with his compliments, and absolutely refused to listen to his complaints and criticisms. That he did not proceed against the offending officer summarily, was due, no doubt, to his fears lest a palace intrigue should be lurking behind this act of insubordination. His apprehensions on this head were somewhat relieved by the receipt of a letter from the favourite, enclosing a secret letter of complaint against Münnich, sent to him by his own cousin, the above-mentioned Magnus, at Homburg's instigation; but Münnich, no longer certain of his own army, now deemed it prudent to retrace his steps, instead of proceeding against Kaffa, so after breaking off the gilded door-heads and half-moons

[1] Manstein: *Mémoires*.
[2] Münnich: *Tagebuch*.

from the mosques and palaces of Bagchaserai as trophies, he set the whole place on fire, and then led his army back to Perekop, where the joyful news reached him of the fall of Kinburn. At Perekop it was decided in a council of war to dismantle the Lines, and blow up the fortress of Or-Kapi, because there were no available means, within a hundred miles, of placing them in a proper condition of defence, whereupon the whole army returned through the steppes to the Lines of the Ukraine.

While Münnich was thus rendering the Crimea defenceless and uninhabitable, Lacy had been equally successful before Azov, though there he had met with a far stouter resistance than his brother-marshal had encountered at Perekop. The garrison consisted of picked men, and the Seraskier defended the place heroically, making sortie after sortie, to the great damage and confusion of the besiegers, who were only kept at their work by the rash gallantry of Lacy. On the 18th June, when the siege had already lasted more than a month, a bomb fell into the powder magazine of the fortress, in the midst of the great square, exploding it and blowing up three hundred houses and five mosques,[1] and, eleven days later, the Commandant sent a *parlementaire* into the Russian camp, offering to surrender if he were permitted to march out with all the honours of war. Lacy insisted on an unconditional surrender. "Rather than accept such conditions," replied the Seraskier, "I'll bury myself beneath the ruins of the place." Then the garrison was allowed to march out with drums beating and colours flying, and the Russians took possession of Azov. They found the walls mounted with 137 cannons and 4 mortars, and a prodigious quantity of muniments of war fell into their hands; but the food supplies of the fortress had run very low, and although no breach had been made

[1] Manstein.

in the walls, the whole interior of the town was little more than a shell. The same evening Lacy sent his eldest son to St. Petersburg, to lay the keys of Azov at the feet of the Empress.[1]

After the fall of Azov, Lacy, as concerted with Münnich, set off for the Crimea with his 7,000 men. On his way, he fell in with the Cossacks of Spiegel's corps which had been sent against Kinburn, and who professed to have lost their way. Surprised to find them in those parts, and not believing them, Lacy arrested the men, but the next day he fell in with six more, who confirmed the story of their fellows, and reported, besides, that Münnich had already quitted the Crimea for the Ukraine, whereupon Lacy turned right about, and retreated in the same direction. But for this accidental encounter, he would have marched straight into the heart of the Crimea, and run a great risk of perishing there with his little army. Lacy was naturally much exasperated at his colleague's neglect to advertise him in time of his retreat, so this incident served to alienate the two Marshals still further.

On his return to the Lines of the Dnieper, Münnich numbered his forces, when the appalling fact came to light that 30,000 men, or more than half of his entire force, had perished, and of these scarcely 2,000 had been slain by the enemy. At court the news of this shocking mortality, the unavoidable result of fatigue, hunger, and exposure in an unhealthy climate, caused a great sensation, and Münnich's many enemies made the most of it. Nor, even in the opinion of impartial critics,[2] was he altogether to be exculpated. He had provided indeed, as best he could, for the proper feeding and maintenance of his troops, and he had carefully

---

[1] Rondeau: *Despatches.*
[2] Manstein, for instance.

consulted beforehand[1] the Cossacks, who knew the whole region well, as to the best season of the year for opening a campaign in those parts. But, on the other hand, he does not seem to have spared the army, as he should have done, for frequently the men had to march for two or three hours at a stretch in the scorching heat of a subtropical sun, instead of at night or in the early morning, in consequence whereof it was no uncommon thing to see the soldiers drop down dead on the road, and many of the officers perished from sheer misery. The Cabinet was also surprised and indignant at the Marshal's premature retreat, so early as August, to the Dnieper, and ordered him to resume the campaign before the summer was over; but Münnich, who, by the way, ungenerously threw the blame of his retreat on Lacy, for not succouring him in time as concerted,[2] declared that disease and murrain had so ravaged the army, that further operations that year were impossible. A Council of War supported the Marshal's views, but people at Court naturally began to ask themselves what was the use of a campaign in which half the army had been lost for next to nothing. Upon the proud and sensitive mind of the Empress, the retreat and partial ruin of her forces, and the discord among her generals, produced a most painful impression. It is pathetic to see how this Princess, whose noble ambition it certainly was to be the mother of her people, chafes and frets beneath the feeling of her own helplessness in the matter. In the extremity of her distress, she turned instinctively to her most prudent counsellor, Ostermann,[3] for assistance, and

---

[1] Solovev.

[2] Lacy replied that he could not send reinforcements by water because the transport galleys were not ready, or by land for want of horses. *See* Solovev.

[3] Ostermann, be it remembered, was the chief author of the war.

asked him in a letter, still preserved, whether an honourable peace was not, after all, preferable to such a devastating war, and how she could best reconcile her generals "who so ill requite our grace and favour by their mutual wranglings." Presently matters were still further complicated by the injudicious action of the Cabinet, who commanded Lacy, on his return from Azov, to inspect, and make a report upon, the condition of Münnich's army, whereupon the latter, deeply hurt, wrote direct to the Empress, desiring, on the plea of ill health, to be relieved of his "overwhelming responsibilities," and requesting, with a somewhat theatrical affectation of magnanimity, that the command-in-chief should be given to his rival. Dissatisfied as she was with Münnich, Anne could not afford to lose him. She therefore took the matter into her own hands, and wrote him a reproachful, yet not unkindly letter,[1] expressing her astonishment at his conduct, reminding him of his duty, and, at the same time, soothing his wounded pride by exhorting him to be as faithful and diligent a servant as heretofore. But Münnich was not so easily mollified. He responded, indeed, in a strain of enthusiastic gratitude, protesting that it was his supreme happiness to serve such a high-minded, divinely appointed and incomparable monarch, but, at the same time, attempting to justify his conduct by pleading the classical example of Aristides, who, for his country's good, was content to resign his command on the eve of Marathon, to his colleague Miltiades. He then reiterated his request that Lacy should supersede him, but was ultimately persuaded to withdraw his resignation, though not till he had received a solemn assurance of the Empress's undivided confidence.

Anne was the more inclined to make peace with the Porte because of the ill success of her actual confederate,

[1] Given in full by Solovev.

Austria, against the Turks, and the evasions and subterfuges of her contingent ally, Kuli Khan, who, shortly after receiving back Daghestan from Russia, had (Feb. 1736) usurped the throne of Persia under the title of Nadir, [1] and now quickly forgot, in the arms of his concubines, not merely his promises to the Empress, but his duties to his own subjects. The Turkish Ministers too, at Ispahan, began to get the upper hand, and the Russian resident, Kalushkin, bitterly complained that, while they scattered their bakshish broadcast, he himself was left so poor that he had not the ghost of a gift wherewith to foil their intrigues. [2] Moreover, the Maritime Powers, headed by England, were insistent in the cause of peace, and offered their mediation repeatedly. It did not escape the attention of the keen sighted Rondeau, that the Russian Ministers, despite their publicly expressed satisfaction at "the great feats" of Marshal Münnich, would have been very glad to see an honourable end put to the war, "but," he adds, "they are yet ashamed to own it after all the great things "they proposed to do." [3] Yet hope quite as much as shame induced the Empress's Government to continue the struggle. It was no secret to the Russian Cabinet that the condition of Turkey was feebler than it had been for at least a century, and the Russian resident at Constantinople, Vishnyakov, never ceased preaching war to the death, with the zeal of a crusader and the emphasis of a prophet. He assured the Vice-Chancellor that there was an absolute dearth of political, military, financial and diplomatic capacity at the Porte; that everything in Turkey was in the utmost confusion,

---

[1] Formerly he has been known as Tahmash Kuli Khan, *i.e.*, Tahmash the Slave of the Khan, now he called himself "The incomparable Shah, Nādir being the Turkish for rare, precious.

[2] Despatches of Kalushkin, cited by Solovev.

[3] Rondeau: *Despatches*.

and that the slightest disaster would bring the crumbling edifice to the ground. The fear of the Turks, he said, rested on an absolute tradition. They were as feeble and faint-hearted now as before they had been valiant and ferocious. "Now is the time," he cries, "not only to extinguish their bestial pride, but also to make a complete end of the lawless horde... There is none capable of resistance, everyone is full of fear. Your Majesty already reigns in the hearts of all the good Christians who still languish beneath the yoke of this expiring barbarism." [1]

At the end of April, 1737, Münnich took the field, and opened the second campaign which was to be the bloodiest of the whole war. His army consisted of 70,000 men, and conspicuous among the generals who accompanied him, were Alexander Rumyantsev, whose outspokenness, it will be remembered, had formerly drawn down upon him the Tsaritsa's displeasure, but who had now been restored to favour and loaded with benefits, and General James Francis Keith, who, during the course of the summer, had brought back Lacy's army from Silesia to the Ukraine. This Keith was a very remarkable man. The youngest child [2] of the 9th Earl Marischal, he was born at the Castle of Inverness, near Peterhead, on June 11th, 1696, and carefully educated at Aberdeen and Edinburgh. In 1715, while on his way to London to seek a commission in the army, he met his elder brother travelling post-haste to Scotland, to take part in the Mar insurrection, and, returning with him, proclaimed James VIII, and, after gallant service at Sheriffmuir, made his escape to Brittany. At Paris he resumed his interrupted studies under Maupertuis, and was chosen

[1] Vishnyakov: Despatches, cited by Solovev.
[2] Dictionary of National Biography, Vol. XXX, pp. 324—326. The article on Keith is excellent, so far as it goes, but unfortunately its author does not seem to have been aware of the existence of Manstein's *Mémoires*, or of Keith's own Diary of the Turkish war.

a member of the *Académie des Sciences*, but, in 1719, his adventurous spirit moved him to take part in Alberoni's futile expedition to the Western Highlands, and, after three months of hiding in his native land, he succeeded in following his brother from Peterhead to Holland. Subsequently he was, for nine years, a Colonel in the Spanish service, and finally, in 1728, entered the Russian service as a Major-General. Anne appointed him Lieutenant-Colonel of the newly formed Ismailov regiment, and Inspector-General of the army of the Ukraine, and he might perhaps have had the honour, instead of Apraksin, of defeating Frederick the Great's army, had not a shameful intrigue, as we shall see in the sequel, driven him to exchange the Russian for the Prussian service, long before the Seven Years' War began. Prince Anthony Ulric of Brunswick-Wolfenbuttel, the destined husband of the Empress's niece,[1] also accompanied the army as a volunteer. Münnich's objective was Ochakov, the ancient Axiake, situated at the confluence of the Dnieper and Bug. It was by far the most considerable fortress in those parts, and was defended by 20,000 of the best troops in Turkey, under the leadership of the valiant Seraskier Tiagya, a pasha of three tails, and son of the late Grand Vizier Ali.[2] On June 29th the Russian army crossed the Bug, and after forming into three huge squares, followed the course of the river to Ochakov, halting, on July 10th, within cannon-shot of the fortress. The field artillery had been left behind under the charge of Prince Trubetskoy, who had had orders to embark them on a fleet of large flat double-sloops, expressly constructed for the purpose, and send them down the Dnieper with all despatch; but when Münnich arrived before the town, he found that the sloops had not arrived, and he therefore had no artillery wherewith to

[1] See Chap. VIII.
[2] Rondeau.

begin the siege. As, moreover, the Tartars had ravaged the whole district for eight leagues round so effectually that not a stick of wood or a drop of water, or a scrap of pasturage, was anywhere to be found, Münnich was driven to the greatest straits, and saw his whole army in danger of perishing. This, too, was the moment chosen by the Prince of Hesse-Homburg to fall so desperately ill, that he was unable to rise from his bed till the afternoon of the day on which Ochakov was taken. The fortress was in the form of an irregular oblong flanked by divers bastions. Three sides of it were surrounded by a parapet, a glacis, and an *avant-fossé* twelve feet wide, but the seaward side was only protected by a low wall in a very indifferent state of defence. Münnich had been informed by one of his spies, who had indeed penetrated into Ochakov, but had had no opportunity of observing its defences, that the place was a hexagon in shape, and equally strong all round, and it was on the report of this man that the Marshal took his measures. He began by occupying a few half-ruined Turkish redoubts in the gardens round the town, and then proceeded to throw bombs into the fortress with such success that whole streets were soon in flames. Anxious to profit by this lucky accident, Münnich ordered Keith, who was posted in the centre of the attacking columns, to advance into the open within gunshot of the glacis, and keep up a continuous fire to distract the attention of the garrison on the ramparts, and at the same time prevent them from extinguishing the flames in the town. Keith represented that such a manœuvre would mean the useless sacrifice of many of his men; but, the Marshal insisting, he promptly obeyed, and led them to the foot of the glacis, where their progress was arrested by the above-mentioned *avant-fossé*, which they were unable to cross, being totally unprovided with ladders or other siege apparatus. For two hours Keith and his men remained in front of this ditch, vainly endeavouring to find a passage across, and exposed all the time to a murderous fire from the walls of the fortress. Finally, they were obliged to retire behind the redoubts in the gardens, and the besiegers rallying forth, massacred all the wounded on the spot. It was now that Münnich, seeing his army retreat, completely lost his head, and, giving way to despair, threw his sword to the ground, and exclaimed to those about him: "All is lost!" In the confusion of his distress, moreover, he sought to lay the blame of failure on Keith's shoulders, insinuating that it was in consequence of that general's excessive impetuosity that the assault had succeeded so ill. Keith, stung to the quick by such an imputation, when he had all along been obeying orders against his own better judgment, at once sent a message to Münnich, begging him to desist from such representations, or else he would demand a court-martial to clear himself, when he would not fail to point out all the blunders that had been committed since the commencement of the siege. If the Seraskier had at that moment ordered a general sortie, the whole Russian army, according to Manstein, must have been "beaten hollow."[1] But the Turkish Commandant had enough to do to try to put out the flames which had now become general within the fortress, and presently the biggest powder magazine in the town exploded, blowing up a large part of the town, and burying beneath the ruins 6,000 men. Almost simultaneously the Cossacks burst into the place from the seaward side. These hardy freebooters had been attracted thither by the sight of the horses of the Spahis, or Turkish light cavalry, quietly feeding in a little plain[2]

[1] Battue à plate couture.
[2] This critical incident is recorded by Rondeau, who heard it from one of the couriers who brought the news of the victory.

just outside the town, and, yielding to their predatory instincts, at once made an attempt to carry the horses off, which the garrison, observing it, sallied forth to prevent, but, instead of succeeding, was repulsed by the Cossacks, who followed close upon its heels to the very walls of the fortress, and, there dismounting, attacked the Turks, sword in hand, with such impetuous valour as to force them back at all points, and follow them into the town, crying: "Nashy, nashy!"[1] On hearing these cries, Münnich, recovering his sang-froid, despatched 6,000 regulars to the assistance of the Cossacks, and they also got into the town, and cut to pieces all who opposed them. The carnage was terrible, no quarter being given on either side. Seventeen thousand Turks perished on the walls, or in the ditches, or under the smoking ruins; 3,000 Spahis were drowned in attempting to swim to the Turkish galleys in the harbour outside, and the Seraskier himself was captured, while making his escape in a little boat, by General Biren, who only with the utmost difficulty prevented the Cossacks from killing him. The courier who brought the news of the victory to St. Petersburg, told Rondeau that so many Turks were slain that nothing but blood and dead bodies were to be seen about the streets, and the corpses caused such an infectious stench that Münnich, after the siege was over, had to march his army fifteen miles away from the scene of action. "Let this affair be related any way," wrote Rondeau to his Court, "it must be confessed that it is a very great and honourable action, but I very much fear that it has cost the Tsaritsa many more brave men than this Court cares to own." And such was indeed the case. At the lowest estimate the Russian loss was 3,000, and the proportion of officers was enormous. Münnich, in a private letter to his son, declared that only

[1] "Ours!" "Ours!"

the mercy of God had got him "out of the scrape."[1] He himself had had a horse killed under him, and five bullets had pierced the folds of his mantle; while Keith was so dangerously wounded in the leg that at first it was feared he would lose it, but his brother came and took him off to Paris where the limb was saved. The grateful Empress raised Keith to the rank of a lieutenant-general, sending him besides a present of 10,000 rubles (£2,500) to pay his travelling expenses and his doctor's bill. Münnich, too, paid him a visit after the storming of the fortress, and congratulated him on his valour. "Monsieur de Keith," added the Marshal, "methinks it is partly to you that we owe the success of this great enterprise."—"Nay, your Excellency," replied Keith, still mindful of Münnich's unjust insinuations the day before, "nay, I don't want to make the least merit out of the affair. What I did was done absolutely in obedience to your orders."

Münnich's detractors and contradictors used always to represent him as the luckiest of commanders, but never had his luck been so wonderful as at the siege of Ochakov. In the opinion of military experts, he had besieged the fortress with so little precaution as to invite and deserve defeat. He had begun to attack without properly reconnoitring the ground; he had directed it against the strongest instead of the weakest side of the fortress, and he had neglected to provide his storming columns with fascines and other necessaries. The place had been captured after all, it is true; but captured contrary to all the rules of warfare, by an acccidental irruption of irregular *cavalry*.

The remainder of the campaign, so far as concerned Münnich, proved uneventful. For the next month the army continued marching and counter-marching along the Bug,

[1] "J'ai tiré mon épingle du feu par un effet de la miséricorde divine." Quoted by Rondeau.

to make the enemy believe it was about to advance on Bender; but its real design was to cover Ochakov, and so prevent the Turks from re-assaulting the place before it had been put into a thorough state of defence. Towards the end of August, Münnich returned to the Lines of the Ukraine, with 24,000 men less than when he started. This terrible mortality was due partly to climatic influences, and partly to the superstitious observance of the ecclesiastical fasts on the part of the common soldiers, who, despite the dispensation granted to them by the Church during actual warfare, preferred to die miserably rather than eat meat.[1] "I doubt whether there are in the whole world any other troops who could sustain such continuous fatigues with so much patience," exclaims Manstein admiringly. The loss of sumpter beasts had also been excessive, 15,000 yoke of artillery-oxen, to say nothing of horses, having perished for want of proper sustenance, mainly owing, it is said, to the criminal negligence of the Prince of Hesse-Homburg.

Whilst Münnich was operating against Ochakov, Lacy, with another army of 40,000 men, had invaded the Crimea from the east, advanced as far south as Baras-Basha, ravaging and burning as he went, without encountering any serious opposition, finally returning to the Ukraine in August, bringing with him 30,000 bullocks and 100,000 sheep, so that a bullock was sold in the Russian camp for half-a-crown, and a sheep for a shilling. The auxiliary Russian flotilla of double sloops, under Bredal, also defeated the Turkish fleet off Cape Kiskow at the mouth of the Don, and, in the late autumn, General Stoffel, who had been left in command at Ochakov, repulsed a large Turkish army which invested the town from Oct. 26th to Nov. 9th, but was forced to abandon the siege, leaving 20,000 dead beneath the walls. Thus, on the whole, the campaign of 1737, though incon-

[1] Manstein.

clusive and very expensive, was decidedly glorious to the Russian arms.

Nevertheless the Empress was very desirous of peace, and as both Austria, who had done even less, and Turkey who had suffered even more, in 1737 than in 1736, were also pacifically inclined, a peace Congress met at the little border town of Nemirov, from July to October, when the Tsaritsa's envoys proposed that Russia should retain all her conquests, including the region between the rivers Dnieper and Don and the Crimea, while Moldavia and Wallachia should be erected into an independent principality, to serve as a barrier state between Russia, Poland, Hungary and Turkey. But to such terms as these the Porte would not listen, and on Oct. 22nd the Congress ended abortively. At the same time there were unmistakable symptoms of a growing coolness between Russia and Austria. The Empress was, not unreasonably, dissatisfied with the imbecility of the Kaiser's strategy, while Austria's adverse criticism of Münnich's peculiar method of storming fortresses, caused great irritation at the Court of St. Petersburg. Great Britain, however, anxious above all things to maintain a good understanding between the Allies, whom she regarded as the only effectual counterpoise to the ambition of France, laboured assiduously, and not unsuccessfully, to preserve the peace between them, and Rondeau was repeatedly instructed to employ his good offices to prevent any misunderstanding between the two Powers, or, better still, with the co-operation of his colleague at Constantinople, Sir Everard Faulkener, to induce the Tsaritsa to magnanimously make peace with the Porte, in spite of her victories.

In the course of the winter, another attempt was made to injure Münnich by one of his enemies in the army, who wrote to the Empress privately, complaining of the quality of the food supplied to her soldiers, a subject on which she was known to have a very decided opinion. Previously to this, the victorious Marshal had come to Court where a perfect ovation awaited him, and he had returned to his head-quarters at Pultawa, highly satisfied with his reception. His wife and family, too, had been petted and enriched, and he was congratulating himself on the pleasant turn his affairs were taking generally, when, at the end of February, he received a rescript from the Tsaritsa, informing him it had been brought to her notice that, during the last campaign, her soldiers had been forced to live, for the most part, on sour dough instead of properly baked bread, which had led to a grievous mortality amongst them, and she commanded him to see to it in the ensuing campaign, that his army was well provided with good biscuits and oaten cakes, so many pounds of which were to be distributed to each man, so that he might have ample provision beforehand. Indignant at what he considered an unwarrantable interference, Münnich, after declaring that he himself had used at his own table the same bread, and no other, that had been served out to the common soldiers, again tendered his resignation; but Anne succeeded in mollifying her sensitive commander by a fresh assurance of her confidence, and by divulging the name of her informant, who was court-martialed forthwith and severely punished.

The campaign of 1738 was almost entirely barren. Münnich had been ordered this year to hasten to the assistance of the Austrians, and accordingly, after crossing the Dnieper, he had marched in the direction of the Bug, whence he followed the Turks, who had assembled to oppose him in considerable force, first to the river Savran on the borders of Poland, and thence to the Dniester, where several smart skirmishes occurred, in which the Russians were uniformly successful. Further than this the Marshal durst not go. The outbreak of the plague in Wallachia and Moldavia, deterred him from proceeding against Bender or Chocim, as originally intended, and, on his return to the Lines of the Ukraine in the late summer, he attempted to console the Empress by assuring her that the finger of God was visibly to be discerned in the failure of the campaign, inasmuch as if he had led the army across the Dniester into the plague-stricken region beyond, not a man would have returned to tell the tale. As it was, he lost more men, horses and bullocks, during this campaign than in any of the others. The Ukraine, ordinarily the granary and "bread-basket" of the empire, had been reduced, by a three years' war of exceptional ferocity, into a howling wilderness, so that the Marshal was obliged to carry all his stores along with him. So encumbered indeed were the Russians with baggage during this campaign, that their army was practically immovable. To give some idea of the enormous quantity of Münnich's impedimenta, I may mention that General Biren alone took with him three hundred oxen and horses, seven asses and three camels, while there was not a sergeant in the Guards who did not have at least sixteen wagons in his train.[1] No wonder then if the huge heavily-laden host covered with difficulty in thirty hours distances that an ordinary army would have traversed in less than four. So overloaded were the beasts of burden that they could scarce drag their limbs along, and the soldiers were so badly looked after, that they "died like flies." Before the campaign was half over 10,000 of the men were down with illness, and in nine cases out of ten, owing to the dearth of doctors and medicine chests, and the neglect of the simplest sanitary precautions, illness meant death. We are told that the sick were thrown together, in batches of five and six, into little carts scarcely large

[1] Relation of Major Paradis, cited by Solovev.

enough to hold two men, and driven by miserable wretches shivering with ague, and more resembling corpses than living beings. From Moldavia the plague spread to the Crimea and the Ukraine, taking off its victims by thousands, and decimating the garrisons of Kinburn and Ochakov to such an extent that the Russians had to dismantle and evacuate both places, and retire precipitately to the healthier districts of the Dnieper. Lacy was scarcely more fortunate than his colleague Münnich. In the beginning of July he had invaded the Crimea for the third time, with the intention of taking its strongest fortress and finest harbour, the great slave mart Kaffa, whither the bulk of the inhabitants of the peninsula had now retired; but he found the whole country so wasted and desolate that he had great difficulty in subsisting, and was obliged to return to the Ukraine without accomplishing his object. Mortified by his ill success, Lacy tendered his resignation, but the Empress assured him in an autograph letter, that she had no fault to find with his conduct, and persuaded him to remain.

Loud and long were the complaints of the Court of Vienna against Münnich, in the course of 1738. During this campaign, indeed, the Austrians had been even less successful than their Russian Allies, inasmuch as they had not only been unable to capture Widdin, but had lost several of their own fortresses, and they laid the blame entirely on the Russian Commander, whom they accused of wilfully withholding his promised co-operation. But Münnich pleaded the existence of the plague in extenuation of his remissness, and observed, besides, with perfect justice, that the Russians had indirectly assisted the Austrians during the last two campaigns, by drawing off the Turks and the whole of the Tartars, and thus bearing the brunt of the conflict. He was warmly supported by the Tsaritsa and her Cabinet, and Biren, who hated the supercilious Court of Vienna even more than the Marshal, openly quarrelled with the Austrian Ambassador, Count Ostein. This gentleman had bitterly complained to Biren on the subject of Münnich's slackness, whereupon the Grand Chamberlain took fire, and laid the whole blame of the bad situation of Austria's affairs on the Imperialists themselves. "If you had had anything like a decent army in the field," cried he, "we should long since have had an honourable peace."—"I do not see," sneered Ostein, "that your Court has done anything very great during the war, beyond making a great noise, and killing a Tartar or two." This reply so irritated Biren that he immediately turned upon his heel and walked away. The same evening he sent his equerry to Ostein, requesting him in future to address himself to Count Ostermann, whom he knew the Ambassador could not endure.[1]

But the Allies had too much need of each other to risk a rupture because of the personal quarrels of their respective Ministers. Besides, there was at last the prospect of an acceptable peace. In the autumn of 1738, the questions arising out of the War of the Polish Succession were definitively settled by the Treaty of Vienna (18 Nov.). By this treaty Augustus III was recognised as King of Poland, whilst his unsuccessful rival, Stanislaus, with the title of King, was compensated with the Duchies of Lorraine and Bar, which, on his death, were to revert to France. The actually reigning Duke, Francis Stephen, was translated to Tuscany, and the Emperor also surrendered the two Sicilies to the Infant Don Carlos, receiving in exchange Parma and Piacenza and the recognition of the Pragmatic Sanction. Now, although this peace was a great diplomatic victory for France, aggrandizing her as it did at the expense of the Kaiser without any corresponding sacrifices or losses to speak of on her part, yet it was felt by her statesmen that

[1] Rondeau.

her triumph was by no means complete. She had amply avenged herself, indeed, for Eugene's victories in the War of the Spanish Succession; but, on the other hand, after instigating Poland to support the cause of Stanislaus, she had abandoned the Republic to the tender mercies of Russia, and her own prestige in the North had proportionately suffered. Her rulers were therefore rightly of opinion that the best way to raise her prestige in the north of Europe was to come forward as a mediator between the belligerents, an office which could not fail to increase her authority and dignity in the eyes of Europe. She had, moreover, the further object of separating Russia and Austria after the conclusion of peace, and even hoped, it is said,[1] ultimately to bring about a revolution in Russia itself against the universally detested foreigners at present ruling there. The Porte is said to have been the first to actually invite the mediation of France, but Austria readily acquiesced in the proposal, and in May, 1738, Ostermann also, on behalf of the Tsaritsa, wrote to Villeneuve, the French Ambassador at Constantinople, authorising him to open pacific negotiations with Turkey, but at the same time, expressly reserving the right of his Imperial Mistress to accept the co-mediation of the Maritime Powers[2] if necessary. The terms now offered by Russia were much more moderate than those of the preceding years, the Tsaritsa declaring that she would be content with Azov and district, if Ochakov and Kinburn were dismantled. But the Turks, relieved of all anxiety from the side of Persia (Nadir Shah having risen from his three

[1] Solovev.

[2] The Maritime Powers, England and Holland, always jealous of France, had endeavoured to anticipate the mediatorial offers of France, but their overtures were received with so much coldness by both Austria and Turkey, that they ultimately withdrew their offers of mediation altogether, in high dudgeon. See Rondeau, where some very interesting details on this head are given.

months' debauch to carry his victorious arms against the Great Mogul, whose forces he was now beseiging in Candahar), and the Turks having, in the meantime, driven the Austrians into Hungary, and captured the fortress of Orsova, would not listen even to these modest proposals, and it became clear to the Russian statesmen that they could only hope to obtain the much desired peace by force of arms—thus another campaign was indispensable.

On March 1st, 1739, an extraordinary cabinet council was held at St. Petersburg, to draw up the plan for the ensuing campaign, the Tsaritsa presiding, and Münnich being in attendance as military adviser. It was unanimously resolved to co-operate energetically with the Austrians, by invading Moldavia and proceeding to invest the fortress of Chocim on the Dniester, Ostermann insisting with irresistible force that unless the Kaiser were actively assisted, the superiority of the Turkish army would compel him to make a separate peace, when the whole force of the enemy would be directed against Russia. But now a difficulty arose. The nearest way to Chocim lay through the Polish Province of Podolia, and the Empress had bound herself by a solemn declaration to the King of Poland, to respect the territories of the Republic. The Russian Cabinet was thus in a dilemma. If it kept faith with Augustus III, it would be obliged to abandon an ally who counted upon its assistance, and yet it could only aid that ally effectually by breaking its solemn promise to a friendly neutral Power. In either eventuality its conduct could scarcely fail to be regarded as infamous. Finally, Ostermann pleaded the necessity of the case for disregarding the Empress's promise to the Poles, especially as the latter would be too weak to resent it, and even proceeded to justify this breach of honour on the ground that the Poles, during the previous campaign, had permitted the Tartar hordes to march through their territory to attack the Lines of the Ukraine, and this was the excuse ultimately made, with many apologies, to the Saxon Minister, Suhm, when he subsequently protested against the violation of Polish territory.[1]

On quitting the Council, Münnich set off for the Ukraine, and, at the end of May, the army, 65,000 strong, quitted its *rendezvous* at Kiev, and, marching straight through Polish territory, on July 29th crossed the Dniester at Sinkowcza, about seven leagues distant from Chocim. Retarded by heavy rains and frequent engagements with the Turks, who had never shown themselves so troublesome, the army did not reach the Pruth till Aug. 16th, and following first the course of that river, and then crossing its tributary, the Walicza, entered the mountains of Moldavia through the celebrated defiles of Perekop, the scene of Sobieski's victories, where a very small force skilfully disposed could have annihilated the whole Russian army, with impunity, in a couple of hours. But here Münnich's proverbial luck again befriended him, for the pass had been left unguarded, and on Aug. 27th, at Stavuchanakh, he came in sight of the Turkish camp commanded by the Seraskier Vali-Pasha, whom the Porte regarded as one of its most capable officers. The Turkish position was so strong that at first sight it seemed absolutely impregnable. In front, their main army, under the Seraskier, occupied the summit of a steep hill, where they had intrenched themselves in a camp flanked by batteries. The Governor of Chocim with the Serdengestis, or mounted Janissaries, was encamped to the left, his rear covered by impenetrable forests on ascending ground; Jenlish Ali Pasha with the Spahis, was on the right, in an equally advantageous position, while the countless Tartar hordes led by their Khan, Islum Gerei, surrounded the Russians on all sides, and harassed them incessantly. A

[1] Compare Solovev and Rondeau.

retreat was impossible. Münnich had no alternative between attacking the enemy on the spot, or perishing miserably; it is due to him to add that he never hesitated a moment, and his conduct on this day, so memorable in the annals of Russian warfare, is the best possible vindication both of his courage as a soldier, and his capacity as a commander. Early on Aug. 28th, the Marshal advanced to attack the Turkish intrenched camp on the hill in front of him, the enemy's batteries keeping up a constant but ineffectual cannonade till midday, by which time they had fired 500 balls and killed one horse! Münnich meanwhile had reconnoitred their camp, and discovered that they had neglected to defend the little river, Shulanets, on their left, in the belief that its morasses would sufficiently protect their position at this point. But Münnich's practised eye perceived that the free use of fascines would give his army a passage, and, by 2 o'clock, the Russian columns had successfully crossed the low-lying swamp, and halted at the foot of the hill. Here they were attacked impetuously on all sides by the Turkish and Tartar cavalry; but the enemy recoiled before the point-blank fire of the steadily advancing Russian squares, which gained ground every moment, and approached nearer and nearer to the Turkish intrenched camp. A still more resolute attack was made, midway up the hill, by the Janissaries, scimitar in hand, many of these gallant fellows even bursting through the *chevaux-de-frise* guarding the squares, but nothing could stop the dogged advance of the Russians, who continued to ascend the hill in the face of a terrible fire, till at last the whole Turkish army, panic-stricken, fled in every direction, so that when the victors reached the heights at 7 o'clock in the evening, they found the camp absolutely deserted, and an immense booty fell into their hands. Never was so complete a victory won with so little loss.

Incredible as it sounds, the Russians only lost 70 men during an action that had lasted 12 hours, while the Turks left 1,000 dead upon the field. The following day Münnich advanced with 30,000 men, and all his siege artillery towards Chocim, for until that place was taken his position was precarious at best. Nowadays Chocim is only a third-rate market town with a local reputation for its bricks and its boots; but a century and a half ago it was one of the first strongholds in Europe. The heroic memories which still haunt the place have been wedded to immortal verse.[1] Situated as it was on the Turko-Polish border, in a curve of the Dniester, whose waters washed its rock-hewn walls on three sides, its possession was disputed for generations by the two Powers. It was here in 1621, that the aged Chodkiewicz, Poland's greatest general, rose from a sick bed to achieve his crowning exploit, and, with only 30,000 Polish noblemen and 30,000 Cossacks, successfully resisted half-a-million of Moslems led by the Padishah in person. It was here too, fifty years later, that John Sobieski won that splendid victory over the Turks, which paved his way to the Polish throne. In 1718 the place was finally captured by the Turks with the assistance of French engineers,[2] and was still further fortified, its walls being mounted with 157 cannons and 22 mortars. Münnich therefore anticipated a siege in form, which would severely exercise his engineering skill; but Fortune had yet another agreeable surprise in store for her favourite, for Chocim surrendered unconditionally at the very first summons, the tidings of the battle of Stavuchanakh having filled the garrison with panic terror. After

---

[1] Ignacy Krasicki and Waclaw Potocki have celebrated the past glories in two heroic poems of marvellous vividness and force, bearing the same title, "Wojna Chocimska," or "War of Chocim."

[2] See Slownik Geograficzny Krolestwa Polskiego. Article "Chocim."

occupying the fortress, Münnich continued his march. On the 9th and 10th September, he crossed the Pruth and advanced upon Jassy, the Hospodar, Gregory Ghika, flying precipitately before him, while the assembled Estates of Moldavia received him with enthusiasm as a deliverer; and voluntarily offered to maintain 20,000 Russians at their own cost. On the 19th September, he was able to report that the Principality of Moldavia had "solemnly submitted to the Empress of all the Russias." On the evening of the very same day, he received from Prince Lobkowitz, the Austrian Commander-in-Chief in Transylvania, "the miserable and desperating" notification of the Peace of Belgrade. By this shameful convention, certainly the most humiliating treaty ever signed by the Court of Vienna, Austria sacrificed the fruits of all Eugene's victories, and purchased peace by the surrender of all her conquests made at the Peace of Passarowitz in 1718, including Servia, the Krajowa Banat, part of Sclavonia and the fortresses of Schabatz, Orsova, and Belgrade itself. Arrested in his triumphant progress, and incensed beyond measure at being so basely deserted by the very man who only twelve months before had dared to deny him, Münnich, the capacity of a simple captain of grenadiers, the Marshal threw all diplomatic reserve to the winds, and sitting down in his wrath, indited on the spot to Lobkowitz, an epistle which reveals a considerable command of sarcasm and a very pretty turn for antithesis. After indignantly protesting that the peace was absolutely contrary to the honour and the interests of the two august Imperial Houses, he thus proceeds: "What has become of the sworn alliance between the two Courts? Whilst the Russians are taking fortresses, the Imperialists are demolishing and ceding them to the enemy! While the Russians are acquiring principalities, the Imperialists are surrendering kingdoms! The Russians reduce the enemy to extremities, the Imperialists allow him everything that can flatter or augment his pride!... May I ask what has become of our indissoluble alliance? I venture to assure your Excellency that even if the army of the Emperor had been at the last gasp, the Court of Vienna, with the assistance of my Imperial Mistress, would undoubtedly have obtained from the Turks a far more honourable peace than the one they have just procured." [1] In his despatches to his own Court, he expressed his readiness to prosecute the war alone to a successful issue, and even proposed to cross the Danube, and penetrate to the heart of the Ottoman Empire. But disgusted as the Russian Ministers were with the conduct of their ally, [2] they knew that it was utterly impossible to continue the struggle single-handed. Münnich was therefore recalled to the Ukraine, and peace negotiations with the Porte were opened simultaneously at Paris and Stambul, under the mediation of France. Vishnyakov was the Russian plenipotentiary at the latter place, and, with the loyal co-operation of the Marquis de Villeneuve, he ultimately succeeded in concluding an honourable peace. Russia was to retain Azov and a small district around it to serve as a boundary between the two States. The fortifications of Azov were to be dismantled, but the Russians, by way of compensation, were permitted to build a new fortress on the isle of Cherkask in the Don. Great and little Kabardia were to remain free and serve as a buffer state between the two Powers in the south-east; but Russia bound herself to relinquish all her other conquests, and engaged not to rebuild the arsenal of Taganrog, or

[1] The letter is given in full in Manstein.

[2] The defeat of Grodska, and the general incapacity and ill-success of his Generals, had induced the Emperor to come to terms with the Porte. When the Russian Minister at Vienna, Lanczynski, protested, the Austrian Ministers only shrugged their shoulders, apologetically declaring that the capture of Chocim came a month too late.

maintain a fleet on the Euxine. The Porte also refused to concede the Imperial Title to the Tsaritsa, although Vishnyakov exhausted all his casuistry to obtain it.

The conclusion of the peace was celebrated by a whole series of brilliant fêtes and spectacles. On Feb. 25th, 1740, the Empress went in state to the chapel of the Winter Palace, where a solemn thanksgiving service was held, and Ambrosius, Archbishop of Vologda, delivered an eloquent but concise discourse, the Tsaritsa having previously given the preacher to understand that he was "to stick to the point and not be over long."[1] In the midst of this function Secretary Bakunin, surrounded by the heralds in gorgeous vestments, advanced to the reading-desk and recited the declaration of peace, whereupon the troops assembled in the great square outside blew their trumpets and rolled their drums, and salutes were fired from the Admiralty, and the Fortress of Peter and Paul. After service, the Empress reviewed 20,000 veterans, drawn up under the command of Gustav Biren, the favourite's brother, along the banks of the Neva and in front of the Winter Palace, the soldiers loudly huzzahing as they marched past "the great mother," who was resplendent in gold brocade and wore a magnificent tiara of diamonds. On returning to the Palace, the Tsaritsa received the congratulations of her ministers and generals, and Marshals Münnich and Lacy and Prince Cherkasky delivered pathetic orations, wherein they piously expressed the wish that all good Russians might follow in the footsteps of their incomparable Empress and "so find acceptance before the Lord." The heralds, preceded by trumpeters, then paraded the principal thoroughfares, proclaiming the peace and scattering gold and silver among the people, and in the evening a general illumination, by order, turned night into day. Even the poorest

[1] "Ne ochen prostrannoe i ne dolgoe."

houses were lit up, and no single window had less than ten candles in it. On the following day there was a masquerade at Court, and more money was scrambled for by the mob, the Tsaritsa, surrounded by her Court, looking on from a balcony, on which occasion "her Majesty was graciously pleased to be right merry." But when the people rushed upon the meat and drink provided for them, the "majestic and most serene spectators" were still more amused. After supper, on the same day, there was a grand display of fireworks on an island in the Neva; but the citizens and muzhiks, unused to such spectacles, were panic-stricken by the explosion of some rockets, and rushed hither and thither in great terror and confusion, blindly fighting with and overturning each other in their efforts to get away, which gave her Majesty and her suite "particular occasion for mirth and amusement."

Thus, after a war which had lasted four years and a half, and cost her a hundred thousand men, and millions of rubles, Russia won but a single city, with a small district at the mouth of the Don. To contemporary observers this seemed but a lame and impotent conclusion, and yet, after all, more had been gained than was immediately apparent. In the first place, this was the only war hitherto waged by Russia against the Turks which had not ended in crushing disaster. Even Peter the Great, victorious everywhere else, had been worsted in his struggle with the Porte. Münnich, whatever his shortcomings, had at least dissipated the illusion of Ottoman invincibility, and taught the Russian soldiers that 10,000 janissaries and spahis were no match in a fair field for half that number of grenadiers and hussars. In the second place, the Tartar hordes had been well-nigh exterminated by the Calmucks and Cossacks, and though these "dog-headed" savages might still perhaps, for a time, continue to be a plague, they had ceased for ever to be a terror. In the third place, Russia's signal and unexpected successes in the steppes, had immensely increased her prestige in Europe. The progress of the Russian arms was followed with intense interest both at London and Paris. Horace Walpole, in acknowledging the receipt of Münnich's map of the Crimea from Rondeau in 1736, remarked that the eyes of all the world were fixed upon the Lines of Perekop, and, a year later, Rondeau himself observes of Russia, with some apprehension, that "this Court begins to have a great deal to say in the affairs of Europe." It was a new thing too, to see the Muscovite Ambassador at Stambul, competing with his French colleague on almost equal terms, and at last both France and England became apprehensive lest the victories of Russia might help her to the monopoly of the Levant trade. But the most striking tribute to the improved position of Russia during this war, was the anxiety displayed by Great Britain, towards the end of it, to enter into a definitive treaty of alliance with her. In 1734, when Ostermann himself had pressed for such a treaty, the English Cabinet had, with scant courtesy, declined to even entertain the idea of such a thing; in 1738, on the contrary, they offered their friendship with almost embarrassing insistence. But it was now the Russian Vice-Chancellor's turn to be diplomatically coy. His own eagerness for the alliance abated in proportion to the growing impatience of Rondeau to conclude it, and, while assuring the English Minister of the unalterable benevolence of the Tsaritsa towards the King of Great Britain, he dextrously eluded every attempt to extract from him a definitive treaty.

AMICONI DEL.             WAGNER SCULP.

Anne, Empress.

*To face p. 277.*

## CHAPTER VIII.

### THE LATTER DAYS OF ANNE.

(1735—1740).

COURT of the Tsaritsa—Her personal appearance and mode of life—Peterhof Amusements—Gorgeousness of the Court—Fairy Fêtes at the Summer Palace and the Winter Palace—The Carnival of the Calmuck Bride and the Ice Mansion—Anne's noble buffoons—Other Jesters—Luxury of the Court—The gaming tables—Morality of Anne's Court—The Tsarevna Elizabeth—Terror-stricken atmosphere of the Court—Servility of the Courtiers—Anecdote of Anne's caustic wit—Malign influence of Biren—He is elected Duke of Courland—A kidnapping anecdote—Biren's cruel persecution of the Russian nobility—Antagonism of Biren, Münnich and Ostermann—Unique position of the latter—Biren's dread of him—Yaguzhinsky—The strange and tragic history of Artemius Voluinsky—Alexius Bestuzhev—European politics—Ascendency of France—Rise of the Hat Party in Sweden—Murder of Major Sinclaire—England and Russia—Anne of Mecklenburg—Birth of Ivan VI—Illness of the Tsaritsa—The Regency question—Intrigues of Biren—Death of the Tsaritsa.

WHILST the energy of Marshal Münnich was defending and extending the limits of the Empire, and the sagacity of Vice-Chancellor Ostermann was consolidating its political greatness, the Grand Chamberlain, Biren, found a more congenial occupation in enriching himself, and at the same time diverting his Imperial Mistress, by prompting her to set on foot a Court, which, for all its Oriental extravagance and bizarre semi-barbarism, was indisputably one of the most gorgeous and picturesque Courts in Europe. But, indeed, in this respect, the Tsaritsa needed but little prompting. She had inherited from her grandfather, Tsar Alexius, a very pronounced liking for pomp and pageantry, and as she had ample leisure, more money than she knew what to do with, a natural love of order and decency, and, to say nothing of religious influences, was averse by temperament to the more sensual forms of dissipation, it soon became her ambition to surround herself with all that could minister to her comfort, flatter her pride, and give the world an exalted idea of her power and greatness. Anne's ordinary life was simple in the extreme—of almost military regularity. She always rose before eight, was ready by nine to work with her secretaries and ministers, and dined at noon in her own private apartments or with the Birens, whose apartments in the palace adjoined her own. Most of her afternoons were spent with her ladies, and, after supping moderately, she would invariably retire to rest between 11 and 12.[1] She certainly appeared at her best in her private circle, and Lady Rondeau, who had many opportunities of studying her there, and, indeed, seems to have been one of the Tsaritsa's favourites, draws a by no means displeasing picture of the Ruler of all the Russias. She is described as a large woman, towering above the tallest cavaliers of her court, but very well shaped for her size, easy and graceful in her person, and of a majestic bearing. She had a brown complexion, black hair, dark-blue eyes, and an awfulness[2] in her countenance that struck

[1] Manstein.
[2] Lady Rondeau.

one at first sight, and indeed revolted those who disliked [1] her; but, whenever she spoke to a friend, she had a smile about her mouth that was inexpressibly sweet. Except when angry, there was so much affability in her address as to make those with whom she was conversing imagine for a time that they were talking to an equal; yet never for a moment did she drop the dignity of a sovereign. At her private *soirées* there were generally five or six ladies and two or three gentlemen present, who conversed together in a familiar manner, the Tsaritsa joining in the conversation from time to time, or now and then sitting down and working at the same frame with one or other of her ladies.[2] Gossip, with a spice of scandal in it, was indeed one of the Empress's favourite distractions, and she loved to be surrounded by lively girls and good-humoured young women whose merry chatter could divert her thoughts from cares of state. Two of Anne's favourite talkers were Eudoxia Zagryazhskaya and Tatiana Novokshchenova, especially the latter, whose death proved an irreparable loss to her, though the Empress very providently tried to find a substitute the moment Tatiana began to ail. "Seek out for me," she wrote to her kinsman Soltuikov, at Moscow, "seek out for me from among the poor young gentlewomen at Pereyaslavl, some who are like unto Tatiana Novokshchenova, for, methinks, she is soon to die, and I want someone to take her place. You know our ways, and that we like such as be about forty and are chatty, like Novokshchenova."[3] On another occasion she requested the same gentleman to

[1] Natalia Sheremeteva, for instance, who said of her that she was terrible to look upon and had a most repulsive expression. See *Solovev*. On the other hand, Lady Rondeau says: "She is what we should call a fine agreeable woman."

[2] Lady Rondeau.

[3] Solovev.

"pick out for us two little Persian or Lesghian girls, good, clean and not foolish, for our amusement."[1] Anne seems to have been a just and very generous mistress; but, if Kostomarov tells truly, her maids of honour must have had some very bitter moments. When tired of hearing them talk, she would often make them sing to her, exclaiming in an imperious voice: "Now, girls! come along! come along!" and it is said that the cheeks of these young ladies frequently flushed and tingled beneath the prompt, and not very gentle correction of their mistress's own imperial hand. Anne had some taste for music and acting, and, at the very beginning of her reign, a very fine *troupe* of comedians was sent from Warsaw to Moscow, to divert the Empress, who for some time afterwards could think of nothing else.[2] The plays that appealed most strongly to her peculiar sense of humour, were those rough-and-tumble farces and burlesques the fun of which consisted in the free distribution of kicks and cuffs. In her latter years, the German comedy at the Winter Palace became a regular institution, and everybody, including the foreign ministers, was expected to visit it.

Anne had always preferred a country life to a town life, and she spent a great deal of her time at the Château of Peterhof, some leagues from the Capital, an inconveniently small residence for so large a Court, but pleasantly situated on the top of a hill sixty feet high, about half a mile from the sea, commanding a view of the harbour of Cronstadt and the coast of Finland. The valley lying between the *château* and the sea is covered by a thick wood which was cut into walks and alleys interspersed with fountains and statues. Here the Empress passed most of the summer months, walking, riding, or shooting stags, boars and other

[1] "Dlya svoei zabavui."—*Kostomarov.*
[2] Rondeau.

animals brought thither for the purpose from great distances; her Majesty's prowess on such occasions being duly chronicled in the gazettes day by day.[1] When the cold weather set in, the Court flitted back to the Capital and resided in the Winter Palace, which, considerably enlarged and beautified during Anne's reign, was the scene of some very curious and magnificent spectacles and pastimes. I have already said that it was the ambition of the Empress to make her Court the most splendid in Europe; but though no expense was spared to promote this object, her efforts were not at first very successful. To begin with, Anne's own taste was by no means perfect. She had a foolish fondness for bright and glaring colours, and could not bear to see sombre hues about her. On ordinary days she used to wear long and ample sky-blue or apple-green garments,[2] with a bright handkerchief tied round her head, and all the other ladies had to wear dresses to match. The consequence was an incongruous and grotesque combination at the Russian Court, at least in its earlier days, of splendour and tawdriness, barbaric luxury and gaudy slovenliness. The richest habits were often accompanied by very badly made perukes, or a fine piece of stuff was spoiled by the clumsiness of the tailor; or, if the dress was successful, it was ruined by the meanness of the equipage. Thus a superbly dressed gentleman was often to be seen in a carriage drawn by the most wretched hacks, and as for the women, where one was really well dressed, there would be a dozen dowdies.[3] Still, when one reflects that the Court of Anne was the first Court, at least in the modern sense of the word, that Russia ever had, it must be admitted that the progress made during her reign in the

[1] Kostomarov.
[2] Do.
[3] Manstein.

direction of polite luxury was truly wonderful. The Empress herself, whose natural love of order and decency quickly taught her to distinguish between true and false taste, was the first to unlearn her own earlier vulgarities. In her latter years she was content to wear stiffened gowns of rich brown and gold, which suited her complexion, and pearls were the only jewels with which she braided her silvering locks.[1] Her court, too, though always somewhat odd and bizarre, and savouring rather of the east than of the west, impressed and astonished the most distinguished *habitués* of other and more civilized courts, by its superior splendour and gorgeousness. Some of the spectacles there as described by eye-witnesses are almost unique of their kind. Thus, on the occasion of the capture of Dantzic, a masquerade ball was given in the gardens of the Summer Palace, a very badly built mansion on the banks of the Neva, when all the ladies were dressed in stiffened bodied gowns covered with white gauze and silver flowers, with quilted petticoats of divers colours, and their head-dresses consisting of their own hair curled into large natural curls adorned with chaplets of flowers. The Empress and the Imperial family dined in a grotto facing a long walk terminated by a fountain, and enclosed on each side by a high hedge of Dutch elms. A long table ran the whole length of the walk, which, at one end, joined the Tsaritsa's table in the grotto. Over the long table was a pavilion of green silk supported by voluted pillars with wreaths of natural flowers twisted round them. Between the pillars, in the niches of the hedges, on both sides, were sideboards, parallel with the table, covered all along one side with silver plate and on the other with rare china. Every voluted pillar was illuminated with very pretty effect. Three hundred people sat down to sup in the pavilion, the gentlemen

[1] Lady Rondeau.

drawing lots for their partners, and every man sitting down by his partner at table. After supper a ball began beneath the same pavilion, the servants of the court converting the supper-room into a ball-room, with astonishing celerity. The music was hidden behind the high hedge of Dutch elms, so that it appeared to the guests as if the genius of the place had supplied that part of the entertainment.[1]—In the winter the large newly built saloon of the Winter Palace, which Lady Rondeau describes as considerably larger than St. George's Hall at Windsor, was used for fêtes and masquerades. In the coldest weather it was kept perfectly warm, and decorated with orange-trees and myrtles in full bloom, ranged in rows that formed a walk on each side of the hall, only leaving room for the dancers in the middle. The beauty, fragrance and warmth of this artificial grove, when nothing but ice and snow could be seen through the windows outside, had the effect of enchantment.[2] The luxury and elegance of such diversions as these could not have been surpassed at Versailles or Schönbrunn; but we hear besides of other less pleasant entertainments which happily were impossible anywhere else but in Annine Russia. The oddest of these Muscovite pastimes was the Carnival of the Ice Palace, a *jeu d'esprit* which cost the Empress a trifle of 30,000 rubles.[3]

Amongst the Russian gentlemen who had incurred the displeasure of the Tsaritsa, was Michal Aleksyeevich Golitsuin who had been guilty of the offence (an unpardonable one in the eyes of so orthodox a Princess as Anne) of not only marrying a Catholic lady during his travels abroad, but also of embracing the Latin heresy himself. On his return

---

[1] Ibid.
[2] Ibid.
[3] £7,500. See Chétardie: *Despatches, Sb. Imp. Ist. Ob.*, Vol. XCII; Manstein: *Mémoires*, Vol. I; Kostomarov: *Russkaya Istoriya*.

he was degraded into a Court buffoon, and compelled, besides, to become one of her Majesty's *pages*, although he was over forty years of age, and had a grown-up son who was a lieutenant in the Guards. Nor did the cruel scorn of the Empress end even here. On the death of Golitsuin's Italian wife, the Empress sent for and commanded him to marry again. "I will choose you a bride myself this time," said she, "and what is more, you shall have a splendid wedding, the like of which has never been seen before, and I'll pay all the expenses myself." She then produced the lady, a hideous Calmuck, Anna Buzheninova by name, whom the unhappy Golitsuin at once accepted, lest a worse thing should befall him. The Empress, with the double purpose of humiliating the native nobility in the person of one of its chief members, and at the same time of impressing the people by an exhibition of the magnitude of her power and the extent of her dominions, then issued a Ukaz, commanding all the provincial governors to send to the Capital representatives of all the native races within the limits of the Empire—Laps, Finns, Kirghiz, Calmucks, Bashkirs, Tartars, Cossacks, Samoyedes, dressed in their native costumes. They came accordingly, and towards the end of the year 1739, the nuptials of Michal Golitsuin and Anna Buzheninova were celebrated with extraordinary mock pomp and ceremony. The bridal pair went to church in a cage placed on the back of an elephant, and after them came the procession of barbarous races in still more barbarous equipages. Some were in carts drawn by oxen, others in carrioles pulled by pigs, goats or dogs. The Laps and Samoyedes, distinguished by their rough sheepskins, drove their own reindeer sledges, while the Tartars and Cossacks rode on bare-backed horses. After the ceremony, the motley crew sat down to supper in the huge riding-school which Biren had had recently erected at enormous cost, where everyone was served with the dishes of his particular country, the wedding pair sitting apart on a dais under a canopy. After supper every tribe danced its national dances, accompanied by their own music, in the presence of the Tsaritsa and her court, the grace and agility of the Zaporogean Cossacks being particularly admired. Then came the crowning jest of the evening. Late at night the wedded couple were conducted in solemn state to a house especially constructed for them out of large cleanly-cut cubes of solid *ice*. It consisted of a stately vestibule and a large dormitory, all the furniture of which, including the bed, the tables, the chairs, the clocks, the candlesticks, down to the very curtains and toilet requisites, was of ice. Still more remarkable, two mortars and nine cannons, also of ice and mounted on ice carriages, were posted in front of the house, and, on the arrival of the bridal party, they fired a salvo, actually resisting a charge of three-quarters of a pound of gunpowder. The bride and bridegroom were stripped naked in this huge refrigerator, and committed to their cold couch, guards being placed at the doors to prevent them from escaping before morning. Whether the unhappy victims of this grimly practical joke survived their nuptials, we are not told; but the incident affords a fair specimen of the Tsaritsa's feline humour, and is unfortunately by no means a solitary instance of it.

Golitsuin was not the only nobleman who was compelled to make sport for the Tsaritsa and her German sycophants. Among her regular buffoons we meet with two other members of ancient and illustrious boyar families, Nikita Thedorovich Volkonsky and Alexius Petrovich Apraksin, who shared that unenviable distinction with Costa, a Portuguese Jew, Pedrillo, an Italian fiddler, and Bakluirev, a Russian dwarf, all three of very lowly origin. Volkonsky, the brother-in-law of the future Chancellor, Alexius Bestuzhev, owed his humiliation to Anne's hatred of his wife Agrafina. He had the charge of the Empress's white rabbit. Apraksin, a relative of the lately deceased Grand Admiral, had become a convert to Catholicism, like Golitsuin, and was therefore punished in the same way. Another unofficial amuser of the imperial leisure was Prince Aleksander Borisovich Kurakin, the only person at Court who was permitted to speak his mind on all occasions. He possessed the additional privilege of getting drunk whenever he liked, a privilege which the abstemious Empress allowed to no other person, except on the anniversary of her accession, when bumpers were emptied in her honour, which amazed the English Minister. These zanies and mountebanks were always at hand to divert the Empress; but she seems to have enjoyed their antics most on Sunday afternoons after divine service. Sometimes they were ordered to sit in a row, with crossed legs, and cackle to imitate sitting hens. At other times the sport was rather more brutal than ridiculous. Thus, very frequently, two of these unfortunate creatures had to mount on the shoulders of two of their colleagues, serving them as steeds, and charge each other till both were unhorsed, when the struggle would be resumed on the floor, the combatants battering each other's faces and tugging at each other's hair, till the blood came, while Anne and her favourites would stand by and laugh till the tears ran down their cheeks. Once the dwarf Bakluirev, now an old man, who had been the favourite jester of Peter the Great and occasionally gave himself airs in consequence, refused to allow himself to be flung on the floor, not reflecting that the wishes of an Empress of all the Russias admit of no denial. He was at once removed and severely chastised with *batogi*.[1] It is superfluous perhaps to add that the smarting wretch never dared to disobey again. The most

---

[1] Long thin sticks.

adroit of these mountebanks was the Italian Pedrillo. He had come to St. Petersburg to play the violin in the orchestra of the Empress's private theatre, but, displaying some talent for buffoonery, was easily induced to change his profession, and did so well as a court jester, that he gained more than 20,000 rubles (£5,000) in nine years, when, like a prudent man, he took the first opportunity of quitting Russia and living at home on his savings.

Odd and repulsive as this menagerie of fools and mountebanks must seem to our modern ideas, it was in those days a time-honoured Muscovite institution. Every Russian household of any standing maintained one or more domestic jesters, and Anne, who prided herself on being a model Russian lady of the old school, only did on a large scale what most of her contemporary patricians did on a smaller. Even such a rigid and conscientious censor of manners as Prince Shcherbatov has no fault to find with her on this score. All the more severe is he, however, on the exotic luxuries that he accuses her of introducing. It was in this reign, he sorrowfully informs us, that champagne and burgundy were first seen at Muscovite banquets; that mahogany, palisander and ebony chairs and tables supplanted the oak and deal furniture of a simpler age; that rich carpets began to be regarded as necessaries instead of luxuries, and that mirrors and pictures became quite common even in second-rate establishments. I have already alluded to the rich liveries and uniforms of the imperial household, but it was not so much the gorgeousness as the variety and mutability of these splendid appointments that made them so extravagant. At the beginning of her reign, the Tsaritsa affected green liveries laced with gold, but towards the end of it she exchanged them all for black and yellow liveries laced with silver.[1] Then, too,

[1] Rondeau.

every function had its own separate uniform. Thus, to take only one instance, on the Monday, Thursday and Saturday afternoons in winter, when the Empress took horse exercise in Biren's sumptuous riding school, everyone invited to share the pastime, including the foreign Ministers, had to wear a uniform of yellow buffalo-skin embroidered with silver galloon, with a blue vest and trimmings to match.[1] If rich men like the French Ambassador, Chétardie, and the English Ambassador, Finch, complained of the cost of living at St. Petersburg, we can readily understand that most of the boyars, who had nothing but their land to depend upon, found it very difficult to keep pace with the growing extravagance of the Tsaritsa's Court. According to Manstein, 2—3,000 rubles (£500—£750) a year went a very little way towards enabling a gentleman to cut a decent figure there, and many ambitious young dandies were utterly ruined in making the attempt. Another mischievous foreign importation were the gaming tables. Manstein tells us that he has seen as much as 20,000 rubles (£5,000) lost in a single night at *Quinze* or *Pharao*. The Empress herself, indeed, played very seldom, and always with the intention of losing. She generally kept the bank, and called upon those she would to punt, paying the winners in coin on the spot, but only accepting worthless counters herself from the losers. Nevertheless the fact remains that she it was who introduced gambling into Russia, and she must therefore be held largely responsible for the infinite damage done thereby. On the other hand, it is universally admitted that the Court of Anne was at least decent and respectable. For all its luxury and extravagance, and the pride, envy and ostentation which followed in their train, it could never be called immoral or even frivolous. No doubt the Russian women, emancipated from

[1] Chétardie: *Despatches.*

their long seclusion, were now encouraged to cultivate a freer and easier intercourse with the other sex, and discarding their semi-conventual robes and rules, began to wear dresses which set off their fine figures, and ornaments which embellished their charms. Nowhere, too, did the cult of western fashion find such enthusiastic devotees as at Peterhof and the Winter Palace, indeed the daughters and granddaughters of the Boyars had such a rage for the latest Parisian modes, that the few French modistes and hairdressers at the Russian Capital were sorely embarrassed by the demands made upon them. Great Russian ladies, we are told, on the eve of presentations and court balls frequently had to have their hair dressed *three days in advance,* and slept upright on chairs during the interval, so as not to imperil the *coiffeur's* delicate masterpieces.[1] But if the Tsaritsa loved to see stylishly dressed young persons around her, she was equally solicitous as to the quality of their morals. It is true that Anne herself was unable to look back on an absolutely clean record. At one time she had sought and found some distraction from the dulness and monotony of a singularly lonely and friendless life in the arms of two, perhaps of three[2] successive paramours. But there is good reason to believe that her guilty liaison with Biren ceased on *his* marriage day, and from the time she ascended the Russian throne, her private conduct seems to have been of an exemplary regularity. Moreover, she had never been absolutely deaf to the calls of religion or the warnings of conscience, and in her latter years she was a great stickler for morality as she understood it. It was difficult, therefore, for the ladies of the Russian Court to trip seriously beneath the watchful eye of an austere mistress, who took care,

---

[1] Shcherbatov: *O povreshdeni nravov v Russyi*
[2] Peter Bestuzhev, Biren and the elder Löwenwolde. The last alleged *liaison,* however, is not proven.

besides, to remove all stumbling-blocks from their path; indeed it was only the Tsarevna Elizabeth who gave her Majesty any real trouble in this respect. The daughter of Peter the Great was now somewhat past her prime, but she was still indisputably the *belle* of her cousin's Court. The Tsaritsa once asked the Chinese Ambassador at a court ball to say who was the prettiest woman present. Without a moment's hesitation he bowed low to the Tsarevna, remarking that she was as the moon among the stars, and if only she had not quite such large eyes, nobody could look upon her and live. Moreover, her affability, sweetness and unaffected gaiety won the hearts of all who approached her. Unfortunately the morals of this engaging Princess were by no means so excellent as her manners. She had as great a partiality for big individual grenadiers as the King of Prussia had for battalions of these same giants, and we frequently hear of her favourites being surprised by the emissaries of the Tsaritsa, and sent to Siberia. Once or twice Anne was so incensed by her cousin's profligacy, that she threatened to shut her up in a convent, and it is said that but for the intercession of Biren, would actually have done so. Still more watchful was the Tsaritsa over her niece, the Princess Anne of Mecklenburg, whom she loved as a daughter and intended for her successor. This young lady, when only seventeen, was suspected of entertaining some tender feeling for the Saxon Minister, Count Lynar, of whose company she was very fond. Nothing criminal had, as yet, passed between them;[1] but, as the Princess was very young, and the Count was, as Rondeau expresses it, "an uncommonly pretty fellow," the circumspect Tsaritsa thought it prudent to interfere, so Lynar took leave of absence and did not return—at least not during the Empress' lifetime.

[1] Rondeau: *Despatches*.

GOKE PINX, 1758.  SCHMIDT, SCULP., 1761.
Elizabeth, Empress.

*To face p.* 290.

Interesting as it must have been to curious foreigners and chance visitors, the Court of the Tsaritsa Anne was not a pleasant or even a safe place to dwell in, for—and here we touch upon its dark side—it was pervaded by an atmosphere of suspicion and terror. In the old days of the Muscovite monarchy the relations between subject and sovereign had been very different. The Boyars, though they bowed low before the Tsar and addressed their earthly sovereign with a reverence due only to the King of Kings, were not mere sycophants, but real counsellors, claiming access to his person as a birthright; and their counsels, freely and fearlessly given, were generally acted upon. Peter the Great substituted for this aristocracy of birth, proud of its long and lofty lineage, a purely official aristocracy absolutely dependent on the will and favour of the Sovereign. Under that great monarch, who always recognised and rewarded merit, the new system worked excellently well, and produced extraordinary results; but under an ordinary monarch, promotion would, naturally, rather be by favour than by merit, especially if that monarch were a woman, and therefore more liable to be swayed by impulse and caprice. When, as was the case with Anne, the Tsaritsa fell under the evil influence of rapacious and unscrupulous aliens, the native nobility would, in the ordinary course of things, become the sycophants instead of the counsellors of the Crown, and slavish fear would be the predominant tone of the Court. Anne herself, despite the frequent brutality of her pastimes and her occasional outbursts of savage vindictiveness, was not naturally cruel. Lady Rondeau, who had many opportunities of observing her in private, declares that she was readily moved to tears by a melancholy story, and had a heart that revolted at cruelty. Manstein describes her as naturally amiable and affectionate, and even the hostile Kostomarov records an anecdote which goes to prove that if her wit was sometimes caustic, she nevertheless had not a bad heart. The Archbishop of Kazan, on one occasion, in reply to an invitation to Court, wrote to the Empress that he would arrive at St. Petersburg on the Feast of the Annunciation, "which," added he, "falls on the 25th March."—"We are much obliged to you," replied Anne, "for teaching us folks at St. Petersburg on what day the Feast of the Annunciation falls. Hitherto we had always imagined that it was on the same day here as it is at Kazan." This sarcasm quite discomposed the poor Archbishop, and he took it as a very bad sign indeed. What if something worse were in store for him? He knew right well that even the archiepiscopal dignity was no safeguard against the Gosudaruinya's displeasure. Was not a still more august pontiff, Vanatovich, Metropolitan of Kiev, actually languishing in a dungeon for having neglected to proclaim the new Empress's accession. The news of his despair reached Anne's ears, however, and she at once hastened to reassure him. "We hear," she wrote to Saltuikov, "that the Archbishop of Kazan is much disquieted. Write a letter therefore to him in my name, saying that my former letter to him was writ of set purpose, not in wrath, but because I would not have him be so silly again. Assure him too of our favour, and after writing out such letter, send it to us and we will sign the same, and send it to him by post."[1] Nevertheless the fact remains that no other Court was even dominated by a spirit of such slavish dread as the Court of the Tsaritsa Anne, and this ever present terror was mainly due to the malign influence of her favourite—Biren. Ambition and anxiety seem to have been the pivots on which this base

[1] Kostomarov. Compare Lady Rondeau who says of Anne: "She has a way of saying a short satirical sentence sometimes that is really witty, but always tempered with so much good nature that it never shocks."

adventurer's conduct constantly turned, the ambition of remaining the Empress's chief counsellor and consequently the leading man in the Empire, and the anxiety lest a turn of Fortune's wheel should cast him back into his original nothingness. During the latter years of Anne's reign, Biren increased so enormously in power and riches that he must have been a marvel to himself as well as to others. His apartments in the Palace adjoined those of the Tsaritsa, and his liveries, his furniture and his equipages were scarcely less costly than hers. Half the bribes intended for the Russian Court passed into his coffers. He had estates in Livonia, Courland, Silesia and the Ukraine. A special Department of State looked after his brood mares and stallions. His riding-school was one of the sights of the Russian Capital, and the *rendezvous* of the *élite* of Russian society. The massive magnificence of his silver plate astonished the French Ambassador, and the diamonds of his Duchess were the envy of Princes. The climax of this wondrous elevation was reached when, in the course of June 1737, the Estates of Courland elected the son of the ostler of Mittau to be their reigning Duke.[1] It is true the fellow was almost as much loathed in Courland as in Russia; but the will of the Tsaritsa was the law of the land, and large sums of money smuggled into Courland in the shape of small bills from a thousand to four or five thousand crowns, payable in Amsterdam to bearer,[2] speedily convinced the electors that nobody was so worthy to rule them as Count Biren. Henceforward his Most Serene Highness received all the honours due to sovereign Princes, and, together with his consort, took his seat at the Imperial table by the side of the Tsarevna Elizabeth and the Princess

[1] In 1737 the line of Kettler became extinct in the person of the long ailing Duke Ferdinand.

[2] Rondeau: *Despatches*.

Anne of Mecklenburg, presumptive heiress to the throne.

Biren's method of governing his principality was every whit as peculiar as the mode by which he acquired it. His post of Grand Chamberlain at the Russian Court being the source of all his power and influence, he durst not quit it for an instant, and so it came about that his Courlanders never beheld their Duke from one year's end to another. But if they never saw his face, they felt his heavy hand. Biren's spies kept him fully informed of all that was going on in the Duchy, and it was soon remarked there that every free-spoken gentleman, sooner or later, mysteriously disappeared. Bands of masked men would pounce upon the offender when he felt most secure, hustle him into a close carriage—and he would not be seen again for years. Many of such abductions took place during the short reign of Duke Ernest John; but perhaps the most remarkable case was that of Herr von Sacken. This gentleman, while standing one day at the door of his country house, was seized from behind by two unknown persons, gagged, and thrown into one of these close carriages. For two whole years he was conveyed from place to place, his conductors never once showing him their faces unmasked. One night the horses were taken out of the traces, and he was left in the carriage, where he remained till break of day, thinking that he would then resume his journey as usual. But when the morning came and he still found himself alone, he ventured to put his head out of the window, and found himself at the door of his own house whence he had been kidnapped two years before. Von Sacken complained to the Duke, who affected the utmost astonishment, and assured the aggrieved gentleman that if only he could recognise his mysterious abductors and bring them to justice, they should be very severely punished.[1]

[1] Manstein: *Mémoires*.

And if Biren allowed himself these pleasantries in a land where he had little to fear, it can readily be conceived to what lengths his apprehensions would be likely to lead him in Russia proper where he knew himself to be cordially detested by all classes of the population. Here all the instruments of repression that minister to tyranny, were at his absolute disposal, and he used them with all the mercilessness of a true tyrant. General Ushakov, the Director of the terrible Secret Chancellery or Torture-Chamber, was his creature, and the records of that ghastly tribunal enable us to understand how even to this day the name of Biren sounds horrible in the ears of all patriotic Russians. It would really seem as if he had the set purpose of gradually exterminating the leaders of the Muscovite aristocracy, so relentless, so persistent was his persecution of them. But nothing is so cruel as fear, and Biren was fearful in the midst of all his triumphs. Amongst his principal victims were the still surviving members of the fallen Dolgoruki family, who were considered dangerous even in their distant Siberian exile. In the course of 1738, all the old charges of treason and sedition, for which they had already been more than sufficiently punished, were revived against them, and at the end of 1739 they were tried by a special commission at Great Novgorod. Ivan Aleksyeevich Dolgoruki, who had confessed, under torture, to using intemperate language against the Tsaritsa, and accusing her of destroying his family, was broken on the wheel and then decapitated. The great diplomatist Vasily Lukich and his cousins Sergius and Ivan Gregorivich, were spared the wheel, but lost their heads; Vasily and Michal Vladimirovich were condemned to solitary confinement for life, and not allowed to quit their dungeons except to go to church. Nor was the aged chief of the equally illustrious House of Golitsuin allowed to die in peace. His attempt to limit the monarchy had been neither forgotten nor forgiven, and, in 1736, he was arraigned before a special commission on charges so frivolous that one wonders how the judges could have kept their countenances during the proceedings.[1] He was condemned to death, but "the clemency of the Empress" mitigated the punishment to imprisonment in the fortress of Schlüsselberg. Another magnate, Prince Alexius Cherkasky, Governor of Smolensk and brother of the Cabinet Minister, was convicted of treason[2] on the unsupported statement of one false witness, who afterwards confessed his perjury and was sent to Siberia. And the aristocracy of intellect suffered as well as the aristocracy of birth. There were two men, still living, of whom Russia had peculiar reason to be proud, Vasily Nikolaevich Tatishchev and Alexius Vasilevich Makarov. Both of them, now old men, were pupils of Peter the Great. Both of them had been intelligent and conscientious pioneers of the new civilization. Their services were undeniable, their zeal and patriotism beyond all dispute. Nevertheless, shortly after the accession of Anne, both of them were deprived of their offices for alleged peculation, and a searching but ultimately abortive enquiry was made into their past careers by the Secret Chancellery, pending which they were kept in jail, in the utmost misery and wretchedness. In the eyes of their fellow-countrymen, the sole crime of these men was that they were Russians, and everyone looked upon Biren as their persecutor. Even women were not safe from the Secret Chancellery. Thus Praskovia Usupova, a well-known friend of the Golitsuins, was indicted

---

[1] One of the charges brought against him was that he had publicly declared that "if Satan came to him from Hell, he would nevertheless ask and accept counsel from him, notwithstanding that he was the enemy of God."—*Solovev*.

[2] Under stress of prolonged torture, the unfortunate man accused himself of crimes he had never committed.

before that terrible tribunal for treasonable language and for practising enchantments with intent to injure the Tsaritsa. She was condemned to be flogged with whips of tow,[1] and forced to take the veil in a Siberian Monastery, her name being changed from Praskovia to Proklya.[2] The unfortunate woman on arriving at her destination, in a paroxysm of rage tore off her nun's robes, declaring that her true name now was Beschinaya,[3] whereupon she was thrown to the ground, and flogged with whips of cords.[4] The natural result of this cruel and systematic persecution was to humble the Russian gentry to the dust. Those of them who still frequented the Court where the abject slaves of the reigning favourite. The issues of life and death depended on his smile or frown. If he were pleased to be merry, everyone was boisterous with mirth; but if he raised his voice in anger, his crowded antechamber emptied itself in an instant.[5] The richest gentlemen, the highest officials quailed before his Most Serene Highness. A word from him could raise the lowliest or bring down the highest. Even Cabinet Ministers solicited his patronage, and Princesses of the blood stooped to flatter him. Nevertheless the terrible, omnipotent man felt ill at ease and insecure. There were two of his own colleagues, foreigners like himself, whom he equally feared and hated because they would not be his tools, though they always treated him with outward deference— Vice-Chancellor Ostermann and Field Marshal Münnich. These three men comprised the so-called "German Party"[6]

[1] *Koski*.
[2] *I.e.*, accursed.
[3] Without rank, unclassed, dishonoured.
[4] *Shelep*.
[5] See Prince Jakob Shakovsky's account of his stormy interview with Biren, cited by Solovev, which is very interesting, but far too long to quote.
[6] Both Solovev and Kostomarov have well pointed out that there was really no such thing as a "German *Party*" in Russia. Cohesion and co-op-

which ruled Russia throughout the reign of Anne, but their views were often divergent and their aims nearly always antagonistic. Biren, who had no head for business and sufficient intelligence to recognise his own incapacity in this respect, very rarely meddled with affairs of State; but this abstention naturally made him somewhat dependent upon the active and responsible administrators, and it galled his pride to be dependent on anybody except his Imperial Mistress. Now both Münnich and Ostermann were absolutely indispensable in their several departments, and Biren loved them none the better in consequence. The Field Marshal was perhaps the more troublesome and offensive, but also the less dangerous, of the two. He had so much conceit and so little tact that he was perpetually showing his hand, and it was therefore not very difficult to be on one's guard against him. Ostermann, too, disliked the pushing soldier almost as much as he disliked the brutal Courlander, while the Empress used to openly ridicule the Marshal's vanity. Once someone remarked to Anne that Münnich was about to ask her for the title of "Prince of the Ukraine." "The Marshal is really too modest," replied the Empress. "I supposed he would have been content with nothing less than the title of Grand Duke of Muscovy!"—The discreet and reticent Vice-Chancellor was much more redoubtable. His position, too, was absolutely unique. For nearly a quarter of a century he had controlled with matchless sagacity the foreign policy of the Empire, and all the foreign diplomatists, chafe as they might and did at his interminable tergiversations, procrastinations and obscurations (he had become, by this time, a past master of the art of darkening coun-

eration are of the very essence of a party or faction, but in point of fact all three of these men were far too egoistical to act loyally together, and were perpetually intriguing against each other.

sel and ingeniously complicating the most simple issues), the foreign diplomatists nevertheless acknowledged among themselves that the Vice-Chancellor was the only man in Russia who understood politics, while abroad he was universally regarded as one of the greatest statesmen in Europe. The Empress seems to have disliked him personally;[1] but he was her sole counsellor in all political matters, and in his latter years he was known at court as "The Oracle." But the responses of the "Oracle" were generally so obscure and ambiguous that it was difficult to get at his meaning. Nobody ever could tell what he thought on any particular subject, or guess what he would do in any particular case. He treated his friends as if they might one day become his enemies, and his enemies as if they might one day become his friends. In short, an atmosphere of impenetrable mystery enveloped the soft-spoken, taciturn old statesman. Now, to a man of Biren's irritable and suspicious nature, the secrecy and the shyness of Ostermann were peculiarly exasperating. He felt that he could never be sure of a minister whom it was impossible either to compromise or to control, and hence there arose in his breast a very natural desire to find someone who could take Ostermann's place and yet remain a willing tool of his own. As no such person was to be found among the foreigners in the Russian service, it was necessary to seek for him among "the fledglings of Peter the Great," and at length he hit upon Paul Yaguzhinsky. It was not indeed in Yaguzhinsky's nature to truckle to any potentate, least of all to an upstart like the Duke of Courland, whom he heartily despised and fearlessly defied; but Biren hoped that the splendid energy of the man and his immense experience would make him a formidable rival to Ostermann, so he was recalled from his honourable exile at

[1] Because she guessed that he detested Biren. See Rondeau: *Despatches*.

Berlin, in April, 1735, and made a Cabinet Minister in the place of the elder Löwenwolde lately deceased. Twelve months later, however, Yaguzhinsky died, to the infinite regret of all lovers of free speaking and hard drinking; the English colony, whom he had always protected, especially lamenting "their good friend." Biren therefore had to find a substitute, and this time his choice fell upon another Russian, Artemius Petrovich Voluinsky. The new Minister was a man of considerable talent, both as an administrator and a diplomatist. He had been sent by Peter the Great as Minister Plenipotentiary to Persia, and had subsequently represented his country at the abortive Congress of Nemirov. He had also risen to the rank of Major-General in the army, and on the accession of Anne, with whom he was distantly related through the Saltuikovs, he held the post of Governor of Kazan. The Foreign Ministers describe him as "an ingenious gentleman" of tried capacity, and he also had some reputation as a composer of memorials, his literary friends assuring him that his performances in this line were "superior to the '*Télémaque*' of Fenelon." But, on the other hand, he was vainglorious, indiscreet, tyrannical, rapacious and thoroughly corrupt, having been guilty during his official career of every conceivable description of fraud and violence. He was in short one of those men of whom a contemporary Russian Archbishop said that their extravagant violence and luxury drove the poor people prematurely out of God's fair world. The keen-sighted Yaguzhinsky, who knew Voluinsky in his earlier days, is said to have foretold both his elevation and his subsequent collapse. "I foresee," remarked he, "that by dint of fawning and intrigue Voluinsky will force his way into the Cabinet, but I also foresee that two years after he will have to be hanged." This prediction was realized in a much more tragic and sudden manner than even the prophet himself imagined. At first, indeed, things went well enough. A minister with as many enemies as the hairs of his head and the fear of the gallows constantly before his eyes, must needs walk very circumspectly, and, for a time, Voluinsky was as subservient to his powerful protector as even that vulgar despot could possibly desire. He contradicted Ostermann publicly, and played the spy upon him in private. He dutifully did the dirty work of the Duke of Courland and ran his messages, in short he was a model Minister—from Biren's point of view. But gradually the patron became aware of a disagreeable change in his client. He began to absent himself from the Duke's audience chamber on petition days, and as time went on these absences became more and more frequent. Biren took this ill of him, and both his anger and his suspicions were aroused. His Serene Highness had of late contracted the bad habit of treating all those about him like lackeys, and on more than one occasion he reproached Voluinsky roundly for his ingratitude and neglect. At first Voluinsky endured the chronic ill-temper of his all-powerful patron with philosophical patience. Still, it was very unpleasant, and as a man generally avoids what is unpleasant to him, it was not very surprising if he tried to see as little of his Most Serene Highness as possible. Moreover, without perhaps being aware of it himself, Voluinsky had grown more sensitive and susceptible since he became a Cabinet Minister. He was now one of the little junto of dignitaries that ruled the Empire. He was consulted on the most important, the most confidential affairs. Most of the work of the Cabinet was thrust upon his shoulders, and he was a busy, active man who liked work, especially when it was as lucrative as the work of the Russian Cabinet. So his present circumstances made him forget his antecedents, and he began to ask himself why he, Voluinsky, a Russian nobleman, a Cabinet Minister, a relative of the Tsaritsa, should put up with the insolence of the son of a Courland ostler! And now a brilliant thought occurred to him; why should he not supplant his patron in the Empress's favour? It was his privilege to present petitions to her Majesty daily, and he was frequently closeted with her for hours, Anne loving gossip above all things, and Voluinsky having a tongue that was never tired of wagging. The infatuated time-server might have known that the eye of the Duke was watching all his movements, and that any tampering with the Tsaritsa would be looked upon by the reigning favourite as an unpardonable offence. But Voluinsky had by this time so completely lost his head that he rushed blindly into ruin. His first folly was to insult another client of his patron in that patron's very antechamber. The incident presents such a curious picture of the manners and customs of the times, that it deserves to be told in full.

In February, 1740, Voluinsky, who had been entrusted with all the arrangements connected with the nuptials of Prince Golitsuin and his fair Calmuck in the Ice Palace, already alluded to, sent a cadet to summon to his presence the poet and imperial academician, Vasily Karlovich Tredyakovsky,[1] who had been ordered to compose some verses on that festal occasion. On their way to the Minister, the cadet and the poet fell out, and, on arriving at the Ivory Hall where Voluinsky was awaiting them, the former accused the latter of having "cursed" him. Voluinsky, without waiting to hear Tredyakovsky's version of the matter, proceeded to soundly box his ears on the spot, and bade the cadet do the same. At last the poet was released, and, on reaching home, washed the blood off his face, and sat up all night to complete his verses; but the remembrance of the indignity he had suffered was too

[1] He subsequently bore the title of "Professor of Eloquence and Poetical Ingenuities."

much for him, and, at break of day, he donned his uniform, and hastened off to the palace of the Duke of Courland, to lay a complaint against Voluinsky. While he was waiting in the antechamber, who should appear but Voluinsky himself, who sharply demanded what he was doing there, and, finding his answer unsatisfactory, ordered the wretched academician to be seized and conveyed to the police-office, where he was deprived of his sword, thrown to the ground, and received 70 strokes with a stout stick on his bare back. On regaining his feet he was so dazed as to be quite unable to understand the questions put to him by Voluinsky, whereupon he received thirty strokes more and was kept under arrest until the morning. The poet employed his leisure at the police-station in endeavouring to finish his ode on the Ice Palace, which he was to read on the morrow in "The Hall of Recreation;" but as he himself plaintively expresses it: "I did not then feel very much up to rhyming." The next morning he was dressed in a masquerading costume, and conveyed to the entertainment, where he declaimed his verses in the presence of the Court, whereupon he was taken back to jail and kept there till the following day, when he was again brought before Voluinsky. "I don't want to part with you," began the Minister, "till I have flogged you once more by way of wishing you adieu," and, despite the sobs and supplications of the trembling and long-suffering bard, he was thrown upon the floor of the Minister's vestibule, and ten more strokes were scrupulously administered to him. "And now," cried Voluinsky, "you may be off and complain of me to whomsoever you will." In the ordinary course of things this outrage would have had no ill consequences for its perpetrator, as in those days an academician was generally regarded as a thing of naught compared with a Cabinet Minister. Unfortunately for Voluinsky, however, he had mortally offended a being standing immeasurably higher than any mere Cabinet Minister. It was in the Duke of Courland's own antechamber that the assault had been committed, and committed too on the person of one of his Highness's petitioners! This was an affront which Biren could not forgive. Yet he did not move in the matter at once. He felt that if Voluinsky were left severely alone, a sense of impunity[1] would infallibly lure him into fresh and more indictable extravagances. Nor had he long to wait. A few weeks after the Tredyakovsky affair, Voluinsky actually took it into his head to write to the Tsaritsa, calling her attention to the unworthiness of those who possessed and abused her confidence. He mentioned no names, but his allusions were so transparent that it was obvious at a glance that Ostermann and Biren were the persons referred to. Now, to insinuate to an autocratic Princess that she is surrounded by evil counsellors is as much as to imply that she has been guilty of an error of judgment in choosing such counsellors. Voluinsky seems to have overlooked this fact, but it did not escape the Tsaritsa, and, sending for her critic, she asked him sharply what he meant by addressing such memorials to her. "Methinks," said she, "you write to me as if I were a Sovereign of very tender years," and her words turned the unfortunate author sick and cold with fear. Many a man had been sent to Siberia for less. Nevertheless even this piece of folly passed unpunished, and on the celebration of the Peace, Voluinsky received a present of 20,000 rubles (£5,000) from Anne's own hand. But the man must have been afflicted with that judicial dementia which the Ancients

---

[1] Kostomarov who records the above anecdote, erroneously assumes that it was this outrage which precipitated Voluinsky's fall, but that this was not the case is perfectly clear from the documents cited by Solovev.

ascribed to the vengeance of the gods. All his warnings were quite thrown away upon him, and he now proceeded to commit the crowning blunder that was to bring him to the block.

At the end of the War the Cabinet had to consider the amount of compensation due to the Polish Republic for the infringement of its territory by Münnich's army in 1739. Biren, who owed nominal fealty to Poland for his Duchy, and wished to stand well with the Polish Senate, had advised the Empress that a liberal idemnity should be given; but in the debates in Council, Voluinsky declared, with obvious allusion to Biren, that as he himself was *no vassal of Poland*, he had consequently no motive for conciliating a nation naturally hostile to Russia, and therefore advised that no more money should be thrown away on the Polacks. This speech was reported to Biren, and fairly transported him with rage. That he, the Tsaritsa's bosom friend, should be represented as injurious to Russia, and that, forsooth! by his own *protégé*, was more than he could endure. He at once petitioned Anne to order an enquiry to be made into Voluinsky's past career, inasmuch as he who criticised others so freely should himself be able to endure criticism. Anne, perceiving that Voluinsky would be lost if she consented to such a step, refused to sanction it. "Then I quit Russia," replied the favourite, "either he or I must go." At these words the Empress burst into tears and yielded. An ukaz issued in her name during Holy Week, forbade Voluinsky the court, and, a week later, he and a number of his friends were arrested, arraigned before a tribunal composed of Biren's creatures, and cruelly tortured. Into the details of that mock trial there is no need to enter. The crimes and follies of the prisoner, who was as abject in adversity as he had been insolent in prosperity, made it an easy matter to ruin him, and he was condemned to be broken on the wheel and then beheaded. When the death-warrant was presented to the Tsaritsa for signature, a feeling of compassion overcame her, and she made another attempt to deliver her fallen kinsman. But Biren again declared that if Voluinsky were allowed to live, he himself must leave St. Petersburg, and again the unhappy woman yielded. Voluinsky, with a gag in his mouth to prevent him from speaking,[1] was dragged rather than led to the scaffold, where the sight of the hideous instruments of his punishment almost paralysed him with terror. Just as he was about to be bound to the wheel, however, an ukaz was read to him, declaring that the "clemency of the Empress" had mitigated his punishment to the severing of his right hand followed by decapitation. Of his associates, some were beheaded, others flogged, one had his tongue torn out, and the rest were banished for life to Siberia.[2]

Hitherto the Grand Chamberlain had been singularly unfortunate in his efforts to raise up rivals against the Vice-Chancellor. His third choice, however, was more successful, though this time he hit upon a man who so far from owing him anything, seemed bound by very nature to abhor him. This new *protégé* was Alexius Petrovich Bestuzhev-Ryumin, the son of that Bestuzhev whom Biren had supplanted in the Empress's favour, and whose family

[1] Kostomarov says that the gag was not to prevent him from talking, but to stop the blood which flooded his mouth after his tongue had been cut out. As, however, he does not give his authority for this hideous mutilation, and Chétardie, Finch and Solovev say nothing about it, I prefer to disbelieve it.

[2] The Russian Government spread abroad the most alarming reports of the sweeping revolutionary designs of Voluinsky and his associates, but the whole business seems to have been purely a piece of vindictiveness on Biren's part. See the *Despatches of Finch* who affects to believe, and the *Despatches of Chétardie* who openly scoffs at, these wild post-factum accusations.

he had mercilessly persecuted ever since. That Alexius Petrovich should accept any favour from the hand that had struck down his father, was monstrous in the opinion of all right-thinking people, nor was the mode in which he had courted such favour likely to raise him in the estimation of patriotic Russians. It was by acting as informer against one of his own race and order, Prince Alexander Cherkasky, that he had ingratiated himself with the Duke of Courland, and his services on that occasion were ultimately rewarded by a seat in the Cabinet. Yet morally despicable as he was, Bestuzhev possessed diplomatic and political talents of a very high, perhaps of the highest order, and he was destined to see and survive the fall of the German Party, to mount to eminence over their ruin, and enjoy, as Grand Chancellor, under the Tsaritsa Elizabeth, a European reputation far less deserved but scarcely inferior to that of Ostermann.

The last years of Anne were disturbed by a political event which threatened the safety of the Empire, and brightened by a domestic event which promised to perpetuate the dynasty. The domestic event was the birth of a male heir to the throne, the political event was the rise of a warlike anti-Russian Party in Sweden. We will take the latter occurrence first.

The Peace of Belgrade, and the circumstances attending it, had established, beyond all contradiction, the momentous fact that the French Monarchy, after an eclipse of a quarter of a century, had become, once again, the paramount Power of Europe. The cardinal motive of her policy for generations, the depression of the House of Hapsburg, had at length been realized, and it was only the accident of the Russian alliance that now gave to Austria even a semblance of independence. To sever that alliance, and, if possible, to drive Russia back into the semi-barbarism from which

was the next object that the French
 "Russia in respect to the
 wrote Cardinal Fleury,[1] "has
 a degree of power, and its union
 extremely dangerous. If
 make 100,000 Muscovites
 might in other circumstances
 Germany with barbarian troops,
 Emperor to her will." The most obvious
 Russian alliance unserviceable to
 Russia in hostilities with
 Sweden was the only other Power
 whose remaining was regarded by the French as
 Sweden, though she had descended
 Power, was still a considerable
 a considerable value. The possession
 within a day's march of the Russian
 possession of Pomerania gave her an entry
 of the maritime *Reich*, and the
 military parties added not a little to
 Even now she was of more account in the
 than either Prussia or Holland. Moreover,
 ever since the Thirty Years' War, a community of interests
 united France and Sweden, and though Charles
 XI, from personal ill-will, and his successor Chancellor
 from political considerations, had reversed the
 traditional policy of Sweden, there had always been a
 strong French Party in Sweden, and, in 1738, that Party
 came to the front. Glory and honour were its watchwords;
 it aimed at nothing less than recovering the lost Baltic
 Provinces, and it was never weary of ridiculing the wise

[1] See the secret instructions of Fleury to the Marquis de Chétardie, the new French Ambassador at the Russian Court, in *Sb. of Imp. Ist. Rus. Ob.*, Tome XCII.

caution of the aged Chancellor, Count Horn, whom they accused of sacrificing everything to perpetuate an inglorious peace. They derisively nicknamed his adherents Night-Caps (a term subsequently softened into Caps), themselves adopting the sobriquet *Hats*. The epithet instantly caught the public fancy. The nickname *Night-cap* seemed exactly to suit the drowsy policy of a peace-loving dotard, while the three-cornered hat, worn by officers and country gentlemen, as happily hit off the manly self-assertion of the Opposition, and when the Estates met in 1738, these party-badges were in general use. This Riksdag marks a turning-point in Swedish history. France, naturally hailing with satisfaction the rise of a faction content to be her armour-bearer in the North, supported the Swedish Opposition with all the might of a long purse, and, after a prolonged struggle, Chancellor Horn, who at first had ridiculed "the frothy fervour of our young men, who have clouded their wits in the French Minister's wine-cellars,"[1] was driven from office, although the Russian Minister, Michael Bestuzhev-Ryumin, Alexius Bestuzhev's brother, had expended immense sums of money to keep him in his seat. Instigated by France, whose ample subsidies, paid three years in advance, replenished their empty coffers, the Hats now indulged in a series of warlike demonstrations to provoke Russia to a rupture. A fleet was equipped; troops were massed in Finland; thousands of muskets were sent as a present to the Sultan, and Baron Sinclaire, a member of the Secret Committee of the Diet, undertook to deliver despatches to the Turkish Commandant at Chocim, and spy upon the condition of the Russian army as he passed through Poland. Michael Bestuzhev at once advised his Government "to suppress" Sinclaire, and give out that he had been waylaid by Polish bandits, and this invitation to highway

[1] M. P. Bestuzhev's Despatches, cited by Solovev.

robbery and murder was promptly acted upon. Münnich, with the connivance of the Cabinets of St. Petersburg and Vienna, ordered three of his officers to intercept Sinclaire on his return from Chocim, and they "executed their commission" by seizing the unfortunate man at Neusiedel, near Breslau, on neutral territory, dragging him into a wood by the roadside, and there murdering him most brutally, after taking away his papers, which proved to be of no value to anybody but himself.[1] This atrocity, which was carefully kept from the knowledge of the Tsaritsa, naturally sent the martial fervour of the Swedes up to fever heat, and for some weeks after the news reached Stockholm, Bestuzhev, the real as well as the suspected promoter of the evil deed, went in terror of his life. But as the actual assassins were smuggled away into Siberia, and the Empress, in perfect good faith, indignantly repudiated any complicity in the outrage, the agitation of the Stockholmers gradually subsided; and when, at the end of 1739, Russia concluded peace with the Porte, even the warlike Hat Ministry hesitated to engage the Tsaritsa single-handed.

Thus the first attempt of France to egg on Sweden against Russia, had failed; but that she should have made the attempt at all, was of itself a disquieting circumstance to all who were interested in the preservation of peace. England was particularly alarmed. She knew from experience that France had never lacked the will to injure her neighbours when she had the power, and never had the power of France seemed so excessive and so menacing as at the beginning of 1740. Early in that year a Minister Plenipotentiary, Mr. Edward Finch, brother of the Earl of Nottingham, was despatched to St. Petersburg, to succeed the late Mr. Rondeau, with special instructions to jealously watch

[1] Compare M. Bestuzhev's Despatches, cited by Solovev, and Manstein's Mémoires.

every movement of the French Plenipotentiary, the Marquis de Chétardie, who had arrived there a few weeks before, and endeavour, at all hazards, to conclude a defensive Alliance with "our good sister, the Czarina of Moscovy," as being "the only other Power in Europe whose weight and strength in conjunction with our own" could be with equal efficacy opposed to the dangerous machinations of France, "whose superior and still increasing power" had caused his Britannic Majesty to conceive the gravest apprehensions lest the balance of power in Europe should be utterly subverted. Finch, with laudable pertinacity, besieged Ostermann's Cabinet night and day; but the Russian Vice-Chancellor listened but coldly to England's overtures, and his answers (when he condescended to answer at all) were so elusive and ambiguous that the Ambassador was at last completely nonplussed.

Ostermann was, indeed, the master of the situation. He knew right well that Russia had need neither of France nor of Great Britain, and that it was her highest wisdom to sit still. In vain the English Ministers again and again tried to frighten him with the bugbear of an invasion from Sweden; he knew there was no real danger on that side, and, besides, he had already taken every necessary precaution. And his eyes were now turned towards another quarter. In the beginning of 1740 Frederick II succeeded his father, Frederick William, as King of Prussia, and, with the prescience of genius, Ostermann seems to have foreseen that the advent of this new monarch introduced a fresh element of danger into European politics. He was now less inclined than ever to tie himself down to a single irrevocable alliance which might both give premature alarm to other States, and, at the same time, prevent Russia from utilizing possible contingencies. "I am very sensible," he observed to Finch, "that the united power of England

and Russia is very great and would be always respected, yet I believe our alliance would be still more formidable if we widened its bottom by forming a more general concert." He was inclined to admit Prussia and Denmark into a general anti-Gallic league, but so far as this the British Government would not go, and so there for the present the matter rested.[1]

The Tsaritsa had been much more perturbed than her Ministers by the Swedish complications. At Peterhof, where she had resided during the summer of 1740, a constant look-out was kept for the approach of hostile frigates; ten battalions of the Guard were encamped round the Palace, and a carriage and four horses were kept in readiness night and day to convey the Empress, at a moment's notice, to a place of greater safety. But all these alarms were forgotten when, in August of the same year, she held in her arms at the font the eagerly expected heir to the throne. This little Prince, Ivan VI of tragic memory (Anne, his sole sponsor, named him after her own father), was the son of the Princess of Mecklenburg, the Empress's niece, whom, on the death of the girl's mother (her own favourite sister, Catherine Ivanovna), she had adopted, and whom she loved like a daughter. The young lady who, in 1733, was received into the Greek Church under the name of Anne Leopoldovna, was anything but beautiful, and those who, like Lady Rondeau, only knew her in her shy awkward girlhood, thought her stupid; but she was a round-faced, pleasant-looking blonde, very easy-tempered and good-natured, if somewhat indolent and lackadaisical, and her aunt had intended[2] from the very first that she should

[1] See *Sb.* of the *Imp. Rus. Ist. Ob.*, Tome LXXXV. Instructions prefixed to Finch's despatches.

[2] Anne was loth to leave the crown to her niece personally, for fear she might fall, as Tsaritsa, under the influence of her disreputable father the Duke of Mecklenburg.

be the mother of the future Tsar. When the girl was still in her earlier teens, the Empress despatched Grand Chamberlain Löwenwolde abroad to select a husband for her, and, by the advice of the Court of Vienna, he fixed upon the youthful Prince Anthony Ulrik of Brunswick-Bevern, who was sent to Russia forthwith, and also educated at the Tsaritsa's expense. Thus the young couple grew up under the very eye of the Empress, but of anything like a mutual inclination there was no trace. Anthony was a very good young man and no coward, but extraordinarily infantile for his years, and the Princess, who looked upon him as a milksop, was heard to declare more than once that she would rather lay her head on the block than marry such a "meek and mild creature." The Princess's visible dislike of her *fiancé*, suggested to the aspiring mind of the Duke of Courland the audacious idea of marrying his own son Peter to the Tsaritsa's niece, although he was only fifteen years of age, and therefore five years the Princess's junior. He durst not indeed propose such a thing to the Empress, but he insinuated the idea to Anne Leopoldovna herself through one of the Tsaritsa's female buffoons, the Princess Shcherbatova. The rebuff he received, however, not only made him abandon altogether his impudent project, but filled him with an inextinguishable hatred of the Princess herself. For Anne treated his overtures as a deliberate insult. She was not inclined, she said, to wait half-a-dozen years till the grandson of an ostler had grown old enough to offer her his hand, and therefore she thought that, after all, she had best comply with the will of the Tsaritsa, and take the *fiancé* already provided for her, who, at any rate, was a gentleman. So in July, 1739, the young people exchanged bridal rings in the Church of Our Lady of Kazan, and, ten months later, the Grand Duchess, as they now called her, was brought to bed of a fine boy, whom the Empress at once appropriated, carrying him off to her own room, where his cradle was henceforth placed, and jealously guarded, nobody being allowed to perform any service for the little gentleman except in the presence of the Tsaritsa or the Duchess of Courland. The Duke of Courland had affected equal delight at the birth of the Imperial Prince, nay, he actually emptied into the hat of the page who brought the news to him all the money he had about him. But, in his heart, he was deeply chagrined, for he knew that Anne Leopoldovna hated him, and, as the mother of the future Tsar, she was now a person to be feared. Six weeks later a still more momentous event brought home to the Duke of Courland the extreme instability of his power. On Sunday the 16th October, the Tsaritsa, while at table, was seized with a fit, and removed insensible to her bed, which she was never to leave again alive. Biren, horribly agitated, summoned Cherkasky and Bestuzhev to the Palace, to advise him what to do; but they could only suggest that Ostermann should first be consulted, and both Ministers proceeded straightway to the Vice-Chancellor's residence, in the same carriage. Ostermann opined that the Grand Duke Ivan should at once be proclaimed successor to the throne, in conformity with the known wishes of the Tsaritsa, but declined to commit himself to any decision as to who should be Regent, well aware that Biren coveted that post for himself. On the return of the two Ministers to the palace, where they now found Münnich and Löwenwolde closeted with the Duke of Courland, they delivered their message, Münnich stepping aside the while so as not to be obliged to speak prematurely; but Biren, determined that his rival should not escape responsibility, called to him: "Count, do you hear what the Cabinet Ministers say about the Government?"—"No, your Highness," replied

Münnich, "I do not hear."—"They say," continued Biren, "that they don't want things here to be as they are in Poland, where many rule instead of one."—This was an obvious hint to those present to declare themselves, and so Bestuzhev took it, for it was now that he pronounced the fateful words which were, ultimately, to prove the ruin of everyone present except himself: "I think," he exclaimed, "that nobody has a better right to be Regent than your Highness!"—"And yet," he added immediately afterwards, as if frightened at his own words, "and yet it will seem strange to foreign Powers if we pass over the father and mother of the Emperor." Biren gloomily admitted as much and fell a-musing, while Cherkasky whispered something in Löwenwolde's ear. "Don't whisper, speak up!" cried the latter, and then Cherkasky said aloud that it was indispensable to elect the Duke of Courland, whereupon Münnich, not to be behindhand with the rest, also acquiesced: "I think myself," continued the Field Marshal boldly, "that it would be very deplorable if the Princess Anne had any share in the government. You know what a brute her father is, and if he came here he would certainly wring all our necks. As for her husband—well, he has served under me for a couple of campaigns, and I don't know to this day whether he is fish or flesh."—This was encouraging for Biren, but as yet he durst not take any further step, and so nothing was decided that evening. A council of magnates, held next day, overawed by the chief dignitaries of the Empire, was easily brought to beg Biren to accept the regency in the name of the Russian nation, and he acceded to their lukewarm entreaties with an affectation of reluctance that deceived nobody. It now remained for him to obtain the sanction of the dying Empress to his appointment, but here he encountered unexpected difficulties. Anne, indeed, readily signed the ukaz appointing the infant Ivan her successor, and early in the morning of the 18th October, the Guards, drawn up in front of the Palace, took the oath of allegiance to the new Sovereign, man by man, while the Tsarevna Elizabeth, the Princess Anne, her husband Prince Anthony, and all the Ministers, Generals, Senators and Prelates did the same in the Chapel of the Winter Palace. But when it came to appointing her favourite Regent, the Tsaritsa hesitated, not from any diminution of affection, but from a true regard for his future safety. Her clear common-sense told her that the only possible way for the man she loved, to disarm the resentment of his innumerable enemies, who were only awaiting her death to fall upon him, was to descend from his already untenable position as speedily and as gracefully as possible. But the infatuated adventurer, blinded by ambition, could not see the abyss already yawning at his feet, imagining that he had only to continue his authority in order to maintain it. Again and again the Empress tried to save him from himself. When he handed her the petition for the Regency, she thrust it impatiently beneath her pillow. "Duke, duke!" she cried piteously, "my heart is sad for thee, for thou art compassing thine own ruin!" Immediately afterwards she sent for Ostermann, who, this time really crippled by gout, was conveyed to the Palace in a sedan chair, to the infinite chagrin of Biren who had surrounded the Tsaritsa with his creatures, and suffered nobody, not even her own family, to approach her without his permission. The unwonted spectacle of the Vice-Chancellor out of doors (he had not quitted his own house for five years) was the first intimation the public had of the dangerous condition of the Tsaritsa, for her illness had hitherto been kept a profound secret, and the mere allusion to the possibility of her decease was treated as a capital offence. What passed between Anne and Ostermann is not known; but the Vice-Chancellor must have confirmed the Empress in her resolution, for she kept all the petitions and other documents presented to her and made no sign. Five anxious days elapsed. At first Anne rallied, and it was hoped that the skill of her Portuguese physician, Sanchez, might prolong her life for some months, though from the nature of her malady, a permanent cure was well-nigh impossible. On the 22nd she was so much better that there was some talk of a complete recovery, and an assembly was held at Court, when Ostermann mendaciously informed the French Ambassador that her Majesty was out of danger, and that during the last three days, when he had had the privilege of conversing with her, he had been struck by the unusual vigour and lucidity of her reasoning. Chétardie made as if he believed the Vice-Chancellor, "but," says he, "I found the comedy a little too tedious." On the 26th, however, the Tsaritsa had a relapse which left no doubt as to her approaching end. Ostermann and Biren were summoned in haste to her bedside, and, in their presence, she signed her will, leaving the throne to her grandnephew, Ivan Antonovich, and a so-called "positive declaration" drawn up by Bestuzhev, in favour of Biren's Regency, and signed by 194 dignitaries in the name of the Russian people. The tears and entreaties of her favourite had prevailed at last against her own better judgment. Anne Ivanovna expired between 9 and 10 o'clock on the evening of the 28th October, 1740.... She had always dreaded the approach of Death; but when, at last, that tremendous visitor knocked at her door, she received him with the calm courage of Christian resignation.

The death of Anne marks the close of what may be called the sub-Petrine period of Russian History, that is to say, the period during which the followers and pupils of the great reforming Tsar, trained beneath his eye and informed by his spirit, continued and consolidated the work of their illustrious master. Much, very much, still remained to be done; many of the details of Peter's gigantic scheme had to be filled in, many of his ideas had to be reconsidered; but, at any rate, Russia had now definitively broken with the past, and had elected to be a European rather than an Asiatic Power. At first, indeed, her progress along the new lines laid down for her, had been so slow as to be almost imperceptible. In the beginning of the reign of Catherine I, for instance, many of the Western Powers regarded it as by no means improbable that Peter's Empire would not long survive its founder, especially when they saw it, at the most critical period of its existence, subjected to the severe strain of a Gynocracy—a form of government known to be monstrous and abominable to the Muscovite mind. But Peter had made the basis of his Empire so broad and strong, that it proved a comparatively easy task for those who came after him to build upon the foundation he had laid. The acquisition of the Baltic Provinces, too, gave to Russia a larger share in the commerce, and therefore in the riches, of the world, while the victories of Münnich and Lacy revealed the fact that in her dogged peasantry she possessed the raw material, in almost inexhaustible quantities, of one of the steadiest soldieries in the world. Henceforward she was generally regarded as an integral part of the continental system, and took her proper place among the great nations of the world.

THE END.

www.ingramcontent.com/pod-product-compliance
Lightning Source LLC
Chambersburg PA
CBHW031848220426
43663CB00006B/543